SELECTIONS

FROM THE CRITICAL WRITINGS OF

EDGAR ALLAN POE

SELECTIONS

FROM THE CRITICAL WRITINGS OF

EDGAR ALLAN POE

EDITED WITH AN INTRODUCTION AND NOTES

BY

F. C. PRESCOTT

New Preface
by
J. Lesley Dameron

New Introduction
by
Eric W. Carlson

GORDIAN PRESS
NEW YORK
1981

Second Edition, 1981

Published by Gordian Press
85 Tompkins Street
Staten Island, N.Y. 10304

Library of Congress Cataloging in Publication Data

Poe, Edgar Allan, 1809-1849.
Selections from the critical writings of Edgar Allan Poe.

Reprint of the 1909 ed. published by Holt, New York, in series: English-readings.
Includes bibliographical references.
1. Poe, Edgar Allan, 1809-1849--Aesthetics--Addresses, essays, lectures. 2. American literature--19th century--History and criticism--Addresses, essays, lectures. I. Prescott, Frederick Clarke, 1871-1957. II. Series: English-readings.
PS2619.A1 1980 818'.309 80-24488
ISBN 0-87752-182-4

CONTENTS

The selections (except the Marginalia) are arranged in the order of their publication.

NEW PREFACE

by
J. Lasley Dameron
Memphis State University

Professor Frederick Clarke Prescott, without the precedent of any previous single-volume edition of Poe's criticism, winnowed out the best of Poe's critical thought for his *Selections from the Critical Writings of Edgar Allan Poe,* published by Henry Holt in 1909 and now being printed by the Gordian Press. Carefully scrutinizing the bulk of Poe's critical writings—including prefaces, reviews, essays, and editorial fillers, Professor Prescott chose Poe's best and his most representative criticism. Designing his volume as a teaching edition for college or secondary school use, he presented selections chronologically, largely for the purpose of acquainting the student with the development of Poe's generic concepts. As yet, no one volume of Poe's criticism offers so much in a workable form.

Among other things, Professor Prescott was no doubt aware of Poe's inclination toward prolixity in composing reviews that had to be of a certain length and ready for printing by a deadline on occasions before Poe had ample time to think about what he was reviewing. Yet any reader who takes the time to examine the eight volumes of Poe's critical writings presented in the Virginia edition (1902) will certainly be aware of Poe's maturation as a critic and his growing mastery of aesthetic principles.

Professor Prescott's critical and editorial capacities are very evident throughout the volume. Teacher, author, and editor—he died at the age of 85 as *Emeritus* Professor of English at Cornell University with an impressive bibliography to his credit. His *Poetry and Dreams* (Boston: R.G. Badger, 1912) and *The Poetic Mind* (New York: Macmillan, 1922) reflect his interest in the psychoanalytical approach to the study of literature. According to July 28, 1957, issue of the New York *Times,* Professor Prescott taught the "Psychology of Poetry" at Cornell for twenty years and was among the first to apply "Freudian psychoanalytic theory to literature." In 1932, the University of Vermont conferred upon him an honorary Doctor of Humane Letters. Examples of his editorial work, aside from his volume of Poe criticism, include *Prose and Poetry of the Revolution* (New York: Thomas Y. Crowell, 1925), coedited with John H. Nelson; and *An Introduction to American Poetry* (New York: F.S. Crofts, 1932), coedited with Gerald D. Sanders. As an accomplished scholar, he was absolutely correct in drawing upon the standard text of Poe's writing, the Virginia edition *(The Complete Works of Edgar Allan Poe.* Edited by James A. Harrison. 17 vols. New York: T.Y. Crowell, 1902) and in selecting the first printed text of some of Poe's articles.

Most importantly, Professor Prescott, at a time when Poe's criticism was neglected, found Poe's reviews and essays to be valid expressions of Poe's artistic credo. He was among the first to emphasize the fact that Poe's criticism both explains and complements his poetry and fiction. Unlike many of his predecessors, he had little to say about Poe's personality and character, but concentrated on his cultural heritage and background. His chief concern was the presentation of Poe as a serious critic whose insights are perceptive, balanced, and largely generic. Except in two instances—Poe's reviews of Drake's *Culprit Fay* and of Bryant's *Poems*—he offers here the complete text of Poe's compositions, which he explicates and enhances by copious and instructive notes. His introduction still stands as a model of meticulous scholarship. His judgments are substantiated by carefully chosen citations from a variety of Poe's works. His cross-references are most helpful in understanding the diversity of Poe's views on several aesthetic questions Poe entertained throughout his career. In all probability, Professor Prescott in preparing this edition largely benefited from the aid he acknowledged from one of Poe's most distinguished biographers and editors—George Edward Woodberry. Woodberry's *The Life of Edgar Allan Poe, Personal and Literary* 2 vols. (Boston: Houghton Mifflin, 1909) and Professor Prescott's edition appeared in the same year—1909, the centennial year of Poe's birth. During 1909, Poe was honored as no other American writer had ever been honored by the Anglo-American world.

But Professor Prescott does not overpraise Poe, nor does he hesitate to point out certain elements of narrowness in some of Poe's critical pronouncements. Like Robert Jacobs in his *Poe: Journalist and Critic* (Baton Rouge: Louisiana State University Press, 1969), he recognized Poe's breadth as a generic critic. Both find Poe to be a hard-working magazinist who stressed the value of criticism for its own sake and who formulated critical principles of art throughout his life.

Since Prescott's edition, scholars have made notable contributions to our understanding of Poe's criticism, especially its influence, origins, and magazine milieu. This scholarship includes the following: (1) Poe's intimate knowledge of and reliance upon current periodical literature (Margaret Alterton, *The Origins of Poe's Critical Theory,* Iowa City: University of Iowa, 1925); (2) his debt to eighteenth-century ideas, especially the common-sense school of Scottish philosophy (Robert D. Jacobs, *Poe: Journalist and Critic);* (3) his importance in the development of literary theory throughout Europe, particularly Symbolism (Célestin P. Cambiaire, P. Cambiaire, *The Influence of Edgar Allan Poe in France,* New York: G.E. Stechert, 1927, and Carl L. Anderson, *Poe in Northlight: The Scandinavian Response to His Life and Work,* Durham, N.C.: Duke University Press, 1973); and his contributions to the theory and practice of short fiction (Arthur H. Quinn, "Edgar Allan Poe and the Establishment of the Short Story," *American Fiction: An Historical and Critical Survey,* New York: D. Appleton-Century, 1936, pp 77-101, and George D. Snell, "Poe," *The Shapers of American*

Fiction, 1798-1947, New York: E.P. Dutton, 1947, pp. 45-60). One recent collection of Poe's critical writings, but not nearly so complete as Prescott's, is *Literary Criticism of Edgar Allan Poe,* edited by Robert L. Hough (Lincoln: University of Nebraska Press, 1965). Two additional works of significant importance in shedding light upon Poe as critic are Sidney P. Moss, *Poe's Literary Battles: The Critic in the Context of His Literary Milieu* (Durham, N.C.: Duke University Press, 1963) and Michael Allen, *Poe and the British Magazine Tradition* (New York: Oxford University Press, 1969). For more references, see *Edgar Allan Poe: A Bibiography of Criticism, 1827-1967* compiled by Irby B. Cauthen, Jr., and J. Lasley Dameron (Charlottesville: University Press of Virginia, 1974) and checklists of criticism on Poe (beginning with the year 1967) presently available in issues of *Poe Studies.*

Bringing Professor Prescott's edition up to date does necessitate a few revisions in his introduction and notes. First, some comments in the introduction concerning Poe's cultural background should be modified. Recent scholars would argue that John Keats and Percy Shelley exerted more influence on Poe's critical thought than did Hazlitt and Wordsworth from whom (along with Coleridge), argues Prescott, Poe learned a great deal about criticism (xxxv). Poe's concept of the short poem was no doubt derived from a variety of sources, including Coleridge's *Biographia Literaria*—the one and only source proposed by Professor Prescott (xxxiii). Poe's reading was not wholly desultory, as Professor Prescott assumes, nor was his learning insufficient (xxvi). The most apparent inaccuracy Professor Prescott makes in his introduction is this blanket indictment of Poe's associates:

> But he [Poe] never had time or opportunity to come broadly in contact with the best, in men or books, and was thrown too much on his own resources. Except for Lowell, "he never met his intellectual equal in the flesh,"[1] being in this respect at a great disadvantage compared with his New England contemporaries, who

formed a mutually helpful group, and had in general greater opportunities both at home and abroad (xxv-xxvi).

To the contrary, recent scholars point to Poe's cultural opportunities and rich associations with people like John Pendleton Kennedy and George R. Graham. See, for example, Robert Jacobs, *Poe: Journalist and Critic,* and *The Courage of a Critic: Edgar Poe as Editor* (Baltimore: The Edgar Allan Poe Society, 1971); Arthur Hobson Quinn, *Edgar Allan Poe: A Critical Biography* (New York: D. Appleton-Century, 1941); and Richard Beale Davis, *Intellectual Life in Jefferson's Virginia* (Chapel Hill: University of North Carolina Press, 1964).

Secondly, in three instances Professor Prescott alludes to specific titles which Poe did not compose. Although included in the standard Virginia edition, the following reviews (see my note "Thomas Ollive Mabbott on the Canon of Poe's Reviews," *Poe Studies,* 5, Dec. 1972, p. 56) should not be attributed to Poe:

Professor Prescott in quoting from John Macy, "The Fame of Poe,"[1] *Atlantic Monthly,* 102 (Dec. 1908), 832. (1) G.W. Featherstonhaugh's *I Promessi Sposi* (xxii); (2) Bryant's *Poems* published in the *Southern Literary Messenger,* January, 1835, and in the Virginia edition, VIII, pp. 1-2 (*Notes,* 32:1, p. 327); and (3) *The Poems of Alfred Tennyson* appearing in *Graham's Magazine,* September, 1842, and in the Virginia edition, XI, pp. 127-131 (*Notes,* 253:23, p. 345).

Remarkably, only a few editorial changes are required to update this functional one-volume edition of Poe's criticism designed for classroom use. As critic, Professor Prescott was a pioneer in perceiving the breadth and independence of Poe's critical mind. At the same time, however, he recognized Poe's limitations and prejudices. In 1909, when his edition appeared, few Americans were aware of Poe's accomplished criticism. Even now, when we revere Poe as a leading American critic, no definitive edition of his essays and reviews exists.

J. Lasley Dameron
November 4, 1980

Mr. Poe is at once the most discriminating, philosophical, and fearless critic upon imaginative works who has written in America.

—James Russell Lowell, 1845

[Poe was] the finest of fine artists...He was the greatest journalistic critic of his time, placing good European work at sight when the European critics were waiting for somebody to tell them what to say.

—George Bernard Shaw, 1909

His literary articles and lectures, in fact,...surely constitute the most remarkable body of criticism ever produced in the United States...His prose is as taut as in his stories, but it has cast off the imagery of his fiction to become simply sharp and precise: our only first-rate classical prose of this period.

—Edmund Wilson, 1942

The aspect of his critical statements as a whole, from their hundred American titles to the inmost structure of his sentences, is that of a single gesture, not avoiding the trivial, to sweep all worthless chaff aside. It is a movement first and last to clear the GROUND...

His concern, the apex of his immaculate attack, was to detach a "method" from the smear of common usage—it is the work of nine tenths of his criticism. He struck to lay low the *"niaiseries"* of form and content with which his world abounded. It was a machine-gun fire; even in the slaughter of banality he rises to a merciless distinction....

—William Carlos Williams, 1925

He was the first committed, and perhaps still the greatest, American literary journalist on the high French model: a critical tradition represented today by Edmund Wilson and Malcolm Cowley...Poe's aesthetic theory has not been over-rated....

—Allen Tate, 1968

NEW INTRODUCTION

by
Eric W. Carlson
University of Connecticut

Every student of Poe will welcome this reprint edition, there being no other one-volume selection of Poe's criticism in print or in prospect for the near future. Both in its generous selection and in its editorial guidance, this anthology far surpasses the now out-of-print *Selections from Poe's Literary Criticism,* ed. John Brooks Moore (New York: F.S. Crofts & Co., 1926, xix, 199 pp.) and *Literary Criticism of Edgar Allan Poe,* ed. Robert L. Hough (Lincoln: University of Nebraska Press, 1965, xxviii, 155 pp.), though each has its special value. Prescott's edition is distinguished also by its long, excellent introduction, the many excerpts quoted therein, and the scholarly Notes. The Notes are particularly helpful: in addition to the customary source notes are definitions, emendations, and cross references, including some to the Harrison and the Stedman-Woodberry editions. Prescott, moreover, cites and freely quotes from the writings of Coleridge, Wordsworth, Hazlitt, Shelley, Longfellow, the Schlegels, and others, thus placing Poe in the context of some of the Romantics most influential on his thinking and writing. Finally, the reader will be pleasantly surprised to discover unsuspected riches under the general titles "Marginalia" and "Detached Passages" (a miscellany of review excerpts), which appear without any interpretative topical headings.

"What, then, is the value of Poe's criticism?" This question posed by Professor Prescott remains a challenge and deserves an answer that reflects the thinking of the past seventy years. No one will quarrel today with Prescott's modest claims that Poe's criticism is part of our literary history; that his theory of poetry and fiction has more than a passing value; and that it "may have a relative value in connection with his own original work." With Andrew Lang, whom he cites, Prescott believed that Poe's aesthetic theory was consistent with his imaginative writings, the latter a product of the former. Only occasionally has this view been questioned, and then chiefly on technical grounds—with reference, for example, to whether Poe's poetry exemplifies his views on meter and rhyme. As the selections in this volume are about evenly divided between theoretical and practical criticism, it is possible to study the relations of these in both directions, with an eye, however, to chronology. The chronological arrangement also encourages a developmental approach and interest.

For most readers the primary question undoubtedly is how much light Poe's criticism throws on his tales and poems. Apart from the Marginalia and the Detached Passages, nine of the thirteen main selections treat poetry; by comparison, Poe had less to say directly about fiction and drama, though that less is not insignificant. From 1831, when "Letter to B---" appeared, until his late lecture, "The Poetic Principle," he thought long and hard about the nature and function of poetry. As so well summarized by Prescott in part IV of his introduction, Poe distinguished true poetry from humorous verse, satiric verse, and verse drama; from "truth" as fact, statement, or moralizing; from "passion" or raw feeling, though he allowed transmuted feeling (cf. Wordsworth's "emotion recollected in tranquillity"). He defined the two fundamentals of poetry: (1) "poetic sentiment" as sensibility and inspiration; (2) artistic skill as the power of expression or craftsmanship. He distinguished fancy from imagination, the latter being synonymous with invention, novelty, and originality, but professed to disagree with Coleridge by claiming all creative imaginative acts to be "novel combinations" of known elements. Through a "chemical combination," or imaginative reaction, those elements are transformed into a new substance, a new realization. This process, he noted in "Letter to B---," took the form of intuitive insight, likened to seeing a star with half-closed eye or to viewing a painting with "the cursory glance of the connoisseur," that is, with the immediate intuitive certainty of the trained expert. Also significant are Poe's attack on didacticism (the "Heresy of the Lake School") and the concluding definition of poetry, with its emphasis on "music" as providing the essential "indefinite" quality of true poetry.

The review of Drake's "The Culprit Fay" (1836) introduces Poe's objections to literary chauvinism, a concern which led to a more mature view of literary nationalism in "Exordium" (1842). The descriptions of the poetic sentiment as a radiant Paradise and of Ideality as the sense of the beautiful, the sublime, the mystical (the Beauty of Earth and of Heaven) suggest the strong link in Poe's mind between poetry and the Neoplatonic, Transcendental conception of Beauty. The creative poet, however, must also have the power of stimulating the poetic sentiment in others through the "organs of Causality and Comparison," making the "poem as means" subject to rational control.

In January of the next year, the review of Bryant's *Poems* appeared. Of the half dozen poems considered, "The Ages" is chiefly critized for being defective in its meter according to the theory of "equalization," which Poe later developed into a long essay, "The Rationale of Verse." At this time, Poe made no reference to Bryant's essays on trisyllabic verse, essays which had helped establish Bryant as the country's foremost prosodist; but in his September 1834 critique of Halleck (*Works* 11:190-204) Poe revived the argument by rejecting Bryant's sensible position on "roughness" and "discords" as forms of variation.

The next review, of Moore's "Alciphron," is one of the most important in the entire Poe critical canon. Fancy and imagination are differentiated in the manner of Coleridge, whose *Biographia Literaria* Poe as well as Emerson had read with the highest admiration. The term "mystic," a borrowing from the Schlegels, is introduced to mean an "under or *suggestive*" current of meaning: "the *moral* of any sentiment is its mystic or secondary expression. It has the vast force of an accompaniment in music. This vivifies the air; that spiritualizes the *fanciful* conception, and lifts into the *ideal.*" Examples follow in the next paragraph (59). Then the analogy to music continues: "With each note of the lyre is heard a ghostly, and not always a distinct, but an august and soul-exalting *echo.* In every glimpse of beauty presented, we catch, through long and wild vistas, dim bewildering visions of a far more ethereal beauty beyond." A final allusion, to "the according tones of the accompaniment," completes the analogy to music as a way of describing the impressionistic effect made possible by the musical elements in poetry. This description is not only central to Poe's conception of poetry but also indicative of the essentially incantatory nature of his own best poems—"To Helen," "The City in the Sea," "Ulalume," "For Annie," "Eldorado"—resonant as they are with tonal, emotive, and thematic overtones. In several of the miscellaneous passages—on Tennyson (308-10), song-writing (295-99), and the older English poetry (308-10)—it is to this tonal impressionism that Poe attributes the "power" of lyric poetry and song.

The essay on Longfellow's *Ballads and Other Poems* (1842), also recognized as a landmark in American criticism, represents a decided advance over the earlier brief but caustic review of *Hyperion: A Romance* (1839) and the critique of *Voices of the Night* (1840), marred by the concluding charge of plagiarism. Objecting to Longfellow's tendency to inculcate a moral, Poe defines poetry as the expression of man's unquenchable "thirst for supernal BEAUTY." Two paragraphs beginning "Dividing the world of mind" (75) not only reinforce the distinction between "truth" and "beauty" in poetry but also define the tripartite self in terms of pure intellect, taste, and moral sense. These paragraphs are fundamental to any understanding of Poe's epistemology, his faith in intuitive insight, and the symbolism of his moral allegories, his poems and tales of psychic conflict. Poesy, Poe writes, is "not forbidden to moralise—in her fashion. She is not forbidden to depict—but to reason and preach of virtue," later adding that "a didactic moral might be happily made the *undercurrent* of a poetical theme" and labeling the error of didacticism as "essentially German." Beauty may be heightened into the sublime by forms of physical loveliness or by terror—the latter one of the few allusions in Poe's criticism to the function of terror in his work.

In "The Poetic Principle," his final and most developed essay on poetry, Poe borrows heavily from the 1842 review. Yet here he speaks with a new assurance on a series of related topics: the epic or long poem as an artistic anomaly, judged by "the effect it produces"; the unduly brief poem as lacking a sustained cumulative effect ("the steady pressing down of the stamp upon the wax"); the heresy of the Didactic; "the world of mind"; music in poetry; beauty as the "pleasurable elevation, or excitement, of *the soul.*" Here the passage on man's immortal instinct and unquenchable thirst for the Beauty above ends with the sad realization of "our inability to grasp *now,* wholly, here on earth, at once and forever, those divine and rapturous joys, of which *through* the poem, or *through* the music, we attain to but brief and indeterminate glimpses." And, he added near the end, it is through the sensuous beauties in nature and in woman that the poet nourishes his soul. As these beauties enable the poet to glimpse a vision of the supernal, so the poem itself stimulates the appreciator to experience, in some measure, the poet's trance-like ecstasy. Is this experience simply an experience, a psychic response that is only felt, with no transferable meaning, no undercurrent of *meaning?* Jacobs, (p. 442). Robert Jacobs further maintains that by 1845 Poe's "ideal" Beauty or Love could be realized only through music and lyric poetry.

The Marginalia essay on "psychal fancies" (275-78) is of first importance as a point of reference for the meaning of "brief, indeterminate glimpses," "dim, bewildering visions," "elevating excitement of the soul," etc. Not only does it clarify the term "psychal," which Poe coined, but also "supernal beauty." Indeed, it opens up a whole network of connections—forward to "The Poetic Principle," "Ulalume," "The Domain of Arnheim," and *Eureka,* and backward to "Ligeia," "Mesmeric Revelation," and the colloquies.

In the passages quoted so far, along with others yet to come, the recurrence-in-context of certain terms suggests their special significance in the criticism: *idea, ideal,* * *mystic, sublime, supernal, ethereal, spiritual, spirit, soul, vision, visionary, dream, sleep, sleep-waking, moral, moral energy, moral sentiment, vitality, Ideality, nature, natural, intense, intensity, fancy, fanciful, beautiful, imaginative, imitative, fantasy, wild,* * *sentiment, poetic sentiment, force, elevation, elevated, identity, truth, passion, original, originality, simplicity, harmony, effect, unity or totality of effect,* * *transcendental, psychal, dim, shadowy, indeterminate glimpses, nature, natural, artificial,* * *inartificial,* * *affectation,* * *hypochondriac,* * *capability,* * *indefinite,* * *vague, metaphysical, indefinitiveness, picturesque, arabesque, grotesque, grotesquerie, bizarre, bizarrerie, point, quaint, impression, totality of impression* (those marked * were discussed by Robert Jacobs in a lecture on Poe's critical vocabulary. See also J. Lasley Dameron and Louis C. Stagg, *An Index to Poe's Critical Vocabulary, 1966).* Many of these are also part of Poe's metaphoric or symbolic vocabulary in the poems, tales, colloquies, and allegories, in which, by repetition, Poe turns certain other words, phrases, and images into motifs or partial symbols—words such as *eye, hand, voice, low voice, hair, angelic, holy, "born again," will, divine.* In the criticism and the imaginative writings, these vocabularies function as a kind of artistic-critical inter-textual fabric or frame of reference.

The "figures in the carpet" of Poe's writings have yet to be fully studied out, especially the subtle patterns weaving in and out of the symbolic gothic stories. (Poe's use of the term and the image of the *arabesque* has been analyzed by David Ketterer in *The Rationale of Deception in Poe,* 1979, actually less for "deception" than for artistic indirection in Poe's visionary quest. See also my "Poe's Vision of Man" in *Papers on Poe,* ed. R.P. Veler, 1972.)

"The Philosophy of Composition" has been called "one of the most masterly examples of literary criticism in the language." Certainly, if measured by its impact on Baudelaire, Mallarmé, Valéry, Par Lagerkvist, Vladimir Mayakovsky, and Gottfried Benn, among many others, it is Poe's most influential essay. Regardless of whether it is "a hoax, or a piece of self-deception, or a more or less accurate record," T.S. Eliot notes, it led Valéry to ask "What am I doing when I write a poem?" Thus Poe's essay acquired "capital importance" for Eliot, as did Poe's work as a whole when seen through the eyes of the three French writers. (T.S. Eliot, "From Poe to Valéry," *Hudson Review,* Autumn 1949, reprinted in *"The Recognition of Edgar Allan Poe,* ed. E.W. Carlson, 1966. See also "E.A. Poe and the Aesthetics of Work" in Carl Fehrman, *Poetic Creation: Inspiration or Craft,* 1980.)

In describing Poe's qualifications as a critic (xii-xvi), Prescott states that Poe was endowed with both the analytical faculty and the poetic gift, that for him criticism and poetry were one. As demonstrated in this introduction also, the creative process to Poe depended on conscious artistry and control as well as sensibility and intuitive insight. When the vulgar theory of romantic inspiration degenerated into a distrust of rational controls, Poe sought to correct the bias or imbalance by extolling disciplined craftsmanship. Unfortunately, he claimed to have reduced the whole process to "the precision and rigid consequence of a mathematical problem." In reality, Poe the polemicist and analyst was not able to suppress Poe the intuitive poet. For example, when he insists that the poem be neither too long nor too short, so that it "intensely excites, by elevating, the soul" and such excitements must, of "psychal necessity," be brief, one wonders how the composing poet realizes this psychal intensity while in a state of cool calculation. Similarly, with his choices of a preconceived effect, of a sad tone, a refrain, and a theme—all seem to be of unconscious origin rather than of any "unquestionably" right conscious decision, the adverb begging the question, in any event.

In "The Rationale of Verse" Poe set forth another problematic theory, this time of versification. Because of its length (167-228), its thesis, and the opposite reactions it has engendered, it deserves more than passing comment. Although Prescott merely quotes the views of Stedman and Woodberry in his introduction (ix), his Notes (337-40) are excellent. Still standard as a critique is the chapter on Poe in Gay Wilson Allen's *American Prosody*. The most scholarly edition by far, complete with textual and critical notes, and cognate documents, is J. Arthur Greenwood's (Princeton: Wolfhart Book Co., 1968). Richard A. Rand, another student of the literature on prosody, in French and Spanish as well as English, has found that Poe's radical system (along with his verse) is "a real thorn in the side of Continental and Anglo-American Formalism and Structuralism."

In his review of Bryant's *Poems* in January 1837, and in his call for a "Prosody Raisonnée" (279), Poe already had conceived his theory of "equalization," although in the review he vacillated between "heresies" and desirable "deviations from the strict rules of prosodial art." Now, in simplifying metrics to a metronomic five-foot line, each foot of equal duration, he attempts to naturalize and rationalize the form of verse (as line) on the basis of quantity rather than stress. Not denying the presence of the "accentual," to a degree, he proposes a quantitative definition of meter within the "flow" of the line, as in music, so that each foot is equal in duration. Therefore, there can be no legitimate trisyllabic feet except as two short syllables (with one long) may be equivalent in time to the one short syllable in an iambic foot; such a foot would be a "bastard" iamb and its reverse a "quick" trochee. In verse, "an inferior or less capable Music, there is, happily, little chance for complexity" (178). In other words, through the incantatory effect of monotone, as in a refrain, "slightly varying the phrase at each repetition," a cumulative expressionism is achieved in the successive waves of distended sound. In his Marginalia essay on Tennyson (262-64, December 1844), Poe defined the suggestiveness of "the true music" in poetry: "a suggestive indefinitiveness of meaning with the view of bringing about a definitiveness of vague and therefore of spiritual effect..." Suggestiveness, of course, became a fundamental tenet of the American transcendental aesthetic as expounded by Emerson and Whitman, and exemplified by Emerson's artistic essays, Whitman's *Leaves of Grass,* Thoreau's *Walden,* and the fiction of Hawthorne and Melville. It became the key concept also of French Symbolist poetics derived from Poe's Ideal Beauty, undertones of meaning *(les symboles* suggesting *les correspondances),* indefiniteness *(la poésie pure),* musical evocativeness *(la magie verbale),* etc. (See Krishna Rayan, "Edgar Allan Poe and 'Suggestiveness'" *British Journal of Aesthetics 9* (1969), 73-79. See also Prescott's note, p. 342, on 236:22. The best analysis is the long chapter on Poe's theory and poetry of the Vague in *The Theory and Practice of the Vague: A Study in a Mode of Nineteenth Century Lyric Poetry* by Joseph B. Cary, Jr. Ph. D. dissertation, New York University, 1962. Cary relates Poe's "poetic mesmerism" of "pure" sound, metrical regularity, echo effects, monotone, and smoothness of flow to the Bergsonian concept of consciousness as "a flux of fleeting shadows merging into each other.")

The essay on Hawthorne's *Twice-Told Tales* (1842), praised by Tate as a brilliant statement of the necessity of organic unity in fiction, is here supplemented by passages on "intended effect" (320), "totality of effect" (312), "totality of beauty" (311), allegory) (318), the qualities of a good plot (306, 310, 311, 320), Dickens' *The Old Curiosity Shop* (313), and Poe's own *Tales* (1845). At a time when criticism of fiction was in its infancy, Poe has some good things to say about the novel and especially the tale in the six volumes of book reviews (Harrison edition), the volume of sketches *(Autography* and *Literati),* the *Marginalia,* and an occasional letter. Poe's Art of Fiction has yet to be assembled from this mass of material, rich with insights on plot, verisimilitude, unity, originality, character, tone, and style.

In his introduction and notes (xlvi-l, 331-32) Prescott offers a cogent summary and comment on this essay. The tale of effect is governed by the same artistic impressionism, the same empirical psychology, as operates in the poem. As a source of unity, plot is secondary and "intended effect" primary, the unity of effect being an "immense force derivable from *totality.*" The "exaltation of the soul cannot be long sustained"; yet "there must be dropping of the water upon the rock." In both poem and tale, intense imaginative consciousness is the mode for glimpsing the supernal (319).

After quoting Poe's famous definition of the tale (xlix; 94-95; cf. 310), Prescott surmises that the method of composition, "strikingly similar" to the method elaborated in "The Philosophy of Composition," probably describes Poe's writing of his own tales. Both essays in method undoubtedly represent "the subsequent analysis of a mental process more or less unconscious and indeliberate" (Prescott, introduction, p. 1). On the face of it, Poe's wording implies a reductionist rational or technical theory of art in that the deliberately preconceived effect is developed by invented and combined incidents until "a picture is at length painted..." In the quoted phrase, however, there is at least a mild suggestion of an organic view, of an unfolding effect—of the picture in the process of becoming. Furthermore, if the "effect" is modal or emotional rather than preconceivedly thematic, then the story may not be wholly predetermined in meaning or in final formal structure. In contrast to his own "romantic expressionism" (Tate's term), Poe complains that Hawthorne's tales (of 1837) lacked variety of tone and subject, and in his 1847 review he deplores Hawthorne's dependence on allegory. On the other hand, from his comments on "Wakefield" and "The Minister's Black Veil," it seems that Poe badly misread some of Hawthorne's tales.

In 1847, after the publication of *Mosses from an Old Manse* (1846), Poe again reviewed Hawthorne's tale-writing. Except for the four paragraphs on "the tale proper," essentially unchanged from the 1842 essay, this critique takes another look at Hawthorne. After an account of Hawthorne's lack of public recognition, it presents a new argument for "legitimate originality" as distinguished from "absolute novelty of combination." Then comes this definition:

> The true originality—true in respect of its purposes—is that which, in bringing out the half-formed, the reluctant, or the unexpressed fancies of mankind, or in exciting the more delicate pulses of the heart's passion, or in giving birth to some universal sentiment or instinct in embryo, thus combines with the pleasurable effect of *apparent* novelty, a real egoistic delight.

By contrast, Poe contends, Hawthorne's allegorical strain "completely overwhelms the greater number of his subjects," unlike the allegory that is "properly handled, judiciously subdued, seen only as a shadow or by suggestive glimpses..." Therefore, Hawthorne is "peculiar and *not* original," with a fondness for allegory and the mystical that is traceable to the influences of New England transcendentalism. Today, most students of Hawthorne, far from deploring "the mysticism of his Goodman Browns and White Old Maids," find the best tales rich with subtle subliminal and moral allusiveness.

Poe's criticism of the novel is here represented by only three review passages on Bulwer-Lytton's *Night and Morning* (312), Dickens' *The Old Curiosity Shop* (313), and plot in Godwin and Bulwer (320). A careful study of Poe's views of the novel as a genre would require a close reading of the review essays in the Harrison edition, among them these: Theodore Fay's *Norman Leslie,* Baron de la Motte Fouqué's *Undine,* Bulwer-Lytton's *Night and Morning, Rienzi,* and *The Last Days of Pompeii,* Scott's *The Bride of Lammermoor,* Dickens' *Barnaby Rudge,* Catherine Sedgwick's *Hope Leslie* and *The Linwoods,* Beverly Tucker's *George Balcombe,* Cooper's *Wyandotté,* Robert Bird's *Calavar, Sheppard Lee,* and *The Hawks of Hawk-Hollow,* Simms *The Partisan* and *The Damsel of Darien,* and John Pendleton Kennedy's *Swallow Barn* and *Horse-Shoe Robinson.* There are also reviews of sketches by Dickens, Washington Irving, and A.B. Longstreet. Beginning with mildly critical appraisals, Poe sometimes descends to personalities (his so-called "tomahawk" criticism), though even in his devastating piecc on Fay's *Norman Leslie,* he also offers a brilliant analysis of Fay's usage. From 1839 to 1842 he weighs the novel for its appeal to a wide, popular audience as well as to the few who appreciate "totality of beauty." He concerns himself with "true construction," achieved by determining first the effect, then the cause (as in his theory of the tale), perfection of plot (not merely "involution of circumstance" or incident), coincidence, character, originality, verisimilitude, tone, diction, metaphor, style, allegory, and grammar. Usually, he supports his judgments, especially if negative, with analysis, specific examples, and comparative estimates. Like Emerson, he favors a clear, functional style over fancy rhetoric, and the novel of character over the novel of intrigue and costume. Unlike present-day writers, he believed in "the commenting power" of the author as the primary source of unity.

Poe's criticism of the drama is represented very generously by the short pieces on Shakespeare's Hamlet (316), the Greek drama (286), and the 42-page essay on the American drama. In his 1839 review of Willis's *Tortesa, the Usurer* Poe charted new ground by taking this literary form seriously and by analyzing technique, incident, character, and language. Poe's reviews of Broadway plays distinguished the theatrical from the dramatic, the conventional from the inventive, the actable play from the closet drama, the plays of character from the plays of intrigue. As a magazinist in touch with the trends of his times, he sensed the need for a new American form based on a new grasp of "the capabilities of the drama" and on a shift in the creative process that would discipline Feeling and Taste with Reason and Common Sense. His call for a guiding "Natural Art" of the drama was tantamount to a plea for a rationale, a principled generic criticism.

In "The American Drama" (1845) Poe's critique of *Tortesa,* after an extended plot synopsis, emphasizes Willis's excessive use of intrigue and underplots, judged by the standard of organic plot. This play is also found deficient in its undeveloped characters, its improbabilities, overuse of asides, and trite conclusion. Only in his final paragraph does he mention its "capital points" and warmly praise its author. Next, Poe analyzes Longfellow's *The Spanish Student* as being weak in its denouement, its poetry, and its claims to originality. An unsparing summary of the author's "utter and radical want of the adapting or constructive power" is followed by a striking series of examples of stock incidents. Among other defects, four examples of bad grammar are cited, on two of which Poe's reasoning is erroneous. In conclusion, Poe finds meritorious only the poetic passages, and objects to the hybrid character of the play: "Let a poem be a poem only; let a play be a play and nothing more." (For Poe's knowledge and criticism of the drama, see Robert Jacobs, 377-87, and N. Bryllion Fagin, *The Histrionic Mr. Poe* (Baltimore, John Hopkins Press, 1949), ch. III.)

"Exordium" (1842) is Poe's best statement on the nature and function of criticism as a genre. Published at midcareer, it was preceded and followed by other statements, satires, and miscellaneous commentaries on the critical function and the low quality of criticism at the time. A few of his commentaries touch on the nature of plagiarism (269), the need for negative criticism (271), the difference between analyzing and enjoying a work of art (306), and "totality of beauty" for the few (311). It was a time when criticism was still a vague field of thought, despite the new ground charted by the Scottish, French, German, and British aesthetic philosophers, Coleridge in particular. To criticize a literary work, Poe held, is to analyze it not for its opinion, as in an essay or philosophical speculation, but for its "mode" or vehicle of expression of those opinions. A true "review" requires an analysis—"a deliberate perusal, with notes, and subsequent generalization," not merely "the cant of *generality.*" In his review of Longfellow's *Ballads,* also 1842, Poe maintained that "every work of art should contain within itself all that is requisite for its own comprehension." Because of this emphasis on the "poem *per se*" and on the analysis of the object of art, Poe has been hailed as "First of the New Critics" by George Snell *(Quarterly Review of Literature,* II, 330-40).

The earlier "Prospectus for the Penn Magazine" (1840) proclaimed the need for "an absolutely independent criticism" guided only by "the purest rules of Art," in contrast to the personal bias and cant of the literary coteries. The mutual puffing of books by editors and reviewers led Poe to praise L.A. Wilmer for "The Quacks of Helicon" (1841), a satiric exposé of the corrupt, clique-ridden system that created and destroyed reputations. In "The Literary Life of Thingum Bob, Esq." (1844), Poe offered his own parody of the quackery and collusion within the literary establishment. And in "The Literati" (1846) he characterized the most popular writers as charlatans and toadies who pestered editors until they received favorable notices totally at odds with private, honest opinions of their work. Sidney Moss, in *Poe's Literary Battles: The Critic in the Context of His Literary Milieu* (1963), describes the long war that Poe waged so militantly in defense of traditional critical standards. He developed "critical principles and practices that, for America, were unprecedented and brilliant—brilliant enough for him to be called our first great critic" (246). In the process, however, because the hucksters of commercialized journalism were then in the ascendant and made Poe the prime target of their venom and the most scurrilous of personal ridicule, they succeeded in inflicting upon him the loss of prestige, employment, and income until he was virtually hounded out of the profession.

As a "magazinist," Poe of course worked as editor, reviewer, critic, and fiction writer for the American weeklies. Under the title "Magazine-Writing—Peter Snook," he praised "the true Magazine spirit" and predicted that magazine literature would become "the *most* influential of all departments of Letters." One of his Marginalia for December 1846 draws a sharp distinction between the Magazine Literature of America and that of the British Quarterly Reviews, the latter described as stilted, verbose, ponderous, inaccessible, and of interest to the few only, whereas the magazines satisfy the need for "the curt, the condensed, the pointed, the readily diffused." As with "the tale of effect" and the poetry of "spiritual effect," here Poe is quick to sense the emergence of a new form and style. That he was also conscious of it as an *American* essay style serving a new audience need underscores the functional test by which he rejected the conventional rhetoric of the British quarterlies. The clarity and incisiveness of Poe's own nonfiction prose brought forth from Edmund Wilson and William Carlos Williams the tributes quoted at the beginning of this introduction. Since Sidney Moss's 1963 account of Poe as critic in the context of this milieu, several other studies have appeared that recognize the influence of the journalistic experience on Poe: Edd Winfield Parks, *Edgar Allan Poe as Literary Critic* (1964); Michael Allen, *Poe and the British Magazine Tradition* (1969); Robert D. Jacobs, *Poe: Journalist and Critic (1969);* Stuart Levine, *Edgar Poe: Seer and Craftsman* (1972); Sidney P. Moss, *Poe's Major Crisis: His Libel Suit and New York's Literary World* (1970);

Roger Forclaz, *Le Monde d'Edgar Poe* (Berne, 1974); Claude Richard, *Edgar Allan Poe: Journaliste et Critique* (Paris, 1978).

It is a mistake, however, to conclude that Poe's imaginative writing also is essentially journalistic or magazinist in purpose and quality. When Poe warned against "the dogma that no work of fiction can fully suit, at the same time, the critical and the popular taste," he was reviewing Dickens' *Barnaby Rudge,* the vast popularity of which he attributed to the author's application of "certain well-understood critical propositions." Neither popularity nor sales success could be an adequate test of literary value. The distinction clearly reflects Poe's awareness of different kinds of audience response and different levels of meaning as consciously or subconsciously "intended." All the evidence points to the fact that in his poems and tales, as well as in his criticism, Poe is not simply literalist or "Gothicist," "Romantic" or German "Romantic Ironist," "Rationalist" or "Demonist," "Idealist" or "Absurdist." No one of these labels or narrow approaches can account for the variety, complexity, and depth, or the symbolic, psychological, and moral dimensions of his imaginative writings. In fact, the reader of this introduction may have noted that, in Poe's aesthetic, elements not only of the classical and romantic, but of the modern as well, are generously represented. His anticipation of a modern, truly creative artistic function has yet to be adequately defined in terms of such elements as the impressionistic use of image, sound, tone, and rhythm, both in the poems and the tales; the organic "unity of effect" or "harmony of elements" in a work of art; the theory of the Vague ("indefinitiveness," "suggestiveness"); motif, symbol, and "subdued" allegory as figures in the carpet; the subconscious or intuitive origin of creative ideas; the aesthetic experience as an intense imaginative realization; psychic conflict as a consequence of disintegration within the individual and within society (see "The Colloquy of Monos and Una"); the mediating function of "Taste" or "poetic intellect" in the "world of mind"; the "moral" or volitional self as crucial to the process of individuation, to the search for the "soul," the reintegrated, primal self; cognitive and moral values as "undercurrents" in poetry and fiction; psychal transcendentalism as a visionary experience; the individual's relation to the organic Whole, "identity with God," with "the universal Ens," "the Divine Will." These are some of the significant emphases that link Poe's writings, critical and imaginative, to authentic modernism in literature, art, and philosophy.

Prescott's conclusion that "his criticism adds something which none but Poe could have added..." seems overmodest in the light of the remarkable consistency, continuity, psychological insight, and philosophic perspective that distinguish the critical writings. Both Poe and Emerson, more than any of their contemporaries, tried to define an aesthetic consonant with the American experience, with the universally human, and with "the general intention of Nature." For them, an honest, principled criticism would help assure the future of democracy and the arts.

Eric W Carlson
November 4, 1980

Index to MARGINALIA (pp. 257-307)

Index to APPENDIX: DETACHED PASSAGES (308-322)

Eric W. Carlson

PREFACE

THE principle of selection in the present volume is to include such reviews and passages as may have interest, first, because they have general critical value; or, secondly, because they throw light on Poe's own poetry or fiction; or, thirdly, because they give interesting estimates of contemporary writers who are still read. Not all that is worth reading for these purposes can be included in one volume. The essays in the text, however, are supplemented by many passages quoted in the Introduction and Notes. In particular Sections IV and V of the Introduction aim to summarize Poe's theories of poetry and fiction mainly by means of quotation.

Whatever, in general, may be the advisability of selection, no apologies need be made in the present case. Poe's critical writings are extensive, those only which have been collected filling several volumes in the standard editions. Of this large mass of material — written by a professional reviewer for periodical publication — much is still interesting, — while perhaps more is ephemeral, trifling, and valueless. The ordinary reader, therefore, will judge Poe's critical faculty less justly in the collected editions than in a selection of the best reviews and passages. Moreover, Poe himself constantly practiced a sort of selection; he tacitly divided his work into two classes, discarding what was ephemeral after one publication, detaching and using again what was of lasting interest. In general material thus used more than once forms the best part of Poe's criticism.

Except in two cases — the reviews of Drake's *Culprit Fay* and of Bryant's *Poems* — the articles are given without omission. From the scraps of the *Marginalia*, however, only those having special critical value are selected. The Appendix includes detached passages which are interesting in themselves or for comparison.

The text, in the case of articles from *Burton's Gentleman's Magazine*, from *Graham's Magazine*, from the *American Review*, and from *Sartain's Union Magazine* — the larger part of the whole — is that of the original periodicals; in the others it is that of the Virginia edition of Poe's Works, — for the use of which grateful acknowledgment is made to the publishers of this edition, Messrs. T. Y. Crowell and Company. Unless otherwise indicated the notes refer to this edition throughout. Since this edition closely follows the originals, the pieces are all here reprinted practically as they were published, obvious misprints alone being corrected. It has been thought best carefully to preserve capitals, italics, and punctuation. In a conventionalized dress Poe loses much of his individuality. He employed capitals and italics freely for emphasis, and punctuated with care. He had his "philosophy of point" and believed that "a sentence may be deprived of half its force — its spirit — by improper punctuation." The punctuation in particular, therefore, is Poe's own.

PREFACE

My thanks are due to Professor G. E. Woodberry for valued information; and to Professor J. M. Hart for access to *Sartain's Magazine*.

F. C. PRESCOTT.

ITHACA, NEW YORK

INTRODUCTION

As a poet and as a writer of prose tales Edgar Allan Poe has a secure position in literature. Though there are objectors and detractors, on the whole this position is recognized by critics, American and foreign; and by the great body of readers too — as frequent new editions of the poems and tales show. As a critic Poe has not found equal recognition. The critical writings which form the third and by far the largest division of his work are little read and seldom reprinted. They are perhaps generally thought of as hack articles which furnished a means of livelihood to Poe the poet; which may have had readers and influence in their time; — but which are now out of date and negligible even by admirers of Poe's poetry and fiction. The critical writings, however, like everything else connected with Poe's life and work, have been the subject of wide differences of opinion. According to Stedman, for example, the *Rationale of Verse* is "a curious discussion of mechanics now well enough understood," and "reads as if addressed to a metrical kindergarten";[1] according to Professor Saintsbury it is "one of the best things ever written on English prosody and quite astonishingly original."[2] In the opinion of Mr. Henry James Poe's critical work is "probably the most complete and exquisite specimen of provincialism

[1] *Works*, Stedman and Woodberry, vol. vi, p. xiv.

[2] *History of Literary Criticism*, vol. iii, p. 635.

ever prepared for the edification of men"[1]; in the opinion of J. M. Robertson it "will better stand critical examination to-day than any similar work produced in America or England in his time."[2] What, then, is the value of Poe's criticism? In the face of opposing views the reader must answer the question for himself. The material in controversy — at least the best and most characteristic parts of it — is presented in the present volume. The following introduction attempts, by discussing Poe's qualifications as a critic and by summarizing his critical theory, to facilitate an answer.

The value of Poe's critical work, whatever it may be, lies in three possible directions. In the first place "as a part of our literary history, it has," Stedman allows, "a very decided value." Poe lived in the first original period of American literature; as a professional critic he reviewed as they came out the works of Bryant, Longfellow, and Hawthorne. His opinion of these writers and even of their less-remembered contemporaries has at least historical interest. Comment on *The Minister's Black Veil* by the author of *William Wilson* is worth having. Again, Poe's expressions on poetry and prose fiction may have absolute as well as historical value. Poe may have made a permanent contribution, not only to the body of poetry, but to the body of poetical theory. A poet's slowly elaborated definition of poetry should not be dismissed lightly. Finally Poe's essays on poetry and fiction may have a relative value in connection with his own original work. One of the foremost authorities on

[1] *Hawthorne*, p. 62.

[2] *New Essays Toward a Critical Method*, p. 111.

Poe, it is true, considers Poe's essays on poetry empty and second-hand, and without important bearing on his own poetry. If, however, Poe developed his poetical theory carefully and independently, and if, as Mr. Andrew Lang believes,[1] Poe, unlike most poet-critics, was true to his theory — then his poetical theory becomes the best commentary on his poetical product. And the same is true of his theory of the prose tale. Before discussing these theories, however, let us try to ascertain Poe's qualifications as a critic.

I

Where are we to look, Wordsworth asks,[2] "for that union of qualifications which must necessarily exist before the decisions of a critic can be of absolute value? — for a mind at once poetical and philosophical?" "Among those, and those only," he replies, "who, never having suffered their youthful love of poetry to remit much of its force, have applied to the consideration of the laws of this art the best power of their understanding." Poe — along it is true with various other qualities untoward — possessed this union of qualifications. He never lost his youthful love of poetry; and he applied to the consideration of the laws of poetry the best power of his understanding. He had in kind, if not in degree, the same

[1] *Letters to Dead Authors*, p. 134.

[2] In the *Essay Supplementary to the Preface;* which, by the way, Poe read; see 4 : 29, 6 : 25, notes. This class, Wordsworth says in the context, includes also the most erroneous and perverse critics — but it includes *all* of the best. Cf. quotations from Poe in 1 : 2, note.

qualities in combination which made great critics of Dryden and Coleridge; he had "a mind at once poetical and philosophical."

Poe was a poet not merely in the sense that he left poetry of enduring value — as we have taken for granted — but also in the sense that poetry was, if not the sole, at least the highest and most lasting interest of his life. Unlike other American writers of his time, he was a man of letters and nothing else. He made his living by literature and devoted his entire energy to it from first to last. And he devoted himself most unreservedly to what he considered highest in literature — that is, to poetry. Though the "events not to be controlled" which played so large a part in his life prevented him from accomplishing what he wished in "the field of his choice," he could say in the Preface of 1845: "With me poetry has been not a purpose, but a passion."[1] Poe himself believed the poetic gift essential to the critic. The poet is not necessarily a critic; but the critic must be a poet. "Poets," he says, "are by no means necessarily judges of poetry, but nothing is more certain than that, to be a judge of poetry, it is necessary at least to have the poetic sentiment, if not the poetic power — the 'vision' if not the 'faculty divine.'"[2]

Combined with and dominating Poe's poetic sentiment was his logical or "ratiocinative" faculty. It is not, ac-

[1] See 149 : 12.

[2] See 1 : 2, and note. "The vision and the faculty divine," occurs in Wordsworth's *Excursion*, Book I. Poe perhaps got it from Coleridge's *Biographia Literaria*, chap. xviii, where it is quoted.

cording to Poe himself, remarkable to find these two powers in combination; indeed "the *truly* imaginative mind," he says, "is never otherwise than analytic."[1] Poe was conscious of possessing this logical faculty; he cultivated it and gloried in it. It was perhaps his most characteristic mental feature. The analytical powers, — he says in a passage in which, as is often the case when he is discussing character even in fiction, he has more than half in mind his own character — the analytical powers "are always to their possessor, when inordinately possessed, a source of the liveliest enjoyment. As the strong man exults in his physical ability, delighting in such exercises as call his muscles into action, so glories the analyst in that moral activity which disentangles."[2] This faculty Poe applied to every subject which he treated. In every subject he sought the philosophy or rationale.[3] "It is the curse of a certain order of mind," says Poe, thinking again of his own mind, "that it can never rest satisfied with the consciousness of its ability to do a thing. Still less is it content with doing it. It must both know and show how it is done."[4] Thus Poe, being a poet,

[1] *Murders in the Rue Morgue*, *Works*, vol. iv, p. 146.

[2] *Ibid.*

[3] Cf. "the philosophy of point," *Works*, vol. xvi, p. 130; "the philosophy of music," vol. x, p. 41; "The Philosophy of Furniture"; "The Philosophy of Composition"; "The Rationale of Verse." *Landor's Cottage* is an analysis or formula of the ideal landscape, *The Cask of Amontillado* of the perfect revenge.

[4] *Works*, vol. xvi, p. 40 (264 : 21). Cf. Coleridge, *Table Talk*, March 1, 1834: "I am by the law of my nature a reasoner. . . . I can take no interest whatever in hearing or saying a thing merely as a fact. . . . I require in everything what for lack of an-

inevitably theorized, or criticised, poetry. Indeed to Poe poetry itself was largely a matter of logic.[1] It was the result of a reconciliation of "genius with artistic skill."[2] The most profound art is "based both in instinct and *analysis*."[3] He would have admitted perhaps that certain effects in poetry and music are "simply out of the reach of analysis."[4] But in a large sense analysis is the highest activity of the mind, and criticism is above poetry itself. Or criticism includes poetry, as the greater the less. "Theory and practice are in so much *one*, that the former implies or includes the latter. If the practice fail it is because the theory is imperfect." "To say that a critic could not have written the work which he criticises, is to put forth a contradiction in terms."[5] What we call poetic "creation" is only poetic practice which should be directed and dominated by the higher theory. Thus Poe was not only a poet, but by the law of his nature a critic of poetry. And there was, in his mind, not the slightest hostility between the creative and the critical

other word, I may call *propriety*, — that is, a reason why the thing *is* at all, and why it is *there* and *then* rather than elsewhere or at another time."

[1] Cf. Coleridge, *Biographia Literaria*, chap. i: "That poetry, even that of the loftiest and, seemingly, that of the wildest odes, had a logic of its own, as severe as that of science," etc. And Wordsworth, *Letters*, vol. ii, p. 313: "The logical faculty has infinitely more to do with poetry," etc.

[2] *Works*, vol. xiii, p. 129.

[3] *Works*, vol. xvi, p. 150 (301 : 31).

[4] *Works*, vol. x, p. 41.

[5] *Works*, vol. xi, p. 39; vol. xvi, p. 69 (268 : 26); cf. vol. xvi, p. 66 (266 : 14).

faculties; "it is nonsense to assert that the highest genius would not be benefited by attention to its modes of manifestation." [1]

The same logical analysis which Poe applied to his own work he employed when he was called upon to criticise the work of others. To him criticism was a science. "Shall we so term it?" he asks in *Graham's Magazine* as early as 1842.[2] He objects to the puffery, vague opinion, and generalization, which formed the staple of the reviews of his day. He believes the criticism of a book to be the "passing of judgment upon its merits or defects." [3] And this judgment must be reasoned. The opinion of Southey, for example, is worth "only just so much as it demonstrates." [4] Wilson again lacks the first requisite for the critic, — viz., principles, analysis, and demonstration.[5] Poe himself endeavors to be "the just critic who reasons his way." He defends himself, in the "Reply to Outis," against the charge of having descended to personal abuse or to "mangling by wholesale." "No man," he boasts, "can point to a single critique, among the very numerous ones which I have written during the last ten years, which is either wholly fault-finding or wholly in approbation; nor is there an instance to be discovered, among all that I have published, of my having set forth, either in praise or censure, a single opinion upon any critical topic of moment, without attempting, at least, to give it authority by something that wore the

[1] *Works*, vol. xiii, p. 195.
[2] *Works*, vol. xi, p. 1 (65 : 12).
[3] *Works*, vol. xi, p. 3 (67 : 19).
[4] *Works*, vol. x, p. 225.
[5] *Works*, vol. xii, p. 241.

semblance of a reason. Now is there a writer in the land," he asks, "who, having dealt in criticism even one-fourth as much as myself, can of his own criticisms conscientiously say the same?"[1] The boast is not an empty one. Allowance must always be made in Poe's reviews (as will appear later) for various kinds of unreasonableness — not so much for deliberate injustice, as for ignorance, and crotchet, and prejudice. One, however, who has read through Poe's critical writings, which extend from 1831 to his death, and which were written in different places and for many different periodicals — which were produced, that is, during a long period and under circumstances very unfavorable to uniformity of judgment — a reader of this mass of material is struck by the remarkable consistency which runs through the whole work.[2] This consistency can only be due to the fact that Poe clearly formulated critical principles and applied them to his varying subjects with precision.

Poe, then, had a rare combination of qualities for criticism: he was a poet and an analyst. And just as his typical tales, for example *The Pit and the Pendulum* and *Ligeia*, are the result of unusual emotional and imaginative states of mind, first experienced and subsequently analyzed and rationalized; so his criticism has interest and value, because it is the work of an imaginative and poetical mind gifted with the strange power of, so to speak, looking coolly on and subjecting its products and processes to logical analysis.

[1] *Works*, vol. xii, p. 85.

[2] References in the notes from one review to another will substantiate this. See, for example, 234 : 2, note.

II

If, to the great natural gifts just mentioned, had been added others of perhaps a lower order —judgment, deliberation, fairness, knowledge — and if, further, circumstances in general had been more favorable, Poe might have become a critic of the first rank. As it was, weaknesses of character and equipment, "events not to be controlled" in his own life, and limitations belonging to the period in which his life was spent, prevented this highest development.

In the first place overweening confidence in his own intellect, in his ability to master everything from a cryptogram to the cosmogony by sheer reasoning power, led Poe to overestimate and abuse a valuable faculty. His intellect was too often untempered by taste, common sense, and human feeling. He often seems blindly and willfully bent on carrying out preconceived theories to conclusions which he himself must have felt to be false. This was a source of critical error. For example, originality was in Poe's theory an indispensable mark of poetic genius. The originality of *The Sinless Child* by Elizabeth Oakes Smith "must forever entitle it," in Poe's judgment, "to the admiration and respect of every competent critic." Longfellow's *Rain in Summer* is "plagiarized" from this admirable poetess.[1] Poe's frequent charges of plagiarism, by the way, were due, not so much to jealousy, or, as Briggs thought,[2] to mere monomania, as to the fact that by a process of reasoning he reached the conclusion

[1] *Works*, vol. xiii, p. 86; vol. xii, p. 233.

[2] Woodberry, *Poe* (1885), p. 228.

that originality was the first requisite of poetry and then resolutely tested each new poem for this quality. There is something wrong in *à priori* reasoning which attributes this mark of genius to Mrs. Smith and denies it to Longfellow.

Again Poe never had quite time to do competent criticism. He took his reviewing seriously, it is true: he was conscientious and painstaking. He objects to the practice of English reviewers who, neglecting to read the book under review, make it the occasion for an original disquisition on the same subject; this is not criticism.[1] He objects to the vagueness and generality of contemporary reviewers,[2] and fills — even overburdens — his own reviews with specific analysis and quotation — in fact this is one of the ear-marks of his work, and leaves no room for doubt as to his having read the book under discussion. "We are patient, and have gone through the whole book with the most dogged determination,"[3] he says of some third-rate novel; and in this and other cases he shows his honesty by giving a careful summary of the plot. At the same time all Poe's criticism was piecework and hackwork — written to order, often hurriedly, on all sorts of books, as the exigencies of his profession demanded. At the close of the excellent article on *Barnaby Rudge* he fears he has written without due deliberation; "for, alas! the hurried duties of the journalist preclude it."[4] For the *Broadway Journal* he had some-

[1] *Works*, vol. xi, pp. 3, 4 (67: 1 *et seq.*).

[2] *Ibid.*

[3] *Works*, vol. ix, p. 185. Cf. vol. x, p. 163.

[4] *Works*, vol. xi, p. 63.

times to supply the entire copy for an issue, and this "when his physique was rapidly running down."[1] First-rate criticism is not written under such conditions. Poe "dealt for the most part with small subjects," as Stedman sums up the matter by saying, "and when he had a large one, he seldom had leisure for treating it in a large and adequate way."[2] The circumstances under which Poe's critical work was produced, as has already been noted, make more remarkable the consistency and unity of principle which run through the whole. They also, however, explain why the best of Poe's criticism is to be found, not in any extended treatise, but in his "suggestions" and "marginalia," and in the brief but brilliant passages which he himself so often extracted for republication from their context of ephemeral commonplace.

Poe's judgment, which in its healthy and best state was fair and independent, was sometimes warped by personal feeling and prejudice. His independence, considering the state of literature and criticism in America in his time, was indeed remarkable. He attempted deliberately to get rid of the prepossessions which ordinarily hinder absolute judgment; he even went too far in freeing himself from the bonds of time and place and received opinion — so that his judgments are often novel and merely individual — too entirely his own. For one thing he tried to rise above national prejudice — and this at a time when America was just beginning to emerge from a state of provincialism into nationality in letters, and when it was particularly hard to avoid undue respect

[1] Robertson, *New Essays*, p. 115, quoting Ingram.

[2] *Works*, Stedman and Woodberry, vol. vi, p. xii.

for British productions on the one hand or undue pride in American productions on the other. He believed that "the world at large is the only proper stage for the literary *histrio*";[1] and that the point of view of the critic must be above national lines. "There is not a more disgusting spectacle under the sun than our subserviency to British criticism. It is disgusting, first, because it is truckling, servile, pusillanimous, — secondly, because of its gross irrationality."[2] But it is only "the *excess* of our subserviency" which is blamable. "In paying, as a nation, a respectful and not undue deference to a supremacy [the literary supremacy of Europe] rarely questioned but by prejudice or ignorance, we should, of course, be doing nothing more than acting in a rational manner." On the other hand he protests against literary chauvinism. "We throw off, with the most presumptuous and unmeaning hauteur, *all* deference whatever to foreign opinion, . . . we get up a hue and cry about the necessity of encouraging native writers of merit . . . and thus often find ourselves involved in the gross paradox of liking a stupid book the better, because, sure enough, its stupidity is American."[3]

The correctness of Poe's attitude in this matter — one of great difficulty at the time, and likewise of great importance in its relation to the development of American literature — should be borne in mind in consideration of Mr. Henry James's dictum (already quoted[4]) upon the provincialism of Poe's critical writings. They were in

[1] Cf. 12 : 20 ; 65 : 24.

[2] *Works*, Stedman and Woodberry, vol. vii, p. 214.

[3] 12 : 6; 12 : 17.

[4] See p. ix.

many respects provincial, — as was everything else in America in their time: they even bore one of the special marks of provincialism in their frequent combination of ignorance with self-sufficiency.[1] Poe, like some later Americans, could not raise himself into cosmopolitanism by his boot-straps. But on the whole he, better than most of his contemporaries, knew where he stood.

To return to the subject of independence, Poe was perhaps less open to national than to sectional bias. But his Southern feeling was never aggressive. In regretting that Simms and Pinkney had been "born too far south," and in ridiculing the "magnanimous cabal" of the *North American Review*, he was not so much unfair himself as ready to resent what he believed to be unfairness on the New England side.

He professed, further, to rise above received opinion in criticism; he had no respect for either traditional or popular reputation. He is fond of quoting the aphorism of Chamfort: *Il y a à parier que toute idée publique, toute convention reçue, est une sottise car elle a convenu au plus grand nombre.* Hence he is not afraid to say that "there is about the *Antigone*, as well as about all the ancient plays, an insufferable *baldness*, or platitude, the inevitable result of inexperience in art"; [2] that *Paradise Lost* has "eminent, although overestimated merits"; [3] that

[1] The best example of this is probably to be found, not in Poe's criticism, but in his serious propounding of *Eureka: an Essay on the Material and Spiritual Universe.*

[2] *Works*, vol. xii, p. 131. Cf. 286: 17.

[3] *Works*, vol. xii, p. 8.

Carlyle is an ass;[1] — or to make other possible mistakes from which ordinary men are saved by timidity. Poe's errors, which are usually explicable and easily allowed for, show his strength as a critic. He was able, moreover, as many instances show, to recognize genius before it had received popular approval.

To illustrate Poe's independence, and his general critical attitude, we may take some examples from the *Southern Literary Messenger* during his first year as a reviewer. He begins in May, 1835, with *Horseshoe Robinson*, by his patron J. P. Kennedy, which he praises justly but not unreservedly. He has an interesting review of an American translation of *I Promessi Sposi*, which he does not "scruple to give great praise." He makes his reputation as a critic by a review — worth reading as an example of his "tomahawk style" — of *Norman Leslie*, by Theodore S. Fay, an American "genius" and associate editor of the New York *Mirror*. He shows this "bepuffed, beplastered, and be-*Mirrored*" popular favorite to be merely silly. He has four pages on a reprint of *Robinson Crusoe* which cannot be improved. He reviews the poems of Joseph Rodman Drake, just posthumously published, — which have been hailed as the work of an "American Keats." After some just observations on provincialism, he shows the *Culprit Fay* to be destitute of true poetic quality, having first as a preliminary to this and later estimates of verse, established critical standards by attempting a definition of poetry. There could not be a better example of sanity

[1] *Works*, vol. xi, p. 177. This is at least as comprehensible as the "dunce" which Wordsworth applied to Byron.

and sound critical method. In June, 1836, he gives high praise to a new English writer in a review of the first American reprint of *Sketches by Boz*, beginning a series of appreciative articles on Dickens which culminate in the famous paper on *Barnaby Rudge*. In the same month he writes on the *Letters, Conversations, and Recollections of S. T. Coleridge*; "with us the most trivial memorial of Coleridge is a treasure of inestimable price."[1] And so on; these are fair examples, and Poe is equally sane throughout, whether the subject be old or new.

Judged by the enlightened opinion of the present day Poe is occasionally wrong. Sometimes, as in the case of *Paradise Lost*, the error, if error it be, is an honest one, due to a mistake in theory. Sometimes unfortunately it is due to unfairness and prejudice. He "cannot point an arrow at any woman," and in particular when they are his friends he is too kind in his notices of the "female poets." Though he calls Cranch "one of our finest poets"[2] he is generally bitter against the transcendentalists, and his tone indicates pique and jealousy. In a scathing review of the poems of Rufus Dawes, of October, 1842, he is supposed to have taken vengeance on Dawes for an unfavorable critique of *Al Aaraaf* printed thirteen years before;[3] and in an equally severe review of W. W. Lord's *Poems* in 1845 he is supposed to have been equally spiteful. In both reviews he is right in his judgment: in both he includes some praise; in both he

[1] For these reviews see *Works*, vols. viii, ix.

[2] *Works*, vol. xiv, p. 236 (195 : 29).

[3] Woodberry, *Poe*, pp. 52, 176, 232.

disclaims personal ill will. But the tone is bad — inexcusably coarse and abusive — and here, as too often elsewhere, Poe is no longer the just judge. The best that can be said in the matter is that he sometimes does not rise above the low standards of his time.

In determining Poe's qualifications as a critic we must finally inquire as to his education, reading, and general training for the office. What was his equipment? On this point there has been the usual difference of opinion. The facts are about as follows. Poe spent five years at school in England, and six years in the English and Classical School at Richmond. In both schools he apparently had good teachers, and in the latter he was noted as one of the two best Latinists.[1] He was at the University of Virginia for nearly a year, during which time he used to visit the library, "in search of old French books, principally histories." He was praised for a translation in verse from Tasso, and in the final examinations "excelled" in the ancient languages and in French.[2] He was for nearly a year at West Point where he stood third in French and seventeenth in mathematics in a class of eighty-seven. During this time he seems to have read the poets. He had on his table a volume of Campbell's *Poems* and characteristically found therein traces of plagiarism.[3] Indeed as he was always fond of poetry, and as he had already published two volumes of

[1] Harrison, *Poe*, vol. i, p. 20.

[2] *Ibid.*, pp. 37, 45, 61.

[3] *Ibid.*, p. 86. Perhaps he had been reading Hazlitt's *English Poets;* see *Nation*, October 8, 1908, p. 335. If so the fact is even more notable.

poetry and was about to publish another, we are not surprised to hear from one of his contemporaries at West Point that "his acquaintance with English literature was extensive and accurate and his verbal memory wonderful. He could repeat both prose and poetry by the hour." The following from the same authority is interesting: "The whole bent of his mind at that time seemed to be toward criticism — or, more properly speaking, caviling. Whether it were Shakespeare or Byron, Addison or Johnson — the acknowledged classic or the latest poetaster — all came in alike for his critical censure. He seemed to take especial delight in caviling at passages that had received the most unequivocal stamp of general approval." [1] Poe's academic education, then, was fairly good but incomplete. In school and college, as later, he was not scholarly, but intelligent; he had a fondness for literature and a bent toward criticism.

Even in school and college, however, Poe probably got less from regular instruction than from pursuing his own intellectual interests. On the whole he was self-taught; and on this account and because of lack of opportunity never quite liberally educated. He had intellectual curiosity, with a judgment and taste of his own, and his reading, as far as it went, was genuine and assimilative. But he never had time or opportunity to come broadly in contact with the best, in men or books, and was thrown too much on his own resources. Except for Lowell, "he never met his intellectual equal in the

[1] T. H. Gibson, *Harper's Magazine*, November, 1867, quoted by Harrison, p. 92. Some allowance may be made; the account was written long after the event.

flesh,"[1] being in this respect at a great disadvantage compared with his New England contemporaries, who formed a mutually helpful group, and had in general greater opportunities both at home and abroad. This intellectual loneliness led to egotism and narrowness. Moreover he did not have taste or opportunity for systematic study. His reading was desultory. He had no library of his own, and his reading was mainly in recent or current literature, — in periodicals and chance books. During the last part of his life he doubtless read little but the magazines of his "competitors" and such books as came to him for review. Poe's mind, then, was not stored with the best that has been known and thought in the world. He lacked the breadth and sanity and flexibility which come from sufficient learning. The best fruits of criticism are traditional and it would be idle to expect them from a self-taught reviewer writing in this new country in the second quarter of the nineteenth century.

Two things may be said, however, in this connection. One is that, with this deficiency of preparation and this disadvantage of time and place, Poe could meet the best minds of other countries and other ages (in their works) without any appearance of inferiority; whoever the writer in question he always speaks in his criticism as an equal of an equal. And secondly, it is possible that if Poe had had the industry to become a scholar he might have lacked or lost something of the originality and independence which are the merit of his criticism.[2] The many

[1] John Macy, *Atlantic Monthly*, December, 1908, p. 836.

[2] "I sometimes find myself wishing, when dealing with these matters of poetical criticism, that my ignorance were even greater

qualities which go to make up the perfect critic are never found combined. Poe was a light-armed combatant in the field of criticism, and had the advantages and disadvantages belonging to that kind.

III

Concerning Poe's actual acquaintance with literature there is some evidence worth collecting. He studied Greek in school, but made little use of it in his maturity and probably read the Greek writers only in translation. He attributes the *Œdipus at Colonos* to Æschylus.[1] He was in youth, as we have seen, a good Latinist, and had some first-hand knowledge of Latin literature. He quotes, sometimes from the minor Latin writers.[2] It is doubtful, however, if he read much Latin, or if the Latin writers formed any essential part of his literary fund. He is said to have known no German.[3] His knowledge

than it is. To handle these matters properly, there is needed a poise so perfect that the least overweight in any direction tends to destroy the balance. Temper destroys it, a crotchet destroys it, even erudition may destroy it."—M. Arnold, *On Translating Homer*, p. 245.

1 *Works*, vol. xii, p. 4; Woodberry, *Poe*, p. 238.

2 *Works*, vol. xiv, p. 214. A quotation from Silius Italicus, however, means little; Poe doubtless drew it from some book on Latin prosody.

3 Woodberry, *Poe*, p. 236, quoting Briggs: "He makes quotations from the German, but he can't read a word of the language." The context shows that Briggs is not entirely to be trusted. See also G. Gruener, *Modern Philology*, vol. ii, p. 125, "Poe's Knowledge of German"; P. Cobb, *The Influence of E. T. A. Hoffmann on the Tales of Edgar Allan Poe*, chap. iii, "Poe's Knowledge of

of Italian and Spanish was slight. French, however, he read easily, and his wide, though unsystematic, reading in French literature undoubtedly had its influence on his critical ideas. Poe's mind, moreover, was quick and intuitive, and from reading in and about literatures in foreign tongues he was able to approach the universality of view which is impossible for the man of one language.[1]

In English literature Poe read widely: his fruitful reading, however, was mainly in the nineteenth century. Of Shakespeare, Milton, the English Bible, and the older literature in general he spoke disparagingly.[2] A passage summarizing his opinion of the poets of the sixteenth and

the German Language." These affirmative arguments are not entirely convincing. In the absence of proof it may be guessed that Poe had a smattering of German but derived his considerable knowledge of German literature mainly from translations and descriptions.

[1] *Pinakidia* and similar articles throw light on Poe's reading and literary habits. These show pretense rather than solidity of learning ; — or, better perhaps, they show the pathetic attempt of a man not broadly educated to make himself at home in universal literature. Too much has been made of their recklessness of citation, etc. (such as the reference to the *Mélanges Littéraires* of "Suard and André") — which shows not so much dishonesty as ignorance and carelessness. Poe was after all not a scholar, but a journalist living on the literary "frontier." These articles show also Poe's interest in the curious and outré in literature, corresponding to his fondness for out-of-the-way matters in geography and science — an interest which perhaps served to give breadth and imagination to his criticism.

[2] Briggs, quoted in Woodberry, *Poe*, p. 238 ; Chivers, in *Century* January, 1903, p. 447.

seventeenth centuries is worth quoting: "Their writings sprang immediately from the soul and partook intensely of the nature of that soul. It is not difficult to perceive the tendency of this glorious *abandon*. To elevate immeasurably all the energies of mind, — but again, so to mingle the greatest possible fire, force, delicacy, and all good things, with the lowest possible bathos, baldness, and utter imbecility, as to render it not a matter of doubt, but of certainty, that the average results of mind in such a school will be found inferior to those results in one (ceteris paribus) more artificial: such, we think, is the view of the older English poetry in which a very calm examination will bear us out." [1] He admired the metrical skill of Pope but would not have called him a poet.[2] He formed his ideas of poetry on that branch of the romantic poetry of the nineteenth century in which Coleridge was the leader. He read Wordsworth, but not sympathetically.[3] For Coleridge he expressed the greatest admiration, calling *Christabel*, the *Ancient Mariner* and *Love* "the purest of all poems." [4] For Poe English poetry seems almost to have begun here. Shelley was pure genius and "profoundly original." [5] Keats was "the sole British poet who has never erred in his themes" and "the greatest of the English poets of the same age, if not of any age." [6] Tennyson developed "the truest and

[1] *Works*, vol. ix, p. 95. This review (of an English anthology) is worth reading.

[2] *Works*, vol. ix, p. 273 (36 : 29); vol. xi, p. 76 (81 : 4).

[3] See *Letter to B——* and notes in this volume.

[4] *Works*, vol. viii, p. 284 (18 : 4).

[5] *Works*, vol. xii, p. 32.

[6] *Works*, vol. xi, p. 76 (81 : 21); *Century*, January, 1903, p. 447.

purest of poetical styles." Miss Barrett narrowly missed uniting the "Tennysonian poetic sense" with the "Shelleyan abandon."[1] These poets Poe read and loved; they (with his own work) formed the basis of his critical theory of poetry. The fact that they are all from one age and kind perhaps accounts for the narrowness in Poe's definition of poetry which will appear later.

Let us inquire, finally, as to Poe's study of earlier critics, to whom he may have been indebted for critical ideas. His reading in this direction in general paralleled his reading of the poets, and led him to the same conclusions. He quotes Aristotle, but at second-hand;[2] it is doubtful if he read the *Poetics* even in translation. He is fond of referring to Bielfeld's *Premiers Traits de l'Érudition Universelle*, 1767, an encyclopedic work which summarizes the critical views of the eighteenth century; and he quotes from it, among other things, a definition of poetry, as *l'art d'exprimer les pensées par la fiction*, to support his belief that poetry involves invention or creation.[3] Of more importance was an early perusal of A. W. Schlegel's *Lectures on Dramatic Art and Literature*, in Black's translation (1815). Traces of this reading run pretty well through his work.[4] Beside miscellaneous

[1] *Works*, vol. xii, p. 34. Cf. also: "I am profoundly excited by music, and by some poems — those of Tennyson especially — whom, with Keats, Shelley, Coleridge (occasionally), and a few others of like thought and expression, I regard as the *sole* poets." — Letter to Lowell, in Woodberry, *Poe*, p. 213.

[2] See 3:31, note.

[3] See 16: note 2; 78:28; and notes.

[4] See 8:23, note.

ideas and curiosities for *Pinakidia*,[1] he got from it some knowledge — perhaps most of his knowledge — of Greek and later dramatic literature, which he discusses often and with assurance. He possibly got also from Schlegel's introductory lecture some important notions in regard to poetry. For example, the following (which he read before 1831) may have started him in developing his poetical theory: "It belongs to the general philosophical theory of poetry, and the other fine arts, to establish the fundamental laws of the beautiful. . . . For this purpose certain scientific investigations are indispensable to the artist. . . . The general theory, on the other hand, seeks to analyze that essential faculty of human nature — the sense of the beautiful. . . . Poetry, taken in its widest acceptation, [is] the power of creating what is beautiful, and representing it to the eye or the ear."[2] From this Poe may have derived his "rhythmical creation of beauty." He may with Schlegel have found "the essence of the northern poetry in melancholy." He undoubtedly got from Schlegel the principle of "unity (or totality) of interest."[3] There is little evidence to show that he read other German critics to whom he refers — Winckelmann, Novalis, Schelling, Goethe, Lessing — except some general remarks on German criticism in the *Marginalia*[4] — in which he prefers "even Voltaire to Goethe," and holds

[1] Woodberry, *Poe*, p. 96. An idea of these gleanings may be got by comparing *Works*, vol. xiv, pp. 39, 41, with Schlegel, Bohn edition, pp. 233, 278, etc.

[2] Bohn edition, pp. 17, 18.

[3] Bohn edition, pp. 26, 243. *Works*, vol. viii, p. 126; vol. xi, p. 79 (84 : 2).

[4] 285 : 20.

"Macaulay to possess more of the true critical spirit than Augustus William and Frederick Schlegel combined."

Poe read to most purpose in the critical writings of the nineteenth century — the best period of English criticism — and, fortunately, he was above all indebted to Coleridge. He read before 1831 Wordsworth's Preface to the *Lyrical Ballads* (1800), the Preface to the *Poems* (1815), with its distinction between fancy and imagination, and the *Essay Supplementary to the Preface* (1815), with its discussion of the relation of poetry and criticism.[1] His expressions on these essays of Wordsworth are mainly in the nature of protest; but he doubtless got from them more than he would admit, and they at least set him thinking. Some time before 1831, also, he read the *Biographia Literaria* (1817); a little later he read the *Table Talk* and *Letters, Conversations, and Recollections.* He speaks of Coleridge, almost without exception, in the tone of highest reverence; "the most trivial memorial of Coleridge is a treasure of inestimable price."[2] He urges the republication in America of the *Biographia*, "the most deeply interesting of the prose writings of Coleridge." To say that Poe derived all his critical ideas from Coleridge is incorrect; it is hardly too much to say that his poetic theory, as expressed throughout his writings from the *Letter to B——* to the *Poetic Principle*, represents the reaction and forming of his own mind after a sympathetic study of Coleridge's work. He derived from Coleridge, for example, the distinction between fancy and imagination; he attempted to analyze and

[1] See *Letter to B——* and notes as evidence.

[2] See Review (June, 1836) in *Works*, vol. ix, p. 51.

clarify it, and used it as a basis for his estimates of Drake and Moore. He believed with Coleridge that "imagination is the soul of poetic genius"; that imagination in man is "a lesser degree of the creative power of God"; or, in the words of Coleridge, "a repetition in the finite mind of the eternal act of creation in the infinite *I am.*"[1] He doubtless found in Coleridge, as in Schlegel, authority for his principle of unity, — as for example in Coleridge's "tone and spirit of unity," — "reducing multitude into unity of effect."[2] From Coleridge's rather enigmatical dictum to the effect that "a poem of any length neither can be, or ought to be, all poetry" he perhaps got his idea that the epic is at best a "series of minor poems," — and that a long poem is really a contradiction in terms.[3] He took Coleridge's definition of a poem, with its distinction between poetry and science, and following a suggestion in the context, undertook to improve on Coleridge, by distinguishing poetry from romance and by clearing up the relation between poetry and metrical form. To show one of Poe's most obvious borrowings, and to show also how he added his own thought to what he borrowed, the two definitions may be placed side by side:

"A poem is that species of composition, which is opposed to works of science, by proposing for its *immediate* object pleasure, not truth; and from all other species (having *this* object in common with it) it is discriminated by proposing to itself such delight from the *whole,* as is

[1] See 16: note 2, and note thereon.

[2] *Biographia*, chap. xiv.

[3] *Ibid.*, chap. xv.

compatible with a distinct gratification from each component *part*." (*Biographia*, chap. xiv.)

"A poem, in my opinion, [as opposed to Coleridge's?] is opposed to a work of science by having, for its *immediate* object, pleasure, not truth; to romance, by having for its object an *indefinite* instead of a *definite* pleasure, being a poem only so far as this object is attained; romance presenting perceptible images with definite, poetry with *in*definite sensations, to which end music is an *essential*, since the comprehension of sweet sound is our most indefinite conception. Music, when combined with a pleasurable idea, is poetry; music without the idea is simply music; the idea without the music is prose from its very definitiveness." (*Letter to B——.*)

Poe got ideas also from an appreciative reading of Hazlitt, whom he characterizes, in a review of the *Characters of Shakespeare*, as "emphatically a critic, brilliant, epigrammatic, startling, paradoxical, and suggestive, rather than accurate, luminous, or profound."[1] The *Lectures on the English Poets* he probably read very early; and in a review of Hazlitt's *Literary Remains*, in 1836, he quotes "a fine passage on the *ideal*," which suited his own conceptions.[2] He speaks of Leigh Hunt's essay on poetry (prefixed to *Imagination and Fancy*, 1844) with contempt — perhaps because it ran counter to some of his favorite ideas.[3] He had high regard for Macaulay, and doubtless learned from the Essay on

[1] *Works*, vol. xii, p. 226.

[2] *Works*, vol. ix, p. 145. For the passage see Hazlitt, *Works*, Waller and Glover, vol. ix, p. 429.

[3] See 179: 4, and note.

Montgomery some of the tricks of the reviewer's trade. An admirable critique of the *Essays*, however, — in which he calls Macaulay a "terse, forcible, and logical writer . . . not a comprehensive or profound thinker" — shows that he did not wrongly estimate Macaulay's abilities.

Poe, then, had read some of the best English critics, and was not entirely unequipped for criticism. He learned from the best masters — Wordsworth, Coleridge, Hazlitt. It is not wrong to say, with Professor Woodberry, that Coleridge was, "taken all in all, the guiding genius of Poe's entire intellectual life," [1] — it being added that Coleridge stands in a similar relation to many of the other poets and critics of the nineteenth century. Much in Poe's poetry goes back to the same original mind. But just as Poe's poetry, while owing much to Coleridge and other predecessors, is still profoundly original, — so Poe's criticism, though founded on the work of Coleridge and earlier critics, develops into something entirely his own.

IV

Poe's critical papers are of two kinds — general essays in poetic theory and specific reviews. The latter, dealing sometimes with valuable, more often with valueless and forgotten books, have various degrees of interest. They are all, however, merely the application to particular cases of general principles which run, as has been said, through the entire work. The main interest, then, is in

[1] *Poe*, p. 93.

the general essays or in such portions of the others as develop definitions and standards; at any rate one who understands Poe's theories needs no further introduction to their particular applications.

Let us take first the theory of poetry. The narrowness of Poe's conception of poetry has frequently been commented upon. It includes only one kind of poetry, being based upon his own poetical work, or upon work very similar thereto. This does not, however, mean that Poe's taste was narrow; or that he saw no merit in such works, outside his definition, as are usually included under the head of poetry. He does not "gainsay the peculiar merits" of the *Essay on Man* or *Hudibras*.[1] He would only say that these works are philosophy or satire in verse, and not poetry. So a drama in verse is not poetry (though it may contain poetry) — because it *is* a drama, and is distinguished by difference of aim.[2] To include all these different things under one term only leads to confusion and obscurity. Poe would in general restrict the word to what is known as "pure poetry." It is well, then, to begin an exposition of Poe's theory with negatives. In the first place the aim of poetry is not to convey truth or to teach a moral lesson. To believe the contrary is the "heresy of the didactic," against which Poe never tires of declaiming.[3] Truth is prosaic and its proper medium is prose. It may, indeed, be introduced into a poem but always as subsidiary — as humbly ministering

[1] *Works*, vol. xi, p. 76 (81 : 7).

[2] *Works*, vol. xiii, p 73 (148 : 15).

[3] See 234 : 2, and note.

to the poetic purpose. "If, through the attainment of a truth, we are led to perceive a harmony where none was apparent before, we experience, at once, the true poetical effect — but this effect is referable to the harmony alone, and not in the least degree to the truth which merely served to render the harmony manifest."[1] It is possible, of course, "to introduce didacticism, with effect, into a poem," as it is "to introduce poetical images and measures, with effect, into a didactic essay." Only, however, by a *tour de force;* thus to attempt "to commingle the obstinate oils and waters of poetry and truth" is "to labor at a disadvantage" and "to be guilty of a fruitless and wasteful expenditure of energy."[2] The trouble with Longfellow, for example, was that he diluted his pure poetry with didacticism. In the same way the aim of poetry is not to convey passion. "Poetry and passion are discordant."[3] "True passion is prosaic — homely." It is only in the subsidence and control of passion that "we are poetic, and it is clear that a poem now written will be poetic in the exact ratio of its dispassion. A passionate poem is a contradiction in terms."[4] "We are willing to permit Tennyson to bring, to the intense *passion* which prompts his *Locksley Hall,* the aid of that terseness and pungency which are derivable from rhythm and from rhyme. The effect he produces, however, is a purely passionate,

[1] *Works*, vol. xiv, p. 290 (255 : 4).

[2] *Works*, vol. xi, p. 255; cf. vol. xiv, p. 198 (155 : 17).

[3] Poe always gives Coleridge as authority for this statement, — which is difficult to find in Coleridge's writings. See 238 : 20, note.

[4] *Works*, vol. xi, p. 277; vol. xvi, p. 56 (265 : 16).

and not, unless in detached passages of this magnificent philippic, a properly poetic effect."[1] Again humorous verse is not poetry. "Humor . . . is directly antagonistical to that which is the soul of the muse proper. . . . The only bond between humorous verse and poetry, properly so called, is that they employ in common a certain tool [rhythm and rhyme]. But this single circumstance has been sufficient to occasion, and to maintain through long ages, a confusion of two very distinct ideas in the brain of the unthinking critic."[2]

If, then, poetry is not concerned with truth or passion or humor, what is its province? Poe's answer is in outline as follows. The world of mind may be divided into the pure intellect, taste, and the moral sense. "Just as the intellect concerns itself with truth, so taste informs us of the beautiful, while the moral sense is regardful of duty." Taste is the arbiter of poetry; and the province of poetry is beauty. The sense of beauty is an immortal instinct, planted deep in the nature of man. This sense finds delight in the manifold forms of nature amid which man exists, and it finds delight, likewise, in a description of these forms. Mere description of actual beauty, however, is not poetry.[3] The immortal mind of man longs for a beauty above and beyond nature, — a beauty not of this world; it strives to anticipate some

[1] *Works*, vol. xi, p. 255. Cf. vol. viii, p. 283 (16 : 4).

[2] *Works*, vol. xi, p. 23. Cf. 81 : 9, and note.

[3] *Works*, vol. xiv, p. 273 (236 : 4). Cf. vol. xvi, p. 102 (279 : 23) : "*Mere* description is not poetry at all. We demand creation — ποίησις." See also 236 : 4, note.

portion of the loveliness which belongs to eternity. It is this "struggle to apprehend the supernal loveliness" which gives rise to poetry. It is this higher and more fleeting beauty which the poet tries to catch and reveal in words, — working to this end through an "elevating excitement of the soul." Music, "in its various modes of meter, rhythm, and rhyme," if not absolutely essential to poetry, is nevertheless so vitally important that no poet would decline its assistance. Indeed "it is in music, perhaps, that the soul most nearly attains the great end for which, when inspired by the poetic sentiment, it struggles — the creation of supernal beauty." In pure music man perhaps *in fact* anticipates (Poe thought) the music of heaven. At any rate the highest effects open to the poet are secured by the union of music with poetry. The poetry of words, then, may be defined, in brief, as the "Rhythmical Creation of Beauty." The poet whose work best answers this definition is Keats. "He is the sole English poet who has never erred in his themes. Beauty is always his aim." [1]

What Poe means by the *beautiful*, as the subject of poetry, is further explained by the fact that he expressly includes under this term,[2] or ordinarily couples with it,[3] the *sublime* and the *mystical*. What he means by the *sublime* he does not explain. The *mystical* he applies to "that class of composition in which there lies beneath the transparent upper current of meaning an under or *suggestive* one. What we vaguely term the *moral* of any

[1] *Works*, vol. xi, p. 76 (81 : 21).

[2] *Works*, vol. xiv, p. 275 (238 : 15); vol. xii, p. 38 (104 : 17).

[3] *Works*, vol. viii, p. 282 (15 : 21); vol. x, p. 65 (58 : 11).

sentiment is its mystic or secondary expression. It has the vast force of an accompaniment in music. This vivifies the air; that spiritualizes the *fanciful* conception, and lifts it into the *ideal.*" *Comus*, the *Ancient Mariner*, the *Sensitive Plant* of Shelley — to take some of Poe's examples — have this *suggestive* character. "In every glimpse of beauty presented [by these poems], we catch, through long and wild vistas, dim bewildering visions of a far more ethereal beauty beyond."[1] Poe's own poems, for example *The Haunted Palace*, perhaps best illustrate his meaning.

Imagination is the soul of poetry;[2] and imagination, like poetry, partakes of the divine. "Imagination in man is, possibly, a lesser degree of the creative power of God." Poetry does not lie in mere reproduction of nature; it demands creation; "the word ποίησις itself speaks volumes upon this point."[3] The poetic beauty is an ideal beauty.

The word poetry has two meanings, which in Poe's theory are carefully distinguished. It means, first, "the poetic sentiment" in the abstract, — that elevating excitement of the soul which comes from contemplation of the highest beauty. It means, secondly, — in its ordinary acceptation — the expression of poetic sentiment in language. Poetry in this ordinary sense is the result of the poetic sentiment in the mind of the poet, and its merit is measured by "its capabilities of exciting the poetic sen-

[1] *Works*, vol. x, p. 65 (58: 11).
[2] *Works*, vol. viii, p 283 (16: 4).
[3] *Works*, vol. xi, p. 74 (78: 26).

timents in others."[1] The poetic sentiment is a divine gift; to this the *poeta nascitur* applies. Poetry in the concrete, however — the poetic effect — is a matter not merely of inspiration, but of reason and calculation as well. "A poem is not the poetic faculty, but the *means* of exciting it in mankind;" and this means is subject to analysis. Hence in the composition of a poem logical acumen is even more important than "the faculty of Ideality"; and Coleridge, who wrote "the purest of all poems," possibly owed his "almost magical pre-eminence rather to metaphysical than poetical powers." Here possibly Poe is led into exaggeration; but he everywhere insists that the highest poetry cannot come from mere inspiration, — that it demands also the coolest calculation. "How few," he says, "are willing to admit the possibility of reconciling genius with artistic skill! Yet this reconciliation is not only possible, but absolutely necessary. It is a mere prejudice which has hitherto prevented the union, by studiously insisting upon a natural repulsion which not only does not exist, but which is at war with all the analogies of nature. The greatest poems will not be written until this prejudice is annihilated."[2] Genius furnishes the material, which "in the hands of the *true* artist . . . is but a mass of clay, of which anything may be fashioned at will, or according to the skill of the workman."[3]

What, then, to the true artist is meant by the mental process which we call imagination? — for even this proc-

[1] *Works*, vol. viii, p. 284 (17 : 12).

[2] *Works*, vol. xiii, p. 129.

[3] *Works*, vol. xvi, p. 99 (279 : 3).

ess, according to Poe, is not beyond analysis. *Imagination* is *creation;* and this in turn is equivalent to *invention*, or *novelty*, or *originality*.[1] The equivalency of these five terms gives the clue to an important, and perhaps neglected, part of Poe's theory. The imagination creates. It cannot, however, produce anything entirely novel, — anything which did not before exist; "if it could it would create not only ideally, but substantially, — as do the thoughts of God."[2] The new is always resoluble into the old; the novelty is one of combination. To create, then, is only to produce novel combinations.[3] The same terms may be applied to invention or originality. "True invention is elaborate. There is no greater mistake than the supposition that a true originality is a mere matter of impulse or inspiration. To originate is carefully, patiently, and understandingly to combine."[4] The possibilities of invention, of originality, are moreover unlimited. "The true invention never exhausts itself. It is mere cant and ignorance to talk of the really imaginative man's 'writing himself out.' As well prate about the aridity of the eternal ocean ἐξ οὗπερ πάντες ποταμοί. So long as the universe of thought shall furnish matter for

[1] *Works*, vol. xi, pp. 73, 110 (78 : 8; 97 : 16).

[2] *Works*, vol. xii, p. 37 (103 : 17).

[3] Poe may have got the word and a hint for the idea from Coleridge: "A poem contains the same elements as a prose composition; the difference, therefore, must consist in a different combination, in consequence of a different object proposed. According to the difference of the object will be the difference of the combination." — *Biographia Literaria*, chap. xiv.

[4] *Works*, vol. xiv, p. 73; cf. vol. xiv, p. 203 (161 : 1).

novel combination, so long will the spirit of true genius be original, be exhaustless — be itself." [1]

Poe's theory is most succinctly stated in the following passage, — which will serve as summary. "The first element [of poetry] is the thirst for supernal BEAUTY — a beauty which is not afforded the soul by any existing collocation of earth's forms — a beauty which, perhaps, no *possible* combination of these forms would fully produce. Its second element is the attempt to satisfy this thirst by *novel* combinations among those forms of beauty which already exist — or by novel combinations *of those combinations which our predecessors, toiling in chase of the same phantom, have already set in order*. We thus clearly deduce the *novelty*, the *originality*, the *invention*, the *imagination*, or lastly the *creation* of BEAUTY, (for the terms as here employed are synonymous) as the essence of all Poesy." [2]

The principle of originality is so important in Poe's criticism that it deserves some further explanation and illustration. The grossest offense under this head is plagiarism. Poe is constantly detecting plagiarism: it is, however, in his eyes less a moral than a literary sin. "The great adversary of invention is imitation." [3] To imitativeness is due the stagnation of the drama. To revive the drama "the first thing necessary is to burn or bury the 'old models,' and to forget, as quickly as possible, that ever a play has been penned. The second thing is to consider *de novo* what are the *capabilities* of the drama — not merely what hitherto have been its conventional purposes.

[1] *Works*, vol. xi, p. 96. [2] *Works*, vol. xi, p. 73 (77 : 30).

[3] *Works*, vol. xiii, p. 33 (107 : 14).

The third and last point has reference to the composition of a play (showing to the fullest extent these capabilities), conceived and constructed with feeling and with taste, but with feeling and taste guided and controlled in every particular by the details of reason — of common sense — in a word, of a natural art."[1] Longfellow errs, not merely in his didacticism, but in his imitativeness. Students of Longfellow's poetry, who understand Poe's theory of originality, will also understand Poe's attitude in this much misunderstood matter. He often praises Longfellow, — and with entire consistency, for "imitators are not, necessarily, unoriginal — except in the exact points of imitation. Mr. Longfellow, decidedly the most audacious imitator in America, is remarkably original, or, in other words, imaginative, upon the whole."[2] Some further elaboration of the theory of originality is to be found in the second paper on Hawthorne, where distinction is made between absolute novelty and novelty of effect. The latter, "the true originality — true in respect to its purposes — is that which, in bringing out the half-formed, the reluctant, or the unexpressed fancies of mankind, or in exciting the more delicate pulses of the heart's passion, or in giving birth to some universal sentiment or instinct in embryo, thus combines with the pleasurable effect of *apparent* novelty, a real egoistic delight. The reader, in the case first supposed (that of absolute novelty), is excited, but embarrassed, disturbed, in some degree even pained at his own want of perception, at his own folly in not having himself hit upon the idea. In

[1] *Works*, vol. xiii, p. 37 (111 : 10).

[2] *Works*, vol. xvi, p. 97.

the second case his pleasure is doubled. He is filled with an intrinsic and extrinsic delight. He feels and intensely enjoys the seeming novelty of the thought, enjoys it as really novel, as absolutely original with the writer — and himself. They two, he fancies, have, alone of all men, thought thus. They two have, together, created this thing." [1]

Finally besides originality (in other words invention or imagination) a poem must have artistic form. It must be a unified and organized whole. From his earliest criticism to his latest Poe insists on "the vastly important artistic element," unity or totality of effect.[2] This explains why, both in theory and in practice, he stands for the short poem. In a poem too long to be read at one sitting totality is lost. A second reason is that in the perusal of a long poem it is impossible to sustain that elevating excitement of the soul which is the essence of poetry; but this second reason is reducible into the first. A poem should be "*unique* in the proper acceptation of that term."

We may close the discussion of Poe's theory of poetry by quoting his shortest definition, — which has usually been overlooked. In his sketch entitled *Landor's Cottage* he speaks of poetry as consisting in "combined novelty and propriety," — "than in the words just employed," he says, "I could scarcely give of poetry in the abstract a more rigorous definition." These words contain, in implication, the larger part of Poe's rationale of poetry.

[1] *Works*, vol. xiii, p. 146.

[2] *Works*, vol. viii, p. 126; vol. xi, p. 106 (93 : 14); vol. xiv, pp. 196, 267 (153 : 26, 229 : 6); vol. xvii, p. 266 (321 : 27).

V

Poe's theory of the prose tale may be disposed of more briefly, since it has much in common with his theory of poetry. The poem and the prose tale are governed by the same artistic principles; the two differ in subject matter and form. The poem is the higher mode of expression; it is concerned alone with beauty, and it employs rhythm as an essential aid. The prose tale is less elevated, but broader in its range. Because it discards rhythm it may use material which would be out of place in poetry. "The writer of the prose tale, in short, may bring to his theme a vast variety of modes or inflections of thought and expression — (the ratiocinative, for example, the sarcastic, or the humorous) which are not only antagonistical to the nature of the poem, but absolutely forbidden by one of its must peculiar and indispensable adjuncts; we allude of course to rhythm. It may be added here, *par parenthèse*, that the author who aims at the purely beautiful in a prose tale is laboring at a great disadvantage. For beauty can be better treated in a poem. Not so with terror, or passion, or horror, or a multitude of such other points."[1]

Allowance being made for this difference in subject matter and mode of expression the principles of composition, already developed for the poem, apply to the prose tale. Here, as "in all cases of fictitious composition," originality "should be the first object."[2] "Mr. Hawthorne's distinctive trait is invention, creation, imagina-

[1] *Works*, vol. xi, p. 109 (95 : 31).

[2] *Works*, vol. xiii, p. 85.

tion, originality — a trait which, in the literature of fiction, is positively worth all the rest."[1] Thus, in fiction as in poetry, originality is equivalent to imagination or creation; and the novelty is again clearly a matter of combination.[2] Dickens's best characters are "*creations* (that is to say original combinations of character)" and "belong to the most august regions of the ideal."[3]

"That vital requisite in all works of art, unity," is of particular importance in fiction, — and unity is a matter of "preconsideration." Most authors sit down to write without fixed design. "Pen should never touch paper until at least a well-digested *general* purpose be established. In fiction the *dénouement*, in all other compositions the intended *effect*, should be definitely considered and arranged, before writing the first word; and *no* word should be then written which does not tend, or form a part of a sentence which tends to the development of the *dénouement*, or to the strengthening of the effect."[4] Plot in fiction means unity and organization. It is by no means mere complexity of incident, or intrigue. "In its most rigorous acceptation, it is *that from which no component atom can be removed, and in which none of the component atoms can be displaced, without ruin to the whole;* and although a sufficiently good plot may be constructed, without attention to the whole rigor of this definition, still it is the definition which the true artist

[1] *Works*, vol. xi, p. 110 (97 : 16). This judgment is curiously reversed in the later critique of Hawthorne, where he is said to be only "peculiar."

[2] *Works*, vol. ix, p. 261. [3] *Works*, vol. x, p. 153.

[4] *Works*, vol. xiv, p. 188 (320 : 14).

should always keep in view, and always endeavor to consummate in his works."[1]

Plot, however, — analogous to sculptural outline — can appeal only to the cultivated reader. "At best it is but a secondary and rigidly artistical merit, for which no merit of a higher class — no merit founded in nature — should be sacrificed."[2] In many of the finest fictions — *Gil Blas*, *Pilgrim's Progress*, *Robinson Crusoe* — plot is wanting. Defoe, however, like Scott, Godwin, Brockden Brown, used another unifying principle — namely that of "autorial comment." The writer of fiction may discuss what is transacting, and shape its effect; this "often gives a species of unity (the unity of the writer's individual thought) to the most random narrations."[3] The binding power of comment should never be neglected.

The highest form of fiction is to be found not in the old-fashioned novel but in the tale, for in this the fullest unity may be realized. The long fiction, like the long poem, loses "the immense force derivable from *totality*." It cannot be read at one sitting; the intervention of worldly affairs — even the mere cessation in reading, destroys the unity of effect. "In the brief tale, however, the author is enabled to carry out the fullness of his intention, be it what it may. During the hour of perusal the soul of the reader is at the writer's control."[4]

Of the principle of unity as it applies to the prose tale

[1] *Works*, vol. xiv, p. 188 (320 : 14).

[2] *Works*, vol. x, p. 121; cf. vol. xiii, p. 47 (121 : 1) for a better but longer statement.

[3] *Works*, vol. x, pp. 200, 218; vol. xii, p. 224.

[4] *Works*, vol. xi, p. 108 (94 : 25).

the best statement occurs in the reviews of Hawthorne: "A skillful literary artist has constructed a tale. If wise, he has not fashioned his thoughts to accommodate his incidents; but having conceived, with deliberate care, a certain unique and single *effect* to be wrought out, he then invents such incidents — he then combines such events as may best aid him in establishing this preconceived effect. If his very initial sentence tend not to the outbringing of this effect, then he has failed in his first step. In the whole composition there should be no word written, of which the tendency, direct or indirect, is not to the one pre-established design. And by such means, with such care and skill, a picture is at length painted which leaves in the mind of him who contemplates it with a kindred art, a sense of the fullest satisfaction. The idea of the tale has been presented unblemished, because undisturbed; and this is an end unattainable by the novel."[1]

The method of composition here outlined for the prose tale is strikingly similar to that more fully elaborated for the poem in the *Philosophy of Composition*: the writer first determines the length of his work and his intended effect; he then proceeds to create or invent — in other words to make such combinations as will establish this effect.

The question then arises whether Poe is here describing the method he actually employed in the composition of his own tales. This question cannot be positively answered: one who has read the tales carefully, however,

[1] *Works*, vol. xi, p. 108 (94 : 31). Cf. vol. xiii, p. 153, for the same paragraph with interesting variations.

in the light of the paragraph just quoted will hesitate to answer it in the negative. And a similar statement may be made concerning the *Philosophy of Composition.* This celebrated piece has been regarded as an afterthought, as fiction, as a hoax. It certainly is not plain autobiography. It is doubtless, like many of Poe's tales, the subsequent analysis of a mental process more or less unconscious and indeliberate. It is doubtless rhetorically dressed and exaggerated for magazine purposes. It is none the less supported by the artificial character of *The Raven;* and it is consistent with Poe's entire critical theory. It is — if in the absence of proof another opinion may be hazarded — fundamentally true.

The originality of Poe's critical theory, which has already been insisted upon, will now be more apparent. Hints and suggestions for it may be found in Wordsworth, Coleridge, and Hazlitt; but in its entirety it is clearly Poe's own. The question remains as to its value. Does it, in the first place, throw light on Poe's original work? Poe's first statement of his poetical creed was contained in the Preface to the *Poems* of 1831. From this early date until his death he developed his theory — with more and more fullness but with practical consistency — and wrote poetry at the same time. It is thus perfectly natural that his poetic theory and poetic practice should be parallel — in other words that his theory should be based on his poetry and that his poetry in turn should be influenced and determined by his theory. An examination of the poetry, moreover, shows it characterized by brevity, music, unity, and form — the qualities insisted upon in the theory — the later poems gaining on the earlier in these respects. The difference between *Tamerlane* and *The Raven* is probably in part due to the fact that Poe's theorizing intervened between the two; indeed *The Raven* is probably the very poem in which the theory is applied most deliberately, if not most successfully — as the *Philosophy of Composition* would suggest. And there is the same correspondence between Poe's tales and his theory of fiction. In other poet-critics — Dryden for example, or Wordsworth — theory and practice may part company. Poe scrupulously makes the one conform to the other: indeed the effort by which this conformity is secured is sometimes apparent. If this be true, then Poe's criticism is important to the study of his poetry in an unusual degree.

What finally is the absolute or permanent value of Poe's criticism? This question has already been answered by implication. If Poe's theory was based on his own poetry and if in turn his theory moulded and determined his poetic expression, then his poetry and his criticism are inseparable; the merit of the one attaches to the other in its different kind. As his poetry has original value and enlarges our conception of the possibilities of the poetic art — so his criticism adds something which none but Poe could have added to our critical knowledge of poetry.

SELECTIONS FROM
EDGAR ALLAN POE

Letter to B——

It has been said that a good critique on a poem may be written by one who is no poet himself. This, according to *your* idea and *mine* of poetry, I feel to be false — the less poetical the critic, the less just the critique, and the converse. On this account, and because there are but few B——'s in the world, I would be as much ashamed of the world's good opinion as proud of your own. Another than yourself might here observe, Shakespeare is in possession of the world's good opinion, and yet Shakespeare is the greatest of poets. It appears then that the world judge correctly, why should you be ashamed of their favorable judgment? The difficulty lies in the interpretation of the word "judgment" or "opinion." The opinion is the world's, truly, but it may be called theirs as a man would call a book his, having bought it; he did not write the book, but it is his; they did not originate the opinion, but it is theirs. A fool, for example, thinks Shakespeare a great poet — yet the fool has never read Shakespeare. But the fool's neighbor, who is a step higher on the Andes of the mind, whose head (that is to say, his more exalted thought) is too far above the fool to be seen or understood, but whose feet (by which I mean his every-day actions) are sufficiently near to be discerned, and by means of which that superiority is ascertained, which *but* for them would never have been discovered — this neighbor asserts that Shakespeare is a great poet — the fool believes him, and it is henceforward his *opinion*. This neighbor's opinion has, in like manner, been adopted from one above *him*, and so, ascendingly, to a few gifted individuals who kneel around the summit, beholding, face to face, the master spirit who stands upon the pinnacle. . . .

You are aware of the great barrier in the path of an American writer. He is read, if at all, in preference to the combined and established wit of the world. I say established; for it is with literature as with law or empire — an established name is an estate in tenure, or a throne in possession. Besides, one might suppose that books, like their authors, improve by travel — their having crossed the sea is, with us, so great a distinction. Our antiquaries abandon time for distance; our very fops glance from the binding to the bottom of the title-page, where the mystic characters which spell London, Paris, or Genoa, are precisely so many letters of recommendation. . . .

I mentioned just now a vulgar error as regards criticism. I think the notion that no poet can form a correct estimate of his own writings is another. I remarked before, that in proportion to the poetical talent, would be the justice of a critique upon poetry. Therefore, a bad poet would, I grant, make a false critique, and his self-love would infallibly bias his little judgment in his favor; but a poet, who is indeed a poet, could not, I think, fail of making a just critique. Whatever should be deducted on the score of self-love, might be replaced on account of his intimate acquaintance with the subject; in short, we have more instances of false criticism than of just, where one's own writings are the test, simply because we have more bad poets than good. There are of course many objections to what I say: Milton is a great example of the contrary; but his opinion with respect to the Paradise Regained, is by no means fairly ascertained. By what trivial circumstances men are often led to assert what they do not really believe! Perhaps an inadvertent word has descended to posterity. But, in fact, the Paradise Regained is little, if at all, inferior to the Paradise Lost, and is only supposed so to be, because men do not like epics, whatever they may say to the contrary, and reading those of Milton in their natural order, are too much wearied with the first to derive any pleasure from the second.

I dare say Milton preferred Comus to either — if so — justly. . . .

As I am speaking of poetry, it will not be amiss to touch slightly upon the most singular heresy in its modern history — the heresy of what is called very foolishly, the Lake School. Some years ago I might have been induced, by an occasion like the present, to attempt a formal refutation of their doctrine; at present it would be a work of supererogation. The wise must bow to the wisdom of such men as Coleridge and Southey, but being wise, have laughed at poetical theories so prosaically exemplified.

Aristotle, with singular assurance, has declared poetry

the most philosophical of all writings[1] — but it required a Wordsworth to pronounce it the most metaphysical. He seems to think that the end of poetry is, or should be, instruction — yet it is a truism that the end of our existence is happiness; if so, the end of every separate part of our existence — everything connected with our existence should be still happiness. Therefore the end of instruction should be happiness; and happiness is another name for pleasure; — therefore the end of instruction should be pleasure: yet we see the above mentioned opinion implies precisely the reverse.

To proceed: ceteris paribus, he who pleases, is of more importance to his fellow men than he who instructs, since utility is happiness, and pleasure is the end already obtained which instruction is merely the means of obtaining.

I see no reason, then, why our metaphysical poets should plume themselves so much on the utility of their works, unless indeed they refer to instruction with eternity in view; in which case, sincere respect for their piety would not allow me to express my contempt for their judgment; contempt which it would be difficult to conceal, since their writings are professedly to be understood by the few, and it is the many who stand in need of salvation. In such case I should no doubt be tempted to think of the devil in Melmoth, who labors indefatigably through three octavo volumes, to accomplish the destruction of one or two souls, while any common devil would have demolished one or two thousand. . . .

Against the subtleties which would make poetry a study — not a passion — it becomes the metaphysician to rea-

[1] Spoudaiotaton kai philosophikotaton genos.

son — but the poet to protest. Yet Wordsworth and Coleridge are men in years; the one imbued in contemplation from his childhood, the other a giant in intellect and learning. The diffidence, then, with which I venture to dispute their authority, would be overwhelming, did I not feel, from the bottom of my heart, that learning has little to do with the imagination — intellect with the passions — or age with poetry. . . .

> "Trifles, like straws, upon the surface flow,
> He who would search for pearls must dive below,"

are lines which have done much mischief. As regards the greater truths, men oftener err by seeking them at the bottom than at the top; the depth lies in the huge abysses where wisdom is sought — not in the palpable places where she is found. The ancients were not always right in hiding the goddess in a well: witness the light which Bacon has thrown upon philosophy; witness the principles of our divine faith — that moral mechanism by which the simplicity of a child may overbalance the wisdom of a man.

We see an instance of Coleridge's liability to err, in his Biographia Literaria — professedly his literary life and opinions, but, in fact, a treatise *de omni scibili et quibusdam aliis*. He goes wrong by reason of his very profundity, and of his error we have a natural type in the contemplation of a star. He who regards it directly and intensely sees, it is true, the star, but it is the star without a ray — while he who surveys it less inquisitively is conscious of all for which the star is useful to us below — its brilliancy and its beauty. . . .

As to Wordsworth, I have no faith in him. That he had, in youth, the feelings of a poet I believe—for there are glimpses of extreme delicacy in his writings—(and delicacy is the poet's own kingdom—his *El Dorado*)—but they have the appearance of a better day recollected; and glimpses, at best, are little evidence of present poetic fire—we know that a few straggling flowers spring up daily in the crevices of the glacier.

He was to blame in wearing away his youth in contemplation with the end of poetizing in his manhood. With the increase of his judgment the light which should make it apparent has faded away. His judgment consequently is too correct. This may not be understood,—but the old Goths of Germany would have understood it, who used to debate matters of importance to their State twice, once when drunk, and once when sober—sober that they might not be deficient in formality—drunk lest they should be destitute of vigor.

The long wordy discussions by which he tries to reason us into admiration of his poetry, speak very little in his favor: they are full of such assertions as this—(I have opened one of his volumes at random) "Of genius the only proof is the act of doing well what is worthy to be done, and what was never done before"—indeed! then it follows that in doing what is *un*worthy to be done, or what *has* been done before, no genius can be evinced; yet the picking of pockets is an unworthy act, pockets have been picked time immemorial, and Barrington, the pick-pocket, in point of genius, would have thought hard of a comparison with William Wordsworth, the poet.

Again — in estimating the merit of certain poems, whether they be Ossian's or M'Pherson's, can surely be of little consequence, yet, in order to prove their worthlessness, Mr. W. has expended many pages in the controversy. *Tantæne animis?* Can great minds descend to such absurdity? But worse still: that he may bear down every argument in favor of these poems, he triumphantly drags forward a passage, in his abomination of which he expects the reader to sympathize. It is the beginning of the epic poem "*Temora.*" "The blue waves of Ullin roll in light; the green hills are covered with day; trees shake their dusky heads in the breeze." And this — this gorgeous, yet simple imagery, where all is alive and panting with immortality — this, William Wordsworth, the author of "Peter Bell," has *selected* for his contempt. We shall see what better he, in his own person, has to offer. Imprimis:

> "And now she's at the pony's head,
> And now she's at the pony's tail,
> On that side now, and now on this,
> And almost stifled her with bliss —
> A few sad tears does Betty shed,
> She pats the pony where or when
> She knows not: happy Betty Foy!
> O, Johnny! never mind the Doctor!"

Secondly:

> "The dew was falling fast, the — stars began to blink,
> I heard a voice; it said —— drink, pretty creature, drink;

And, looking o'er the hedge, be — fore me I espied
A snow-white mountain lamb, with a — maiden at its side.
No other sheep were near, the lamb was all alone,
And by a slender cord was — tether'd to a stone."

Now, we have no doubt this is all true; we *will* believe it, indeed, we will, Mr. W. Is it sympathy for the sheep you wish to excite? I love a sheep from the bottom of my heart. . . .

But there *are* occasions, dear B——, there are occasions when even Wordsworth is reasonable. Even Stamboul, it is said, shall have an end, and the most unlucky blunders must come to a conclusion. Here is an extract from his preface—

"Those who have been accustomed to the phraseology of modern writers, if they persist in reading this book to a conclusion (*impossible!*) will, no doubt, have to struggle with feelings of awkwardness; (ha! ha! ha!) they will look round for poetry (ha! ha! ha! ha!) and will be induced to inquire by what species of courtesy these attempts have been permitted to assume that title." Ha! ha! ha! ha! ha!

Yet let not Mr. W. despair; he has given immortality to a wagon, and the bee Sophocles has transmitted to eternity a sore toe, and dignified a tragedy with a chorus of turkeys. . . .

Of Coleridge I cannot speak but with reverence. His towering intellect! his gigantic power! He is one more evidence of the fact "que la plupart des sectes ont raison dans une bonne partie de ce qu'elles avancent, mais non pas en ce qu'elles nient." He has imprisoned his own conceptions by the barrier he has erected against those of others. It is lamentable to think that such a mind should be buried in metaphysics, and, like the Nyctanthes, waste its perfume upon the night alone. In reading his poetry, I tremble, like one who stands upon a volcano, conscious, from the very darkness bursting from the crater, of the fire and the light that are weltering below.

. . . .

What is Poetry? — Poetry! that Proteus-like idea, with as many appellations as the nine-titled Corcyra! Give me, I demanded of a scholar some time ago, give me a definition of poetry. "Très-volontiers," and he proceeded to his library, brought me a Dr. Johnson, and overwhelmed me with a definition. Shade of the immortal Shakespeare! I imagine to myself the scowl of your spiritual eye upon the profanity of that scurrilous Ursa Major. Think of poetry, dear B——, think of poetry, and then think of — Dr. Samuel Johnson! Think of all that is airy and fairy-like, and then of all that is hideous and unwieldy; think of his huge bulk, the Elephant! and then — and then think of the Tempest — the Midsummer Night's Dream — Prospero — Oberon — and Titania! . . .

A poem, in my opinion, is opposed to a work of science by having, for its *immediate* object, pleasure, not truth; to romance, by having for its object an *indefinite* instead of a *definite* pleasure, being a poem only so far as this object is attained; romance presenting perceptible images with definite, poetry with *indefinite* sensations, to which end music is an *essential*, since the comprehension of sweet sound is our most indefinite conception. Music, when combined with a pleasurable idea, is poetry; music without the idea is simply music; the idea without the music is prose from its very definitiveness.

What was meant by the invective against him who had no music in his soul? . . .

To sum up this long rigmarole, I have, dear B——, what you no doubt perceive, for the metaphysical poets, *as* poets, the most soveregn contempt. That they have followers proves nothing —

> The Indian prince has to his palace
> More followers than a thief to the gallows.

Drake's Culprit Fay

BEFORE entering upon the detailed notice which we propose of the volumes before us, we wish to speak a few words in regard to the present state of American criticism. It must be visible to all who meddle with literary matters, that of late years a thorough revolution has been effected in the censorship of our press. That this revolution is infinitely for the worse we believe. There was a time, it is true, when we cringed to foreign opinion — let us even say when we paid a most servile deference to British critical dicta. That an American book could, by any possibility, be worthy perusal, was an idea by no means extensively prevalent in the land; and if we were induced to read at all the productions of our native writers, it was only after repeated assurances from England that such productions were not altogether contemptible. But there was, at all events, a shadow of excuse, and a slight basis of reason for a subserviency so grotesque. Even now, perhaps, it would not be far wrong to assert that such basis of reason may still exist. Let us grant that in many of the abstract sciences — that even in Theology, in Medicine, in Law, in Oratory, in the Mechanical Arts, we have no competitors whatever, still nothing but the most egregious national vanity would assign us a place, in the matter of Polite Literature, upon a level with the elder and riper climes of Europe, the earliest steps of whose children are among the groves of magnificently endowed Academies, and whose innumerable men of leisure, and of consequent learning, drink daily from those august fountains of inspiration which burst around them everywhere from out the tombs of their immortal dead, and from out their hoary and trophied monuments of chivalry and song. In paying then, as a nation, a respectful and not undue deference to a supremacy rarely questioned but by prejudice or ignorance, we should, of course, be doing nothing more than acting in a rational manner. The *excess* of our subserviency was blamable — but, as we have before said, this very excess might have found a shadow of excuse in the strict justice, if properly regulated, of the principle from which it issued. Not so, however, with our present follies. We are becoming boisterous and arrogant in the pride of a too speedily assumed literary freedom. We throw off, with the most presumptuous and unmeaning hauteur, *all* deference whatever to foreign opinion — we forget, in the puerile inflation of vanity, that *the world* is the true theatre of the biblical histrio — we get up a hue and cry about the necessity of encouraging native writers of merit — we blindly fancy that we can accomplish this by indiscriminate puffing of good, bad, and indifferent, without taking the trouble to consider that what we choose to denominate encouragement is thus, by its general application, rendered precisely the reverse. In a word, so far from being ashamed of the many disgraceful literary failures to which our own inordinate vanities and misapplied patriotism have lately given birth, and so far from deeply lamenting that these daily puerilities are of home manufacture, we adhere pertinaciously to our original blindly conceived idea, and thus often find ourselves involved in the gross paradox of liking a stupid book the better, because, sure enough, its stupidity is American.[1]

Deeply lamenting this unjustifiable state of public feeling, it has been our constant endeavor, since assuming the Editorial duties of this Journal, to stem, with what little abilities we possess, a current so disastrously undermining the health and prosperity of our literature.

. . . .

Who will deny that in regard to individual poems no definitive opinions can exist, so long as to Poetry in the abstract we attach no definitive idea? Yet it is a common thing to hear our critics, day after day, pronounce, with a positive air, laudatory or condemnatory sentences, *en masse*, upon material works of whose merits or demerits they have, in the first place, virtually confessed an utter ignorance, in confessing ignorance of all determinate principles by which to regulate a decision. Poetry has never been defined to the satisfaction of all parties. Perhaps, in the present condition of language it never will be. Words cannot hem it in. Its intangible and purely spiritual nature refuses to be bound down within the widest horizon of mere sounds. But it is not, therefore, misunderstood — at least, not by all men is it misunderstood. Very far

[1] This charge of indiscriminate puffing will, of course, only apply to the *general* character of our criticism — there are some noble exceptions. We wish also especially to discriminate between those *notices* of new works which are intended merely to call public attention to them, and deliberate criticism on the works themselves.

from it. If, indeed, there be any one circle of thought distinctly and palpably marked out from amid the jarring and tumultuous chaos of human intelligence, it is that evergreen and radiant Paradise which the true poet knows, and knows alone, as the limited realm of his authority — as the circumscribed Eden of his dreams. But a definition is a thing of words — a conception of ideas. And thus while we readily believe that Poesy, the term, it will be troublesome, if not impossible to define — still, with its image vividly existing in the world, we apprehend no difficulty in so describing Poesy, the Sentiment, as to imbue even the most obtuse intellect with a comprehension of it sufficiently distinct for all the purposes of practical analysis.

To look upwards from any existence, material or immaterial, to its *design*, is, perhaps, the most direct, and the most unerring method of attaining a just notion of the nature of the existence itself. Nor is the principle at fault when we turn our eyes from Nature even to Nature's God. We find certain faculties, implanted within us, and arrive at a more plausible conception of the character and attributes of those faculties, by considering, with what finite judgment we possess, the *intention* of the Deity in so implanting them within us, than by any actual investigation of their powers, or any speculative deductions from their visible and material effects. Thus, for example, we discover in all men a disposition to look with reverence upon superiority, whether real or supposititious. In some, this disposition is to be recognized with difficulty, and, in very peculiar cases, we are occasionally even led to doubt its existence altogether, until circumstances beyond the common routine bring it accidentally into development. In others again it forms a prominent and distinctive feature of character, and is rendered palpably evident in its excesses. But in all human beings it is, in a greater or less degree, finally perceptible. It has been, therefore, justly considered a primitive sentiment. Phrenologists call it Veneration. It is, indeed, the instinct given to man by God as security for his own worship. And although, preserving its nature, it becomes perverted from its principal purpose, and although swerving from that purpose, it serves to modify the relations of human society — the relations of father and child, of master and slave, of the ruler and the ruled — its primitive essence is nevertheless the same, and by a reference to primal causes, may at any moment be determined.

Very nearly akin to this feeling, and liable to the same analysis, is the Faculty of Ideality — which is the sentiment of Poesy. This sentiment is the sense of the beautiful, of the sublime, and of the mystical.[1] Thence spring immediately admiration of the fair flowers, the fairer forests, the bright valleys and rivers and mountains of the Earth — and love of the gleaming stars and other burning glories of Heaven — and, mingled up inextricably with this love and this admiration of Heaven and of Earth, the unconquerable

[1] We separate the sublime and the mystical — for, despite of high authorities, we are firmly convinced that the latter *may* exist, in the most vivid degree, without giving rise to the sense of the former.

desire — *to know.* Poesy is the sentiment of Intellectual Happiness here, and the Hope of a higher Intellectual Happiness hereafter.[1]

Imagination is its soul.[2] With the *passions* of mankind — although it may modify them greatly — although

[1] The consciousness of this truth was possessed by no mortal more fully than by Shelley, although he has only once especially alluded to it. In his *Hymn to Intellectual Beauty* we find these lines.

> While yet a boy I sought for ghosts, and sped
> Through many a listening chamber, cave and ruin,
> And starlight wood, with fearful steps pursuing
> Hopes of high talk with the departed dead :
> I called on poisonous names with which our youth is fed:
> I was not heard : I saw them not.
> When musing deeply on the lot
> Of life at that sweet time when birds are wooing
> All vital things that wake to bring
> News of buds and blossoming,
> Sudden thy shadow fell on me—
> I shrieked and clasped my hands in ecstasy !
>
> I vow'd that I would dedicate my powers
> To thee and thine: have I not kept the vow ?
> With beating heart and streaming eyes, even now
> I call the phantoms of a thousand hours
> Each from his voiceless grave : they have in vision'd bowers
> Of studious zeal or love's delight
> Outwatch'd with me the envious night :
> They know that never joy illum'd my brow,
> Unlink'd with hope that thou wouldst free,
> This world from its dark slavery,
> That thou, O awful *Loveliness*,
> Wouldst give whate'er these words cannot express.

[2] Imagination is, possibly in man, a lesser degree of the creative power in God. What the Deity imagines, *is*, but *was not* before. What man imagines, *is*, but *was* also. The mind of man cannot imagine what *is not*. This latter point may be demonstrated.—See *Les Premiers Traits de L'Erudition Universelle, par M. Le Baron de Bielfield, 1767.*

it may exalt, or inflame, or purify, or control them — it would require little ingenuity to prove that it has no inevitable, and indeed no necessary co-existence. We have hitherto spoken of poetry in the abstract: we come now to speak of it in its every-day acceptation — that is to say, of the practical result arising from the sentiment we have considered.

And now it appears evident, that since Poetry, in this new sense, *is* the practical result, expressed in language, of this Poetic Sentiment in certain individuals, the only proper method of testing the merits of a poem is by measuring its capabilities of exciting the Poetic Sentiments in others.

And to this end we have many aids — in observation, in experience, in ethical analysis, and in the dictates of common sense. Hence the *Poeta nascitur*, which is indisputably true if we consider the Poetic Sentiment, becomes the merest of absurdities when we regard it in reference to the practical result. We do not hesitate to say that a man highly endowed with the powers of Causality — that is to say, a man of metaphysical acumen — will, even with a very deficient share of Ideality, compose a finer poem (if we test it, as we should, by its measure of exciting the Poetic Sentiment) than one who, without such metaphysical acumen, shall be gifted, in the most extraordinary degree, with the faculty of Ideality. For a poem is not the Poetic faculty, but the *means* of exciting it in mankind. Now these means the metaphysician may discover by analysis of their effects in other cases than his own, without even conceiving the nature of these effects — thus arriving at a result which the unaided

Ideality of his competitor would be utterly unable, except by accident, to attain. It is more than possible that the man who, of all writers, living or dead, has been most successful in writing the purest of all poems — that is to say, poems which excite most purely, most exclusively, and most powerfully the imaginative faculties in men — owed his extraordinary and almost magical pre-eminence rather to metaphysical than poetical powers. We allude to the author of Christabel, of the Rime of the Auncient Mariner, and of Love — to Coleridge — whose head, if we mistake not its character, gave no great phrenological tokens of Ideality, while the organs of Causality and Comparison were most singularly developed.

Perhaps at this particular moment there are no American poems held in so high estimation by our countrymen, as the poems of Drake, and of Halleck. The exertions of Mr. George Dearborn have no doubt a far greater share in creating this feeling than the lovers of literature for its own sake and spiritual uses would be willing to admit. We have indeed seldom seen more beautiful volumes than the volumes now before us. But an adventitious interest of a loftier nature — the interest of the living in the memory of the beloved dead — attaches itself to the few literary remains of Drake. The poems which are now given to us with his name are nineteen in number; and whether all, or whether even the best of his writings, it is our present purpose to speak of these alone, since upon this edition his poetical reputation to all time will most probably depend.

It is only lately that we have read *The Culprit Fay*.

This is a poem of six hundred and forty irregular lines, generally iambic, and divided into thirty-six stanzas, of unequal length. The scene of the narrative, as we ascertain from the single line,

> The moon looks down on old *Cronest*,

is principally in the vicinity of West Point on the Hudson.

. . . .

It is more than probable that from ten readers of the *Culprit Fay*, nine would immediately pronounce it a poem betokening the most extraordinary powers of imagination, and of these nine, perhaps five or six, poets themselves, and fully impressed with the truth of what we have already assumed, that Ideality is indeed the soul of the Poetic Sentiment, would feel embarrassed between a half-consciousness that they *ought* to admire the production, and a wonder that they *do not*. This embarrassment would then arise from an indistinct conception of the results in which Ideality is rendered manifest. Of these results some few are seen in the *Culprit Fay*, but the greater part of it is utterly destitute of any evidence of imagination whatever. The general character of the poem will, we think, be sufficiently understood by any one who may have taken the trouble to read our foregoing compendium of the narrative. It will be there seen that what is so frequently termed the imaginative power of this story, lies especially — we should have rather said is thought to lie — in the passages we have quoted, or in others of a precisely similar nature. These passages embody, principally, mere specifications of qualities, of habiliments, of punishments, of occupations, of circumstances, &c., which the poet has believed in unison with the size, firstly, and secondly with the nature of his Fairies. To all which may be added specifications of other animal existences (such as the toad, the beetle, the lance-fly, the fire-fly and the like) supposed also to be in accordance. An example will best illustrate our meaning upon this point — we take it from page 20.

> He put his acorn helmet on;
> It was plumed of the silk of the thistle down:
> The corslet plate that guarded his breast
> Was once the wild bee's golden vest;
> His cloak of a thousand mingled dyes,
> Was formed of the wings of butterflies;
> His shield was the shell of a lady-bug queen,
> Studs of gold on a ground of green;[1]
> And the quivering lance which he brandished bright
> Was the sting of a wasp he had slain in fight.

We shall now be understood. Were any of the admirers of the *Culprit Fay* asked their opinion of these lines, they would most probably speak in high terms of the *imagination* they display. Yet let the most stolid and the most confessedly unpoetical of these admirers only try the experiment, and he will find, possibly to his extreme surprise, that he himself will have no difficulty whatever in substituting for the equipments of the Fairy, as assigned by the poet, other equipments equally com-

[1] Chestnut color, or more slack,
Gold upon a ground of black.

Ben Jonson.

fortable, no doubt, and equally in unison with the preconceived size, character, and other qualities of the equipped. Why we could accoutre him as well ourselves — let us see.

His blue-bell helmet, we have heard
Was plumed with the down of the humming-bird,
The corslet on his bosom bold
Was once the locust's coat of gold,
His cloak, of a thousand mingled hues,
Was the velvet violet, wet with dews,
His target was the crescent shell
Of the small sea Sidrophel,
And a glittering beam from a maiden's eye
Was the lance which he proudly wav'd on high.

The truth is, that the only requisite for writing verses of this nature, *ad libitum*, is a tolerable acquaintance with the qualities of the objects to be detailed, and a very moderate endowment of the faculty of Comparison — which is the chief constituent of *Fancy* or the powers of combination. A thousand such lines may be composed without exercising in the least degree the Poetic Sentiment, which is Ideality, Imagination, or the creative ability. And, as we have before said, the greater portion of the *Culprit Fay* is occupied with these, or similar things, and upon such, depends very nearly, if not altogether, its reputation. We select another example from page 25.

But oh! how fair the shape that lay
  Beneath a rainbow bending bright,

She seem'd to the entranced Fay
  The loveliest of the forms of light;
Her mantle was the purple rolled
  At twilight in the west afar;
'Twas tied with threads of dawning gold,
  And button'd with a sparkling star.
Her face was like the lily roon
  That veils the vestal planet's hue;
Her eyes, two beamlets from the moon
  Set floating in the welkin blue.
Her hair is like the sunny beam,
And the diamond gems which round it gleam
Are the pure drops of dewy even,
That ne'er have left their native heaven.

Here again the faculty of Comparison is alone exercised, and no mind possessing the faculty in any ordinary degree would find a difficulty in substituting for the materials employed by the poet other materials equally as good. But viewed as mere efforts of the Fancy and without reference to Ideality, the lines just quoted are much worse than those which were taken from page 20. A congruity was observable in the accoutrements of the Ouphe, and we had no trouble in forming a distinct conception of his appearance when so accoutred. But the most vivid powers of Comparison can attach no definitive idea to even "the loveliest form of light," when habited in a mantle of "rolled purple tied with threads of dawn and buttoned with a star," and sitting at the same time under a rainbow with "beamlet" eyes and a visage of "lily roon."

But if these things evince no Ideality in their author, do they not excite it in others? — if so, we must conclude, that without being himself imbued with the Poetic Sentiment, he has still succeeded in writing a fine poem — a supposition as we have before endeavored to show, not altogether paradoxical. Most assuredly we think not. In the case of a great majority of readers the only sentiment aroused by compositions of this order is a species of vague wonder at the writer's *ingenuity*, and it is this indeterminate sense of wonder which passes but too frequently current for the proper influence of the Poetic power. For our own part we plead guilty to a predominant sense of the ludicrous while occupied in the perusal of the poem before us — a sense whose promptings we sincerely and honestly endeavored to quell, perhaps not altogether successfully, while penning our compend of the narrative. That a feeling of this nature is utterly at war with the Poetic Sentiment, will not be disputed by those who comprehend the character of the sentiment itself. This character is finely shadowed out in that popular although vague idea so prevalent throughout all time, that a species of melancholy is inseparably connected with the higher manifestations of the beautiful. But with the numerous and seriously-adduced incongruities of the Culprit Fay, we find it generally impossible to connect other ideas than those of the ridiculous. We are bidden, in the first place, and in a tone of sentiment and language adapted to the loftiest breathings of the Muse, to imagine a race of Fairies in the vicinity of West Point. We are told, with a grave air, of their camp, of their king, and especially of their sentry, who is a wood-tick. We are informed that an Ouphe of about an inch in height has committed a deadly sin in falling in love with a mortal maiden, who may, very possibly, be six feet in her stockings. The consequence to the Ouphe is — what? Why, that he has "dyed his wings," "broken his elfin chain," and "quenched his flame-wood lamp." And he is therefore sentenced to what? To catch a spark from the tail of a falling star, and a drop of water from the belly of a sturgeon. What are his equipments for the first adventure? An acorn-helmet, a thistle-down plume, a butterfly cloak, a lady-bug shield, cockle-seed spurs, and a fire-fly horse. How does he ride to the second? On the back of a bull-frog. What are his opponents in the one? "Drizzly-mists," "sulphur and smoke," "shadowy hands and flame-shot tongues." What in the other? "Mailed shrimps," "prickly prongs," "blood-red leeches," "jellied quarls," "stony star fishes," "lancing squabs" and "soldier crabs." Is that all? No — Although only an inch high he is in imminent danger of seduction from a "sylphid queen," dressed in a mantle of "rolled purple," "tied with threads of dawning gold," "buttoned with a sparkling star," and sitting under a rainbow with "beamlet eyes" and a countenance of "lily roon." In our account of all this matter we have had reference to the book — and to the book alone. It will be difficult to prove us guilty in any degree of distortion or exaggeration. Yet such are the puerilities we daily find ourselves called upon to admire, as among the loftiest efforts of the human mind, and which not to assign a rank with the proud trophies of the matured and vigorous genius of

England, is to prove ourselves at once a fool, a maligner, and no patriot.[1]

As an instance of what may be termed the sublimely ridiculous we quote the following lines from page 17.

With sweeping tail and quivering fin,
  Through the wave the sturgeon flew,
And like the heaven-shot javelin,
  He sprung above the waters blue.

Instant as the star-fall light,
  He plunged into the deep again,
But left an arch of silver bright
  The rainbow of the moony main.

It was a strange and lovely sight
  To see the puny goblin there ;
He seemed an angel form of light
  With azure wing and sunny hair,
  Throned on a cloud of purple fair
Circled with blue and edged with white
  And sitting at the fall of even
  Beneath the bow of summer heaven.

The verses here italicized, if considered without their context, have a certain air of dignity, elegance, and chastity of thought. If however we apply the

[1] A review of Drake's poems, emanating from one of our proudest Universities, does not scruple to make use of the following language in relation to the *Culprit Fay.* "*It is, to say the least, an elegant production, the purest specimen of Ideality we have ever met with, sustaining in each incident a most bewitching interest. Its very title is enough,*" &c. &c. We quote these expressions as a fair specimen of the general unphilosophical and adulatory tenor of our criticism.

context, we are immediately overwhelmed with the grotesque. It is impossible to read without laughing, such expressions as "It was a strange and lovely sight" — "He seemed an angel form of light" — "And sitting at the fall of even, beneath the bow of summer heaven" to a Fairy — a goblin — an Ouphe — half an inch high, dressed in an acorn helmet and butterfly-cloak, and sitting on the water in a muscle-shell, with a "brown-backed sturgeon" turning somersets over his head.

In a world where evil is a mere consequence of good, and good a mere consequence of evil — in short where all of which we have any conception is good or bad only by comparison — we have never yet been fully able to appreciate the validity of that decision which would debar the critic from enforcing upon his readers the merits or demerits of a work by placing it in juxtaposition with another. It seems to us that an adage based in the purest ignorance has had more to do with this popular feeling than any just reason founded upon common sense. Thinking thus, we shall have no scruple in illustrating our opinion in regard to what *is not* Ideality or the Poetic Power, by an example of what *is*.[1]

[1] As examples of entire poems of the purest ideality, we would cite the *Prometheus Vinctus* of Æschylus, the *Inferno* of Dante, Cervantes' *Destruction of Numantia*, the *Comus* of Milton, Pope's *Rape of the Lock*, Burns' *Tam O' Shanter*, the *Auncient Mariner*, the *Christabel*, and the *Kubla Khan* of Coleridge; and most especially the *Sensitive Plant* of Shelley, and the *Nightingale* of Keats. We have seen American poems evincing the faculty in the highest degree.

We have already given the description of the Sylphid Queen in the *Culprit Fay*. In the *Queen Mab* of Shelley a Fairy is thus introduced —

> Those who had looked upon the sight
>   Passing all human glory,
> Saw not the yellow moon,
> Saw not the mortal scene,
> Heard not the night wind's rush,
> Heard not an earthly sound,
> Saw but the fairy pageant,
> Heard but the heavenly strains
> That filled the lonely dwelling —

and thus described —

> The Fairy's frame was slight; yon fibrous cloud
> That catches but the faintest tinge of even,
> And which the straining eye can hardly seize
> When melting into eastern twilight's shadow,
> Were scarce so thin, so slight; but the fair star
> That gems the glittering coronet of morn,
> *Sheds not a light so mild, so powerful,*
> *As that which, bursting from the Fairy's form,*
> *Spread a purpureal halo round the scene,*
> *Yet with an undulating motion,*
> *Swayed to her outline gracefully.*

In these exquisite lines the Faculty of mere Comparison is but little exercised — that of Ideality in a wonderful degree. It is probable that in a similar case the poet we are now reviewing would have formed the face of the Fairy of the "fibrous cloud," her arms of the "pale tinge of even," her eyes of the "fair stars," and her body of the "twilight shadow." Having so done, his admirers would have congratulated him upon his *imagination*, not taking the trouble to think that they themselves could at any moment *imagine* a Fairy of materials equally as good, and conveying an equally distinct idea. Their mistake would be precisely analogous to that of many a schoolboy who admires the imagination displayed in *Jack the Giant-Killer*, and is finally rejoiced at discovering his own imagination to surpass that of the author, since the monsters destroyed by Jack are only about forty feet in height, and he himself has no trouble in imagining some of one hundred and forty. It will be seen that the Fairy of Shelley is not a mere compound of incongruous natural objects, inartificially put together, and unaccompanied by any *moral* sentiment — but a being, in the illustration of whose nature some physical elements are used collaterally as adjuncts, while the main conception springs immediately *or thus apparently springs*, from the brain of the poet, enveloped in the moral sentiments of grace, of color, of motion — of the beautiful, of the mystical, of the august — in short of *the ideal.* [1]

It is by no means our intention to deny that in the *Culprit Fay* are passages of a different order from those to which we have objected — passages evincing a degree of imagination not to be discovered in the plot, conception, or general execution of the poem. The opening stanza will afford us a tolerable example.

[1] Among things, which not only in our opinion, but in the opinion of far wiser and better men, are to be ranked with the mere prettinesses of the Muse, are the positive similes so abundant in the writings of antiquity, and so much insisted upon by the critics of the reign of Queen Anne.

'Tis the middle watch of a summer's night—
The earth is dark but the heavens are bright
Naught is seen in the vault on high
But the moon, and the stars, and the cloudless sky,
And the flood which rolls its milky hue
A river of light on the welkin blue.
The moon looks down on old Cronest,
She mellows the shades of his shaggy breast,
And seems his huge gray form to throw
In a silver cone on the wave below;
His sides are broken by spots of shade,
By the walnut bow and the cedar made,
And through their clustering branches dark
Glimmers and dies the fire-fly's spark—
Like starry twinkles that momently break
Through the rifts of the gathering tempest rack.

There is Ideality in these lines—but except in the case of the words italicized—it is Ideality *not of a high order*. We have, it is true, a collection of natural objects, each individually of great beauty, and, if actually seen as in nature, capable of exciting in any mind, through the means of the Poetic Sentiment more or less inherent in all, a certain sense of the beautiful. But to view such natural objects as they exist, and to behold them through the medium of words, are different things. Let us pursue the idea that such a collection as we have here will produce, of necessity, the Poetic Sentiment, and we may as well make up our minds to believe that a catalogue of such expressions as moon, sky, trees, rivers, mountains, &c., shall be capable of exciting it,—it is merely an extension of the principle. But in the line "the earth is dark, *but* the heavens are bright" besides the simple mention of the "dark earth" "and the bright heaven," we have, directly, the moral sentiment of the brightness of the sky compensating for the darkness of the earth — and thus, indirectly, of the happiness of a future state compensating for the miseries of the present. All this is effected by the simple introduction of the word *but* between the "dark earth" and the "bright heaven" — this introduction, however, was prompted by the Poetic Sentiment, and by the Poetic Sentiment alone. The case is analogous in the expression "glimmers and dies," where the imagination is exalted by the moral sentiment of beauty heightened in dissolution.

In one or two shorter passages of the *Culprit Fay* the poet will recognize the purely ideal, and be able at a glance to distinguish it from that baser alloy upon which we have descanted. We give them without farther comment.

> The winds *are whist*, and the owl is still,
>   The bat in the shelvy rock *is hid*
> And naught is heard on the *lonely* hill
> But the cricket's chirp and the answer *shrill*
>   Of the gauze-winged katydid ;
> And the plaint of the *wailing* whippoorwill
>   Who mourns *unseen*, and ceaseless sings
> Ever a note of wail and wo —
>
> Up to the vaulted firmament
> His path the fire-fly courser bent,
> And at every gallop on the wind
> *He flung a glittering spark behind.*
>
> He blessed the force of the charmed line
>   And he banned the water-goblins' spite,

For he saw around in the *sweet moonshine,*
Their little wee faces above the brine,
Giggling and laughing with all their might
At the piteous hap of the Fairy wight.

. . . . . .

Bryant's Poems

Mr. Bryant's poetical reputation, both at home and abroad, is greater, we presume, than that of any other American. British critics have frequently awarded him high praise; and here, the public press have been unanimous in approbation. We can call to mind no dissenting voice. Yet the nature, and, most especially the manner, of the expressed opinions in this case, should be considered as somewhat equivocal, and but too frequently must have borne to the mind of the poet doubts and dissatisfaction. The edition now before us may be supposed to embrace all such of his poems as he deems not unworthy his name. These (amounting to about one hundred) have been "carefully revised." With the exception of some few, about which nothing could well be said, we will speak briefly of them one by one, but in such order as we may find convenient.

The Ages, a didactic piece of thirty-five Spenserian stanzas, is the first and longest in the volume. It was originally printed in 1821, with about half a dozen others now included in this collection. The design of the author in this poem is "from a survey of the past ages of the world, and of the successive advances of mankind in knowledge and virtue, to justify and confirm the hopes of the philanthropist for the future destinies of the human race." It is, indeed, an essay on the perfectibility of man, wherein, among other better arguments some in the very teeth of analogy, are deduced from the eternal *cycles* of physical nature, to sustain a hope of *progression* in happiness. But it is only as a poem that we wish to examine *The Ages.* Its commencement is impressive. The four initial lines arrest the attention at once by a quiet dignity of manner, an air of placid contemplation, and a versification combining the extremes of melody and force —

> When to the common rest that crowns our days,
> Called in the noon of life, the good man goes,
> Or full of years, and ripe in wisdom, lays
> His silver temples in their last repose —

The five concluding lines of the stanza, however, are not equally effective —

> When, o'er the buds of youth, the death-wind blows,
> And blights the fairest; when our bitter tears
> Stream, as the eyes of those that love us close,
> We think on what they were, with many fears
> Lest goodness die with them, and leave the coming years.

The defects, here, are all of a metrical and of course minor nature, but are still defects. The line

> When o'er the buds of youth the death-wind blows,

is impeded in its flow by the final *th* in *youth*, and especially in *death* where *w* follows. The word *tears* cannot readily be pronounced after the final *st* in *bit-*

terest; and its own final consonants, *rs*, in like manner render an effort necessary in the utterance of *stream* which commences the next line. In the verse

> We think on what they were, with many fears

the word *many* is, from its nature, too rapidly pronounced for the fulfilment of the *time* necessary to give weight to the foot of two syllables. All words of two syllables do not necessarily constitute a foot (we speak now of the Pentameter here employed) even although the syllables be entirely distinct, as in *many*, *very*, *often*, and the like. Such as, without effort, cannot employ in their pronunciation the *time* demanded by each of the preceding and succeeding feet of the verse, and occasionally of a preceding verse, will never fail to offend. It is the perception of this fact which so frequently forces the versifier of delicate ear to employ feet exceeding what are unjustly called legitimate dimensions. For example. At page 21 of the volume before us we have the following lines —

> Lo! to the smiling Arno's classic side
> The emulous nations of the West repair!

These verses are exceedingly forcible, yet, upon scanning the latter we find a syllable too many. We shall be told possibly that there should be an elision of the *e* in *the* at the commencement. But no — this was not intended. Both *the* and *emulous* demand a perfect accentuation. The verse commencing *Lo!*

> Lo! to the smiling Arno's classic side,

has, it will be observed, a Trochee in its first foot. As is usually the case, the whole line partakes, in consequence, of a stately and emphatic enunciation, and to equalize the time in the verse succeeding, something more is necessary than the succession of Iambuses which constitute the ordinary English Pentameter. The equalization is therefore judiciously effected by the introduction of an additional syllable. But in the lines

> Stream, as the eyes of those that love us close,
> We think on what they were with many fears,

lines to which the preceding observations will equally apply, this additional syllable is wanting. Did the rhyme admit of the alteration, everything necessary could be accomplished by writing

> We think on what they were with *many a* fear,
> Lest goodness die with them and leave the coming year.

These remarks may be considered hypercritical — yet it is undeniable that upon a rigid attention to minutiæ such as we have pointed out, any great degree of metrical success must altogether depend. We are more disposed, too, to dwell upon the particular point mentioned above, since, with regard to it, the American Monthly, in a late critique upon the poems of Mr. Willis, has evidently done that gentleman injustice. The reviewer has fallen into what we conceive the error of citing, *by themselves*, (that is to say insulated from the context) such verses as

The night-wind with a *desolate* moan swept by.
. . . . . .
With *difficult* energy and when the rod.
. . . . . .
Fell through, and with the *tremulous* hand of age.
. . . . . .
With super*natural* whiteness loosely fell.

for the purpose of animadversion. "The license" he says "of turning such words as 'passionate' and 'desolate' into two syllables could only have been taken by a pupil of the Fantastic School." We are quite sure that Mr. Willis had no purpose of turning them into words of two syllables — nor even, as may be supposed upon a careless examination, *of pronouncing them in the same time* which would be required for two ordinary, syllables. The excesses of measure are here employed (perhaps without any definite design on the part of the writer, who may have been guided solely by ear) with reference to the proper equalization, of *balancing*, if we may so term it, of time, *throughout an entire sentence.* This, we confess, is a novel idea, but, we think, perfectly tenable. Any musician will understand us. Efforts for the relief of monotone will necessarily produce fluctuations in the time of any metre, which fluctuations, if not subsequently counterbalanced, affect the ear like unresolved discords in music. The deviations then of which we have been speaking, from the strict rules of prosodial art, are but improvements upon the rigor of those rules, and are a merit, not a fault. It is the nicety of this species of equalization more than any other metrical merit, which elevates Pope as a versifier above the mere couplet-maker of his day; and, on the other hand, it is the extension of the principle to *sentences of greater length* which elevates Milton above Pope. Knowing this, it was, of course, with some surprise that we found the American Monthly (for whose opinions we still have the highest respect,) citing Pope in opposition to Mr. Willis upon the very point to which we allude. A few examples will be sufficient to show that Pope not only made free use of the license referred to, but that he used it for the reasons, and under the circumstances which we have suggested.

> Oh thou! whatever title please thine ear,
> Dean, Drapier, Bickerstaff, or Gulliver!
> Whether thou choose Cervantes' serious air,
> Or laugh and shake in *Rabelais'* easy chair.

Any person will here readily perceive that the third line

> Whether thou choose Cervantes' serious air,

differs in time from the usual course of the rhythm, and requires some counterbalance in the line which succeeds. It is indeed precisely such a verse as that of Mr. Bryant's upon which we have commented,

> Stream, as the eyes of those that love us close,

and commences in the same manner with a Trochee. But again, from Pope we have —

> Hence hymning Tyburn's elegiac lines
> Hence Journals, Medleys, *Mercuries*, Magazines.

Else all my prose and verse were much the same,
This prose on stilts, that *poetry* fallen lame.

And thrice he lifted high the birth-day brand
And thrice he dropped it from his *quivering* hand.

Here stood her opium, here she nursed her owls,
And here she planned the *imperial* seat of fools.

Here to her chosen all her works she shows;
Prose swell'd to verse, verse *loitering* into prose.

Rome in her Capitol saw Querno sit
Throned on *seven* hills, the Antichrist of wit.

And his this drum whose hoarse heroic bass
Drowns the loud *clarion* of the braying ass.

But such a bulk as no twelve bards could raise,
Twelve *starveling* bards of these *degenerate* days.

These are all taken at random from the first book of the *Dunciad*. In the last example it will be seen that the *two* additional syllables are employed with a view of equalizing the time with that of the verse,

But such a bulk as no twelve bards could raise,

a verse which will be perceived to labor in its progress — and which Pope, in accordance with his favorite theory of making sound accord with sense, evidently intended so to labor. It is useless to say that the words should be written with elision — *starv' ling* and *degen' rate*. Their *pronunciation* is not thereby materially affected

—and, besides, granting it to be so, it may be as well to make the elision also in the case of Mr. Willis. But Pope had no such intention, nor we presume, had Mr. W. It is somewhat singular, we may remark, en passant, that the American Monthly, in a subsequent portion of the critique alluded to, quotes from Pope as a line of "sonorous grandeur" and one beyond the ability of our American poet, the well known

> Luke's iron crown and Damien's bed of steel.

Now this is indeed a line of "sonorous grandeur" —but it is rendered so principally if not altogether by that very excess of metre (in the word Damien) which the reviewer has condemned in Mr. Willis. The lines which we quote below from Mr. Bryant's poem of *The Ages* will suffice to show that the author we are now reviewing fully appreciates the force of such occasional excess, and that he has only neglected it through oversight in the verse which suggested these observations.

> Peace to the just man's *memory*—let it grow
> Greener with years, and blossom through the flight
> Of ages—let the mimic canvass show
> His calm *benevolent* features.

> Does *prodigal* Autumn to our age deny
> The plenty that once swelled beneath his sober eye?

> Look on this beautiful world and read the truth
> In her fair page.

Will then the *merciful* One who stamped our race
With his own image, and who gave them sway
O'er Earth and the glad dwellers on her face,
Now that our *flourishing* nations far away
Are spread, where'er the moist earth drinks the day,
Forget the ancient care that taught and nursed
His latest offspring?

He who has tamed the *elements* shall not live
The slave of his own passions.

When liberty awoke
New-born, amid those *beautiful* vales.

Oh Greece, thy *flourishing* cities were a spoil
Unto each other.

And thou didst drive from thy *unnatural* breast
Thy just and brave.

Yet her *degenerate* children sold the crown.

Instead of the pure heart and *innocent* hands—

Among thy gallant sons that guard thee well
Thou laugh'st at *enemies*. Who shall then declare—

Far like the comet's way thro' *infinite* space.

The full region leads
New *colonies* forth.

Full many a horrible worship that, of old,
Held o'er the *shuddering* realms unquestioned sway.

All these instances, and some others, occur in a poem of

but thirty-five stanzas — yet, in only a very few cases is the license improperly used. Before quitting this subject it may be as well to cite a striking example from Wordsworth —

> There was a youth whom I had loved so long,
> That when I loved him not I cannot say.
> Mid the green moun*tains many and many* a song
> We two had sung like gladsome birds in May.

Another specimen, and one still more to the purpose may be given from Milton whose accurate ear (although he cannot justly be called the best of versifiers) included and balanced without difficulty the rhythm of the longest passages.

> But say, if our *Deliverer* up to heaven
> Must re-ascend, what will betide the few
> His faithful, left among the unfaithful herd,
> The enemies of truth ? who then shall guide
> His people, who defend ? Will they not deal
> More with his *followers* than with him they dealt ?
> Be sure they will, *said the Angel.*

The other metrical faults in *The Ages* are few. Mr. Bryant is not always successful in his Alexandrines. Too great care cannot be taken, we think, in so regulating this species of verse as to admit of the necessary pause at the end of the third foot — or at least as not to render a pause necessary elsewhere. We object, therefore, to such lines as

> A palm like his, and catch from him the hallowed flame.
>
> . . . . . .
>
> The truth of heaven, and kneel to Gods that heard them not.

That which concludes Stanza X, although correctly cadenced in the above respect, requires an accent on the monosyllable *the*, which is too unimportant to sustain it. The defect is rendered the more perceptible by the introduction of a Trochee in the first foot.

> The sick untended then
> Languished in *the* damp shade, and died afar from men.

We are not sure that such lines as

> A boundless sea of blood and *the* wild air.
> . . . . .
> The smile of heaven, till *a* new age expands.

are in any case justifiable, and they can be easily avoided. As in the Alexandrine mentioned above, the course of the rhythm demands an accent on monosyllables too unimportant to sustain it. For this prevalent heresy in metre we are mainly indebted to Byron, who introduced it freely, with the view of imparting an abrupt energy to his verse. There are, however, many better ways of relieving a monotone.

Stanza VI is, throughout, an exquisite specimen of versification, besides embracing many beauties both of thought and expression.

> Look on this beautiful world and read the truth
> In her fair page; see every season brings
> New change, to her, of everlasting youth;
> Still the green soil with joyous living things
> Swarms; the wide air is full of joyous wings;
> And myriads, still, are happy in the sleep
> Of ocean's azure gulfs, and where he flings
> The restless surge. Eternal love doth keep
> In his complacent arms the earth, the air, the deep.

The cadences, here, at the words *page*, *swarms*, and *surge* respectively, cannot be surpassed. We shall find, upon examination, comparatively few consonants in the stanza, and by their arrangement no impediment is offered to the flow of the verse. Liquids and the most melodious vowels abound. *World*, *eternal*, *season*, *wide*, *change*, *full*, *air*, *everlasting*, *wings*, *flings*, *complacent*, *surge*, *gulfs*, *myriads*, *azure*, *ocean*, *sail*, and *joyous*, are among the softest and most sonorous sounds in the language, and the partial line after the pause at *surge*, together with the stately march of the Alexandrine which succeeds, is one of the finest imaginable of finales —

> Eternal love doth keep
> In his complacent arms, the earth, the air, the deep.

The higher beauties of the poem are not, we think, of the highest. It has unity, completeness, — a beginning, middle and end. The tone, too, of calm, hopeful, and elevated reflection, is well sustained throughout. There is an occasional quaint grace of expression, as in

> Nurse of full streams, and lifter up of proud
> Sky-mingling mountains that o'erlook the cloud —

or of antithetical and rhythmical force combined, as in

> The shock that hurled
> To dust in many fragments dashed and strewn
> The throne whose roots were in another world
> And whose far-stretching shadow awed our own.

But we look in vain for something more worthy commendation. At the same time the piece is especially free from errors. Once only we meet with an unjust metonymy, where a sheet of water is said to

> *Cradle*, in his soft *embrace*, a gay
> Young group of grassy islands.

We find little originality of thought, and less imagination. But in a poem essentially didactic, of course we cannot hope for the loftiest breathings of the Muse.

. . . .

The *Waterfowl* is very beautiful, but still not entitled to the admiration which it has occasionally elicited. There is a fidelity and force in the picture of the fowl as brought before the eye of the mind, and a fine sense of *effect* in throwing its figure on the background of the "crimson sky," amid "falling dew," "while glow the heavens with the last steps of day." But the merits which possibly have had most weight in the public estimation of the poem, are the melody and strength of its versification, (which is indeed excellent) and more particularly its *completeness*. Its rounded and didactic termination has done wonders :

> on my heart,
> Deeply hath sunk the lesson thou hast given
> And shall not soon depart.
>
> He, who, from zone to zone,
> Guides through the boundless sky thy certain flight
> In the long way that I must tread alone
> Will lead my steps aright.

There are, however, points of more sterling merit. We fully recognize the poet in

Thou 'rt gone — the abyss of heaven
Hath swallowed up thy form.

There is a power whose care
Teaches thy way along that pathless coast —
The desert, and illimitable air —
Lone, wandering, but not lost.

The Forest Hymn consists of about a hundred and twenty blank Pentameters of whose great rhythmical beauty it is scarcely possible to speak too highly. With the exception of the line

The solitude. Thou art in the soft winds,

no fault, in this respect, can be found, while excellencies are frequent of a rare order, and evincing the greatest delicacy of ear. We might, perhaps, suggest, that the two concluding verses, beautiful as they stand, would be slightly improved by transferring to the last the metrical excess of the one immediately preceding. For the appreciation of this, it is necessary to quote six or seven lines in succession.

Oh, from these sterner aspects of thy face
Spare me and mine, nor let us need the wrath
Of the mad unchained elements, to teach
Who rules them. Be it ours to meditate
In these calm shades thy milder majesty,
And to the beautiful order of thy works
Learn to conform the order of our lives.

There is an excess of one syllable in the first of the lines italicized. If we discard this syllable here, and adopt it in the final line, the close will acquire strength, we think, in acquiring a fuller volume.

> Be it ours to meditate
> In these calm shades thy milder majesty,
> And to the perfect order of thy works
> Conform, if we can, the order of our lives.

Directness, boldness, and simplicity of expression, are main features in the poem.

> Oh God! when thou
> Dost *scare* the world with tempests, set on fire
> The heavens with falling thunderbolts, or fill
> With all the waters of the firmament
> The swift dark whirlwind that uproots *the* woods,
> And drowns *the* villages.

Here an ordinary writer would have preferred the word *fright* to *scare*, and omitted the definite article before *woods* and *villages*.

To the Evening Wind has been justly admired. It is the best specimen of that *completeness* which we have before spoken of as a characteristic feature in the poems of Mr. Bryant. It has a beginning, middle, and end, each depending upon the other, and each beautiful. Here are three lines breathing all the spirit of Shelley.

> Pleasant shall be thy way, *where meekly bows*
> *The shutting flower, and darkling waters pass,*
> *And 'twixt the o'ershadowing branches and the grass.*

The conclusion is admirable —

Go — but the circle of eternal change,
Which is the life of Nature, shall restore,
With sounds and scents from all thy mighty range,
Thee to thy birth-place of the deep once more;
Sweet odors in the sea air, sweet and strange,
Shall tell the home-sick mariner of the shore,
And, listening to thy murmur, he shall deem
He hears the rustling leaf and running stream.

Thanatopsis is somewhat more than half the length of *The Forest Hymn*, and of a character precisely similar. It is, however, the finer poem. Like *The Waterfowl*, it owes much to the point, force, and general beauty of its didactic conclusion. In the commencement, the lines

To him who, *in the love of nature*, holds
Communion with her visible forms, &c.

belong to a class of vague phrases, which, since the days of Byron, have obtained too universal a currency. The verse

Go forth under the open sky and list —

is sadly out of place amid the forcible and even Miltonic rhythm of such lines as

Take the wings
Of morning, and the Barcan desert pierce,
Or lose thyself in the continuous woods
Where rolls the Oregon.

But these are trivial faults indeed and the poem embodies a great degree of the most elevated beauty. Two of its passages, passages of the purest ideality, would alone render it worthy of the general commendation it has received.

So live, that when thy summons comes to join
The innumerable caravan that moves
To that mysterious realm where each shall take
His chamber in the silent halls of death,
Thou go not, like the quarry slave at night,
Scourged to his dungeon; but, sustained and soothed
By an unfaltering trust, approach thy grave
Like one who wraps the drapery of his couch
About him, and lies down to pleasant dreams.

The hills
Rock-ribbed and ancient as the sun — the vales
Stretching in pensive quietude between —
The venerable woods — rivers that move
In majesty, and the complaining brooks
That make the meadows green — and, poured round all,
Old Ocean's gray and melancholy waste —
Are but the solemn decorations all
Of the great tomb of man.

Oh, fairest of the Rural Maids! is a gem, of which we cannot sufficiently express our admiration. We quote in full.

Oh, fairest of the rural maids!
Thy birth was in the forest shades;
Green boughs and glimpses of the sky
Were all that met thine infant eye.

Thy sports, thy wanderings when a child
Were ever in the sylvan wild;
And all the beauty of the place
Is in thy heart and on thy face.

The twilight of the trees and rocks
Is in the light shade of thy locks,
Thy step is as the wind that weaves
Its playful way among the leaves.

Thine eyes are springs, in whose serene
And silent waters Heaven is seen;
Their lashes are the herbs that look
On their young figures in the brook.

The forest depths by foot impressed
Are not more sinless than thy breast;
The holy peace that fills the air
Of those calm solitudes, is there.

A rich simplicity is a main feature in this poem — simplicity of design and execution. This is strikingly perceptible in the opening and concluding lines, and in *expression* throughout. But there is a far higher and more strictly *ideal* beauty, which it is less easy to analyze. The original conception is of the very loftiest order of true Poesy. A maiden is born in the forest —

Green boughs and glimpses of the sky
Are all which meet her infant eye —

She is not merely *modelled in character* by the associations of her childhood — this were the thought of an ordinary poet — an idea that we meet with every day in rhyme — but she imbibes, in her physical as well as moral being, the traits, the very features of the delicious scenery around her — *its loveliness becomes a portion of her own —*

The twilight of the trees and rocks
Is in the light shade of her locks,
And all the beauty of the place
Is in her heart and on her face.

It would have been a highly poetical idea to imagine the tints in the locks of the maiden deducing *a resemblance* to the "twilight of the trees and rocks," from the constancy of her associations — but the spirit of Ideality is immeasurably more apparent when the "twilight" is represented as becoming *identified* with the shadows of her hair.

The twilight of the trees and rocks
Is in the light shade of her locks,
And all the beauty of the place
Is in her heart and on her face.

Feeling thus, we did not, in copying the poem, italicize the lines, although beautiful,

Thy step is *as* the wind that weaves
Its playful way among the leaves,

nor those which immediately follow. The two concluding verses, however, are again of the most elevated species of poetical merit.

The forest depths by foot impressed
Are not more sinless than thy breast —
The holy peace that fills the air
Of those calm solitudes, *is there.*

The image contained in the lines

Thine eyes are springs in whose serene
And silent waters Heaven is seen —

is one which, we think, for appropriateness, completeness,

and every perfect beauty of which imagery is susceptible, has never been surpassed — but *imagery* is susceptible of *no* beauty like that we have designated in the sentences above. The latter idea, moreover, is not original with our poet.

In all the rhapsodies of Mr. Bryant, which have reference to the beauty or the majesty of nature, is a most audible and thrilling tone of love and exultation. As far as he appreciates her loveliness or her augustness, no appreciation can be more ardent, more full of heart, more replete with the glowing soul of adoration. Nor, either in the moral or physical universe coming within the periphery of his vision, does he at any time fail to perceive and designate, at once, the legitimate items of the beautiful. Therefore, could we consider (as some have considered) the mere enjoyment of the beautiful when perceived, or even this enjoyment when combined with the readiest and truest perception and discrimination in regard to beauty presented, as a sufficient test of the poetical sentiment, we could have no hesitation in according to Mr. Bryant the very highest poetical rank. But something more, we have elsewhere presumed to say, is demanded. Just above, we spoke of "objects in the moral or physical universe coming within the periphery of his vision." We now mean to say, that the relative extent of these peripheries of poetical vision must ever be a primary consideration in our classification of poets. Judging Mr. B. in this manner, and by a *general* estimate of the volume before us, we should, of course, pause long before assigning him a place with the spiritual Shelleys, or Coleridges, or Wordsworths, or with Keats, or even Tennyson, or Wilson, or with some other burning lights of our own day, to be valued in a day to come. Yet if his poems, as a whole, will not warrant us in assigning him this grade, one such poem as the last upon which we have commented, is enough to assure us that he may attain it.

The writings of our author, as we find them *here*, are characterized by an air of calm and elevated contemplation more than by any other individual feature. In their mere didactics, however, they err essentially and primitively, inasmuch as such things are the province rather of Minerva than of the Camenæ. Of imagination, we discover much — but more of its rich and certain evidences, than of its ripened fruit. In all the minor merits Mr. Bryant is pre-eminent. His *ars celare artem* is most efficient. Of his "completeness," unity, and finish of style we have already spoken. As a versifier, we know of no writer, living or dead, who can be said greatly to surpass him. A Frenchman would assuredly call him "*un poëte des plus correctes.*"

Between Cowper and Young, perhaps, (with both of whom he has many points of analogy,) would be the post assigned him by an examination at once general and superficial. Even in this view, however, he has a juster appreciation of the beautiful than the one, of the sublime than the other — a finer taste than Cowper — an equally vigorous, and far more delicate imagination than Young. In regard to his proper rank among American poets there should be no question whatever. Few — at least few who are fairly before the public, have more than very shallow claims to a rivalry with the author of *Thanatopsis*.

Moore's Alciphron

Amid the vague mythology of Egypt, the voluptuous scenery of her Nile, and the gigantic mysteries of her pyramids, Anacreon Moore has found all of that striking *matériel* which he so much delights in working up, and which he has embodied in the poem before us. The design of the story (for plot it has none) has been a less consideration than its facilities, and is made subservient to its execution. The subject is comprised in five epistles. In the first, Alciphron, the head of the Epicurean sect at Athens, writes, from Alexandria, to his friend Cleon, in the former city. He tells him (assigning a reason for quitting Athens and her pleasures) that, having fallen asleep one night after protracted festivity, he beholds, in a dream, a spectre, who tells him that, beside the sacred Nile, he, the Epicurean, shall find that Eternal Life for which he had so long been sighing. In the second, from the same to the same, the traveller speaks, at large, and in rapturous terms, of the scenery of Egypt; of the beauty of her maidens; of an approaching Festival of the Moon; and of a wild hope entertained that amid the subterranean chambers of some huge pyramid lies the secret which he covets, the secret of Life Eternal. In the third letter, he relates a love adventure at the Festival. Fascinated by the charms of one of the nymphs of a procession, he is first in despair at losing sight of her, then overjoyed at again seeing her in Necropolis, and finally traces her steps until they are lost near one of the smaller pyramids. In epistle the fourth (still from the same to the same) he enters and explores the pyramid, and, passing through a complete series of Eleusinian mysteries, is at length successfully initiated into the secrets of Memphian priestcraft; we learning this latter point from letter the fifth, which concludes the poem, and is addressed by Orcus, high priest of Memphis, to Decius, a prætorian prefect.

A new poem from Moore calls to mind that critical opinion respecting him which had its origin, we believe, in the dogmatism of Coleridge — we mean the opinion that he is essentially the poet of *fancy* — the term being employed in contradistinction to *imagination*. "The fancy," says the author of the "Auncient Mariner," in his *Biographia Literaria*, "the fancy combines, the imagination creates." And this was intended, and has been received, as a distinction. If so at all, it is one without a difference; without even a difference of *degree*. The fancy as nearly creates as the imagination; and neither creates in any respect. All novel conceptions are merely unusual combinations. The mind of man can *imagine* nothing which has not really existed; and this point is susceptible of the most positive demonstration — see the Baron de Bielfeld, in his *Premiers Traits de L'Erudition Universelle*, 1767. It will be said, perhaps, that we can imagine a *griffin*, and that a griffin does not exist. Not the griffin certainly, but its component parts. It is a mere compendium of known limbs and features — of known qualities. Thus with all which seems to be *new* — which appears to be a *creation* of intellect. It is resoluble into the old. The wildest and most vigorous effort of mind cannot stand the test of this analysis.

We might make a distinction, *of degree*, between the fancy and the imagination, in saying that the latter is the former *loftily employed*. But experience proves this distinction to be unsatisfactory. What we *feel* and *know* to be fancy, will be found still only *fanciful*, whatever be the theme which engages it. It retains its idiosyncrasy under all circumstances. No *subject* exalts it into the ideal. We might exemplify this by reference to the writings of one whom our patriotism, rather than our judgment, has elevated to a niche in the Poetic Temple which he does not becomingly fill, and which he cannot long uninterruptedly hold. We allude to the late Dr. Rodman Drake, whose puerile abortion, "The Culprit Fay," we examined, at some length, in a *critique* elsewhere; proving it, we think, beyond all question, to belong to that class of the pseudo-ideal, in dealing with which we find ourselves embarrassed between a kind of half-consciousness that we ought to admire, and the certainty that we do not. Dr. Drake was employed upon a good subject — at least it is a subject precisely identical with those which Shakespeare was wont so happily to treat, and in which, especially, the author of "Lilian" has so wonderfully succeeded. But the American has brought to his task a mere *fancy*, and has grossly failed in doing what many suppose him to have done — in writing an ideal or imaginative poem. There is not one particle of the true ποίησις about "The Culprit Fay." We say that the subject, even at its best points, did not aid Dr. Drake in the slightest degree. He was never more than *fanciful.* The passage, for example, chiefly cited by his admirers, is the account of the "Sylphid Queen"; and to show the difference between the false and true ideal, we collated, in the review just alluded to, this, the most admired passage, with one upon a similar topic by Shelley. We shall be pardoned for repeating here, as nearly as we remember them, some words of what we then said.

The description of the Sylphid Queen runs thus:

> But oh, how fair the shape that lay
>   Beneath a rainbow bending bright;
> She seemed to the entranced Fay,
>   The loveliest of the forms of light;
> Her mantle was the purple rolled
>   At twilight in the west afar;
> 'Twas tied with threads of dawning gold,
>   And buttoned with a sparkling star.
> Her face was like the lily roon
>   That veils the vestal planet's hue;
> Her eyes two beamlets from the moon
>   Set floating in the welkin blue.
> Her hair is like the sunny beam,
> And the diamond gems which round it gleam
> Are the pure drops of dewy even
> That ne'er have left their native heaven.

In the "Queen Mab" of Shelley, a Fairy is thus introduced:

> Those who had looked upon the sight,
>   Passing all human glory,
> Saw not the yellow moon,
> Saw not the mortal scene,
> Heard not the night-wind's rush,

Heard not an earthly sound,
Saw but the fairy pageant,
Heard but the heavenly strains
That filled the lonely dwelling —

And thus described —

The Fairy's frame was slight; yon fibrous cloud
That catches but the palest tinge of even,
And which the straining eye can hardly seize
When melting into eastern twilight's shadow,
Were scarce so thin, so slight; but the fair star
That gems the glittering coronet of morn,
Sheds not a light so mild, so powerful,
As that which, bursting from the Fairy's form,
Spread a purpureal halo round the scene,
Yet with an undulating motion,
Swayed to her outline gracefully.

In these exquisite lines the faculty of mere comparison is but little exercised — that of ideality in a wonderful degree. It is probable that in a similar case Dr. Drake would have formed the face of the fairy of the "fibrous cloud," her arms of the "pale tinge of even," her eyes of the "fair stars," and her body of the "twilight shadow." Having so done, his admirers would have congratulated him upon his *imagination*, not taking the trouble to think that they themselves could at any moment *imagine* a fairy of materials equally as good, and conveying an equally distinct idea. Their mistake would be precisely analogous to that of many a schoolboy who admires the imagination displayed in Jack the Giant-Killer, and is finally rejoiced at discovering his own imagination to surpass that of the author, since the monsters destroyed by Jack are only about forty feet in height, and he himself has no trouble in imagining some of one hundred and forty. It will be seen that the fairy of Shelley is not a mere compound of incongruous natural objects, inartificially put together, and unaccompanied by any *moral* sentiment — but a being, in the illustration of whose nature some physical elements are used collaterally as adjuncts, while the main conception springs immediately, *or thus apparently springs*, from the brain of the poet, enveloped in the moral sentiments of grace, of color, of motion — of the beautiful, of the *mystical*, of the august — in short, of the ideal.

The truth is that the just distinction between the fancy and the imagination (and which is still but a distinction *of degree*) is involved in the consideration of the *mystic*. We give this as an idea of our own, altogether. We have no authority for our opinion — but do not the less firmly hold it. The term *mystic* is here employed in the sense of Augustus William Schlegel, and of most other German critics. It is applied by them to that class of composition in which there lies beneath the transparent upper current of meaning, an under or *suggestive* one. What we vaguely term the *moral* of any sentiment is its mystic or secondary expression. It has the vast force of an accompaniment in music. This vivifies the air; that spiritualizes the *fanciful* conception, and lifts it into the *ideal*.

This theory will bear, we think, the most rigorous tests which can be made applicable to it, and will be acknowledged as tenable by all who are themselves imaginative. If we carefully examine those poems, or portions of poems, or those prose romances, which mankind have been accustomed to designate as *imaginative*, (for an instinctive feeling leads us to employ properly the term whose full import we have still never been able to define,) it will be seen that all so designated are remarkable for the *suggestive* character which we have discussed. They are strongly *mystic*—in the proper sense of the word. We will here only call to the reader's mind, the *Prometheus Vinctus* of Æschylus; the *Inferno* of Dante; the *Destruction of Numantia* by Cervantes; the *Comus* of Milton; the *Auncient Mariner*, the *Christabel*, and the *Kubla Khan* of Coleridge; the *Nightingale* of Keats; and, most especially, the *Sensitive Plant* of Shelley, and the *Undine* of De La Motte Fouqué. These two latter poems (for we call them both such) are the finest possible examples of the purely *ideal.* There is little of fancy here, and everything of imagination. With each note of the lyre is heard a ghostly, and not always a distinct, but an august and soul-exalting *echo.* In every glimpse of beauty presented, we catch, through long and wild vistas, dim bewildering visions of a far more ethereal beauty *beyond.* But not so in poems which the world has always persisted in terming *fanciful.* Here the upper current is often exceedingly brilliant and beautiful; but then men *feel* that this upper current *is all.* No Naiad voice addresses them *from below.* The notes of the air of the song do not tremble with the according tones of the accompaniment.

It is the failure to perceive these truths which has occasioned that embarrassment which our critics experience while discussing the topic of Moore's station in the poetic world — that hesitation with which we are obliged to refuse him the loftiest rank among the most noble. The popular voice, and the popular heart, have denied him that happiest quality, imagination — and here the popular voice (*because* for once it has gone with the popular heart) is right, but yet only relatively so. Imagination is not the leading feature of the poetry of Moore; but he possesses it in no little degree.

We will quote a few instances from the poem now before us — instances which will serve to exemplify the distinctive features which we have attributed to ideality.

It is the *suggestive* force which exalts and etherealizes the passages we copy.

> Or is it that there lurks, indeed,
> Some truth in man's prevailing creed,
> And that our guardians from on high
> Come, in that pause from toil and sin,
> To put the senses' curtain by,
> And on the wakeful soul look in!

Again —

> The eternal pyramids of Memphis burst
> Awfully on my sight — standing sublime
> 'Twixt earth and heaven, the watch-towers of time,
> From whose lone summit, when his reign hath past,
> From earth for ever, he will look his last.

And again —

> Is there for man no hope — but this which dooms
> His only lasting trophies to be tombs!
> But 'tis not so — earth, heaven, all nature shows
> He *may* become immortal, *may* unclose
> The wings within him wrapt, and proudly rise
> Redeemed from earth a creature of the skies!

And here —

> The pyramid shadows, stretching from the light,
> Look like the first colossal steps of night,
> Stalking across the valley to invade
> The distant hills of porphyry with their shade!

And once more —

> Their Silence, thoughtful God, who loves
> The neighbourhood of Death, in groves
> Of asphodel lies hid, and weaves
> His hushing spell among the leaves.

Such lines as these, we must admit, however, are not of frequent occurrence in the poem — the sum of whose great beauty is composed of the several sums of a world of minor excellencies.

Moore has always been renowned for the number and appositeness, as well as novelty, of his similes; and the renown thus acquired is strongly indicial of his deficiency in that nobler merit — the noblest of them all. No poet thus distinguished was ever richly ideal. Pope and Cowper are remarkable instances in point. Similes (so much insisted upon by the critics of the reign of Queen Anne) are never, in our opinion, strictly in good taste, whatever may be said to the contrary, and certainly can never be made to accord with other high qualities, except when naturally arising from the subject in the way of illustration — and, when thus arising, they have seldom the merit of novelty. To be novel, they must fail in essential particulars. The higher minds will avoid their frequent use. They form no portion of the ideal, and appertain to the fancy alone.

We proceed with a few random observations upon

"Alciphron." The poem is distinguished throughout by a very happy facility which has never been mentioned in connection with its author, but which has much to do with the reputation he has obtained. We allude to the facility with which he recounts a poetical story in a *prosaic* way. By this is meant that he preserves the tone and method of arrangement of a prose relation, and thus obtains great advantages over his more stilted compeers. His is no poetical *style* (such, for example, as the French have—a distinct style for a distinct purpose,) but an easy and ordinary prose manner, *ornamented into poetry*. By means of this he is enabled to enter, with ease, into details which would baffle any other versifier of the age, and at which Lamartine would stand aghast. For anything that we see to the contrary, Moore might solve a cubic equation in verse or go through with the three several demonstrations of the binomial theorem, one after the other, or indeed all at the same time. His facility in this respect is truly admirable, and is, no doubt, the result of long practice after mature deliberation. We refer the reader to page 50, of the pamphlet now reviewed; where the minute and conflicting incidents of the descent into the pyramid are detailed with absolutely *more* precision than we have ever known a similar relation detailed with in prose.

In general dexterity and melody of versification the author of Lalla Rookh is unrivalled; but he is by no means at all times accurate, falling occasionally into the common foible of throwing accent upon syllables too unimportant to sustain it. Thus, in the lines which follow, where we have italicized the weak syllables:

And mark 'tis nigh; already *the* sun bids —
While hark from all the temples *a* rich swell
I rush in*to* the cool night-air —

He also too frequently draws out the word Heaven into two syllables — a protraction which it *never* will support.

His English is now and then objectionable, as, at page 26, where he speaks of

lighted barks
That down Syene's cataract *shoots*,

making *shoots* rhyme with flutes, below; also, at page 6, and elsewhere, where the word *none* has improperly a singular, instead of a plural force. But such criticism as this is somewhat captious, for in general he is most highly polished.

At page 27, he has stolen his "woven snow" from the *ventum textilem* of Apuleius.

At page 8, he either himself has misunderstood the tenets of Epicurus, or wilfully misrepresents them through the voice of Alciphron. We incline to the former idea, however; as the philosophy of that most noble of the sophists is habitually perverted by the moderns. Nothing could be more spiritual and less sensual than the doctrines we so torture into wrong. But we have drawn out this notice at somewhat too great length, and must conclude. In truth, the exceeding beauty of "Alciphron" has bewildered and detained us. We could not point out a poem in any language which, as a whole, greatly excels it. It is far superior to "Lalla Rookh." While Moore does not reach, except in rare snatches, the height of the loftiest qualities of some whom we have named, yet he has written finer poems than any, of equal length, by the greatest of his rivals. His radiance, not always as bright as some flashes from other pens, is yet a radiance of equable glow, whose total amount of light exceeds, by very much, we think, that total amount in the case of any cotemporary writer whatsoever. A vivid fancy; an epigrammatic spirit; a fine taste; vivacity, dexterity and a musical ear; have made him very easily what he is, the most popular poet now living — if not the most popular that ever lived — and, perhaps, a slight modification at birth of that which phrenologists have agreed to term *temperament*, might have made him the truest and noblest votary of the muse of any age or clime. As it is, we have only casual glimpses of that *mens divinior* which is assuredly enshrined within him.

Exordium

In commencing, with the New Year, a New Volume, we shall be permitted to say a very few words by way of *exordium* to our usual chapter of Reviews, or, as we should prefer calling them, of Critical Notices. Yet we speak *not* for the sake of the *exordium*, but because we have really something to say, and know not when or where better to say it.

That the public attention, in America, has, of late days, been more than usually directed to the matter of literary criticism, is plainly apparent. Our periodicals are beginning to acknowledge the importance of the science (shall we so term it?) and to disdain the flippant *opinion* which so long has been made its substitute.

Time was when we imported our critical decisions from the mother country. For many years we enacted a perfect farce of subserviency to the *dicta* of Great Britain. At last a revulsion of feeling, with self-disgust, necessarily ensued. Urged by these, we plunged into the opposite extreme. In throwing *totally* off that "authority," whose voice had so long been so sacred, we even surpassed, and by much, our original folly. But the watchword now was, "a national literature!" — as if any true literature *could be* "national" — as if the world at large were not the only proper stage for the literary *histrio*. We became, suddenly, the merest and maddest *partizans* in letters. Our papers spoke of "tariffs" and "protection." Our Magazines had habitual passages about that "truly native novelist, Mr. Cooper," or that "staunch American genius, Mr. Paulding." Unmindful of the spirit of the axioms that "a prophet has no honor in his own land" and that "a hero is never a hero to his *valet-de-chambre*" — axioms founded in reason and in truth — our reviews urged the propriety — our booksellers the necessity, of strictly "American" themes. A foreign subject, at this epoch, was a weight more than enough to drag down into the very depths of critical damnation the finest writer owning nativity in the States; while, on the reverse, we found ourselves daily in the paradoxical dilemma of liking, or pretending to like, a stupid book the better because (sure enough) its stupidity was of our own growth, and discussed our own affairs.

It is, in fact, but very lately that this anomalous state of feeling has shown any signs of subsidence. Still it *is* subsiding. Our views of literature in general having expanded, we begin to demand the use — to inquire into the offices and provinces of criticism — to regard it more as an art based immovably in nature, less as a mere system of fluctuating and conventional dogmas. And, with the prevalence of these ideas, has arrived a distaste even to the home-dictation of the bookseller-*coteries*. If our editors are not as yet *all* independent of the will of a publisher, a majority of them scruple, at least, *to confess* a subservience, and enter into no positive combinations against the minority who despise and discard it. And this is a *very* great improvement of exceedingly late date.

Escaping these quicksands, our criticism is nevertheless in some danger — some very little danger — of falling into the pit of a most detestable species of cant — the cant of *generality*. This tendency has been given it, in the first instance, by the onward and tumultuous spirit of the age. With the increase of the thinking-material comes the desire, if not the necessity, of abandoning particulars for masses. Yet in our individual case, as a nation, we seem merely to have adopted this bias from the British Quarterly Reviews, upon which our own Quarterlies have been slavishly and pertinaciously modelled. In the foreign journal, the review or criticism properly so termed, has gradually yet steadily degenerated into what we see it at present — that is to say, into anything but criticism. Originally a "review" was not so called as *lucus a non lucendo*. Its name conveyed a just idea of its design. It reviewed, or surveyed the book whose title formed its text, and, giving an analysis of its contents, passed judgment upon its merits or defects. But, through the system of anonymous contribution, this natural process lost ground from day to day. The name of a writer being known only to a few, it became to him an object not so much to write well, as to write fluently, at so many guineas per sheet. The analysis of a book is a matter of time and of mental exertion. For many classes of composition there is required a deliberate perusal, with notes, and subsequent generalization. An easy substitute for this labor was found in a digest or compendium of the work noticed, with copious extracts — or a still easier, in random comments upon such passages as accidentally met the eye of the critic, with the passages themselves copied at full length. The mode of reviewing most in favor, however, because carrying with it the greatest *semblance* of care, was that of diffuse essay upon the subject matter of the publication, the reviewer (?) using the facts alone which the publication supplied, and using them as material for some theory, the sole concern, bearing, and intention of which, was mere difference of opinion with the author. These came at length to be understood and habitually practised as the customary or conventional *fashions* of review; and although the nobler order of intellects did not fall into the full heresy of these fashions — we may still assert that even Macaulay's nearest approach to criticism in its legitimate sense, is to be found in his article upon Ranke's "History of the Popes" — an article in which the whole strength of the reviewer is put forth *to account* for a single fact — the progress of Romanism — which the book under discussion has established.

Now, while we do not mean to deny that a good essay is a good thing, we yet assert that these papers on general topics have nothing whatever to do with that *criticism* which their evil example has nevertheless infected *in se.* Because these dogmatizing pamphlets, which *were once* "Reviews," have lapsed from their original faith, it does not follow that the faith itself is extinct — that "there shall be no more cakes and ale" — that criticism, in its old acceptation, does not exist. But we complain of a growing inclination on the part of our lighter journals to believe, on such grounds, that such is the fact — that because the British Quarterlies, through supineness, and our own, through a degrading imitation, have come to merge all varieties of vague generalization in the one title of "Review," it therefore results that criticism, being everything in the universe, is, consequently, nothing whatever in fact. For to this end, and to none other conceivable, is the tendency of such propositions, for example, as we find in a late number of that very clever monthly magazine, Arcturus.

> "But *now*" (the emphasis on the *now* is our own) — "but now," says Mr. Mathews, in the preface to the first volume of his journal, "criticism has a wider scope and a universal interest. It dismisses errors of grammar, and hands over an imperfect rhyme or a false quantity to the proof-reader; it looks *now* to the heart of the subject and the author's design. It is a test of opinion. Its acuteness is not pedantic, but philosophical; it unravels the web of the author's mystery to interpret his meaning to others; it detects his sophistry, because sophistry is injurious to the heart and life; it promulgates his beauties with liberal, generous praise, because this is his true duty as the servant of truth. Good criticism may be well asked for, since it is the type of the literature of the day. It gives method to the universal inquisitiveness on every topic relating to life or action. A criticism, *now*, includes every form of literature, except perhaps the imaginative and the strictly dramatic. It is an essay, a sermon, an oration, a chapter in history, a philosophical speculation, a prose-poem, an art-novel, a dialogue; it admits of humor, pathos, the personal feelings of autobiography, the broadest views of statesmanship. As the ballad and the epic were the productions of the days of Homer, the review is the native characteristic growth of the nineteenth century."

We respect the talents of Mr. Mathews, but must dissent from nearly all that he here says. The species of "review" which he designates as the "characteristic growth of the nineteenth century" is only the growth of the last twenty or thirty years *in Great Britain.* The French Reviews, for example, which are *not* anonymous, are very different things, and preserve the *unique* spirit of true criticism. And what need we say of the Germans? — what of Winckelmann, of Novalis, of Schelling, of Goethe, of Augustus William, and of Frederick Schlegel? — that their magnificent *critiques raisonnées* differ from those of Kames, of Johnson, and of Blair, in principle not at all, (for the principles of these artists will not fail until Nature herself expires,) but solely in their more careful elaboration, their greater thoroughness, their more profound analysis and application of the principles themselves. That a criticism "*now*" should be different in spirit, as Mr. Mathews supposes, from a criticism at any previous period, is to insinuate a charge of variability in laws that cannot vary — the laws of man's heart and intellect — for these are the sole basis upon which the true critical art is established. And this art "*now*" no more than in the days of the "Dunciad," can, without neglect of its duty, "dismiss errors of grammar," or "hand over an imperfect rhyme or a false quantity to the proof-reader." What is meant by a "test of opinion" in the connection here given the words by Mr. M., we do not comprehend as clearly as we could desire. By this phrase we are as completely enveloped in doubt as was Mirabeau in the castle of *If.* To our imperfect appreciation it seems to form a portion of that general vagueness which is the *tone* of the whole philosophy at this point: — but all that which our journalist describes a criticism to be, is all that which we sturdily maintain it *is not.* Criticism is *not,* we think, an essay, nor a sermon, nor an oration, nor a chapter in history, nor a philosophical speculation, nor a prose-poem, nor an art-novel, nor a dialogue. In fact, it *can be* nothing in the world but — a criticism. But if it were all that Arcturus imagines, it is not very clear why it might not be equally "imaginative" or "dramatic" — a romance or a melodrama, or both. That it would be a farce cannot be doubted.

It is against this frantic spirit of *generalization* that we protest. We have a word, "criticism," whose import is sufficiently distinct, through long usage, at least; and we have an art of high importance and clearly-ascertained limit, which this word is quite well enough understood to represent. Of that conglomerate science to which Mr. Mathews so eloquently alludes, and of which we are instructed that it is anything and everything at once — of this science we know nothing, and really wish to know less; but we object to our contemporary's appropriation in its behalf, of a term to which we, in common with a large majority of mankind, have been accustomed to attach a certain and very definitive idea. Is there no word but "criticism" which may be made to serve the purposes of "Arcturus"? Has it any objection to Orphicism, or Dialism, or Emersonism, or any other pregnant compound indicative of confusion worse confounded?

Still, we must not pretend a total misapprehension of the idea of Mr. Mathews, and we should be sorry that he misunderstood *us*. It may be granted that we differ only in terms — although the difference will yet be found not unimportant in effect. Following the highest authority, we would wish, in a word, to limit literary criticism to comment upon *Art*. A book is written — and it is only *as the book* that we subject it to review. With the opinions of the work, considered otherwise than in their relation to the work itself, the critic has really nothing to do. It is his part simply to decide upon *the mode* in which these opinions are brought to bear. Criticism is thus no "test of opinion." For this test, the work, divested of its pretensions as an *art-product*, is turned over for discussion to the world at large — and first, to that class which it especially addresses — if a history, to the historian — if a metaphysical treatise, to the moralist. In this, the only true and intelligible sense, it will be seen that criticism, the test or analysis of *Art*, (*not* of opinion,) is only properly employed upon productions which have their basis in art itself, and although the journalist (whose duties and objects are multiform) may turn aside, at pleasure, from the *mode* or vehicle of opinion to discussion of the opinion conveyed — it is still clear that he is "*critical*" only in so much as he deviates from his true province not at all.

And of the critic himself what shall we say? — for as yet we have spoken only the *proem* to the true *epopea*. What *can* we better say of him than, with Bulwer, that "he must have courage to blame boldly, magnanimity to eschew envy, genius to appreciate, learning to compare, an eye for beauty, an ear for music, and a heart for feeling." Let us add, a talent for analysis and a solemn indifference to abuse.

Longfellow's Ballads

In our last number we had some hasty observations on these "Ballads" — observations which we now propose, in some measure, to amplify and explain.

It may be remembered that, among other points, we demurred to Mr. Longfellow's *themes*, or rather to their general character. We found fault with the too obtrusive nature of their *didacticism*. Some years ago we urged a similar objection to one or two of the longer pieces of Bryant; and neither time nor reflection has sufficed to modify, in the slightest particular, our convictions upon this topic.

We have said that Mr. Longfellow's conception of the *aims* of poesy is erroneous; and that thus, laboring at a disadvantage, he does violent wrong to his own high powers; and now the question is, what *are* his ideas of the aims of the Muse, as we gather these ideas from the *general* tendency of his poems? It will be at once evident that, imbued with the peculiar spirit of German song (a pure conventionality) he regards the inculcation of a *moral* as essential. Here we find it necessary to repeat that we have reference only to the *general* tendency of his compositions; for there are some magnificent exceptions, where, as if by accident, he has permitted his genius to get the better of his conventional prejudice. But didacticism is the prevalent *tone* of his song. His invention, his imagery, his all, is made subservient to the elucidation of some one or more points (but rarely of more than one) which he looks upon as *truth*. And that this mode of procedure will find stern defenders should never excite surprise, so long as the world is full to overflowing with cant and conventicles. There are men who will scramble on all fours through the muddiest sloughs of vice to pick up a single apple of virtue. There are things called men who, so long as the sun rolls, will greet with snuffling huzzas every figure that takes upon itself the semblance of truth, even although the figure, in itself only a "stuffed Paddy," be as much out of place as a toga on the statue of Washington, or out of season as rabbits in the days of the dog-star.

Now with as deep a reverence for "the true" as ever inspired the bosom of mortal man, we would limit, in many respects, its modes of inculcation. We would limit to enforce them. We would not render them impotent by dissipation. The demands of truth are severe. She has no sympathy with the myrtles. All that is indispensable in song is all with which she has nothing to do. To deck her in gay robes is to render her a harlot. It is but making her a flaunting paradox to wreathe her in gems and flowers. Even in stating this our present proposition, we verify our own words — we feel the necessity, in enforcing this *truth*, of descending from metaphor. Let us then be simple and distinct. To convey "the true" we are required to dismiss from the attention all inessentials. We must be perspicuous, precise, terse. We need concentration rather than expansion of mind. We must be calm, unimpassioned, unexcited — in a word, we must be in that peculiar mood which, as nearly as possible, is the exact converse of the poetical. He must be blind indeed who cannot perceive the radical and chasmal difference between the truthful and the poetical modes of inculcation. He must be grossly wedded to conventionalisms who, in spite of this difference, shall still attempt to reconcile the obstinate oils and waters of Poetry and Truth.

Dividing the world of mind into its most obvious and immediately recognizable distinctions, we have the pure intellect, taste, and the moral sense. We place *taste* between the intellect and the moral sense, because it is just this intermediate space which, in the mind, it occupies. It is the connecting link in the triple chain.

It serves to sustain a mutual intelligence between the extremes. It appertains, in strict appreciation, to the former, but is distinguished from the latter by so faint a difference, that Aristotle has not hesitated to class some of its operations among the Virtues themselves. But the *offices* of the trio are broadly marked. Just as conscience, or the moral sense, recognizes duty; just as the intellect deals with *truth;* so is it the part of taste alone to inform us of BEAUTY. And Poesy is the handmaiden but of Taste. Yet we would not be misunderstood. This handmaiden is not forbidden to moralize — in her own fashion. She is not forbidden to depict — but to reason and preach, of virtue. As, of this latter, conscience recognizes the obligation, so intellect teaches the expediency, while taste contents herself with displaying the beauty: waging war with vice merely on the ground of its inconsistency with fitness, harmony, proportion — in a word with τὸ καλόν.

An important condition of man's immortal nature is thus, plainly, the sense of the Beautiful. This it is which ministers to his delight in the manifold forms and colors and sounds and sentiments amid which he exists. And, just as the eyes of Amaryllis are repeated in the mirror, or the living lily in the lake, so is the mere *record* of these forms and colors and sounds and sentiments — so is their mere oral or written repetition a duplicate source of delight. But this repetition is not Poesy. He who shall merely sing with whatever rapture, in however harmonious strains, or with however vivid a truth of imitation, of the sights and sounds which greet him in common with all mankind — he, we say, has yet failed to prove his divine title. There is still a longing unsatisfied, which he has been impotent to fulfil. There is still a thirst unquenchable, which to allay he has shown us no crystal springs. This burning thirst belongs to the *immortal* essence of man's nature. It is equally a consequence and an indication of his perennial life. It is the desire of the moth for the star. It is not the mere appreciation of the beauty before us. It is a wild effort to reach the beauty above. It is a forethought of the loveliness to come. It is a passion to be satiated by no sublunary sights, or sounds, or sentiments, and the soul thus athirst strives to allay its fever in futile efforts at *creation*. Inspired with a prescient ecstasy of the beauty beyond the grave, it struggles by multiform novelty of combination among the things and thoughts of Time, to anticipate some portion of that loveliness whose very elements, perhaps, appertain solely to Eternity. And the result of such effort, on the part of souls fittingly constituted, is alone what mankind have agreed to denominate Poetry.

We say this with little fear of contradiction. Yet the spirit of our assertion must be more heeded than the letter. Mankind have *seemed* to define Poesy in a thousand, and in a thousand conflicting definitions. But the war is one only of words. Induction is as well applicable to this subject as to the most palpable and utilitarian; and by its sober processes we find that, in respect to compositions which have been really received as poems, the *imaginative*, or, more popularly, the creative portions *alone* have ensured them to be so received. Yet these works, on account of these portions, having once been so received and so named, it has happened, naturally and inevitably, that other portions totally unpoetic have not only come to be regarded by the popular voice as poetic, but have been made to serve as false standards of perfection, in the adjustment of other poetical claims. Whatever has been found in whatever has been received as a poem, has been blindly regarded as *ex statu* poetic. And this is a species of gross error which scarcely could have made its way into any less intangible topic. In fact that license which appertains to the Muse herself, it has been thought decorous, if not sagacious to indulge, in all examination of her character.

Poesy is thus seen to be a response — unsatisfactory it is true — but still in some measure a response, to a natural and irrepressible demand. Man being what he is, the time could never have been in which Poesy was not. Its first element is the thirst for supernal BEAUTY — a beauty which is not afforded the soul by any existing collocation of earth's forms — a beauty which, perhaps, *no possible* combination of these forms would fully produce. Its second element is the attempt to satisfy this thirst by *novel* combinations among those forms of beauty which already exist — or by novel combinations, *of those combinations which our predecessors, toiling in chase of the same phantom, have already set in order.* We thus clearly deduce the *novelty*, the *originality*, the *invention*, the *imagination*, or lastly the *creation* of BEAUTY, (for the terms as here employed are synonymous) as the essence of all Poesy. Nor is this idea so much at variance with ordinary opinion as, at first sight, it may appear. A multitude of antique dogmas on this topic will be found, when divested of extrinsic speculation, to be easily resoluble into the definition now proposed. We do nothing more than present tangibly the vague clouds of the world's idea. We recognize the idea itself floating, unsettled, indefinite, in every attempt which has yet been made to circumscribe the conception of "Poesy" in words. A striking instance of this is observable in the fact that no definition exists, in which either "the beautiful," or some one of those qualities which we have above designated synonymously with "creation," has not been pointed out as the *chief* attribute of the Muse. "Invention," however, or "imagination," is by far more commonly insisted upon. The word ποίησις itself (creation) speaks volumes upon this point. Neither will it be amiss here to mention Count Bielfeld's definition of poetry as "*L'art d'exprimer les pensées par la fiction.*" With this definition (of which the philosophy is profound to a certain extent) the German terms *Dichtkunst*, the art of fiction, and *Dichten*, to feign, which are used for "*poetry*" and "*to make verses*," are in full and remarkable accordance. It is, nevertheless, in the *combination* of the two omni-prevalent ideas that the novelty and, we believe, the force of our own proposition is to be found.

So far, we have spoken of Poesy as of an abstraction alone. As such, it is obvious that it may be applicable in various moods. The sentiment may develop itself in Sculpture, in Painting, in Music, or otherwise. But our present business is with its development in words — that development to which, in practical acceptation, the world has agreed to limit the term. And at this point there is one consideration which induces us to pause. We cannot make up our minds to admit (as some have admitted) the inessentiality of rhythm. On the contrary, the universality of its use in the earliest poetical efforts of all mankind would be sufficient to assure us, not merely of its congeniality with the Muse, or of its adaptation to her purposes, but of its elementary and indispensable importance. But here we must, perforce, content ourselves with mere suggestion; for this topic is of a character which would lead us too far. We have already spoken of Music as one of the moods of poetical development. It is in Music, perhaps, that the soul most nearly attains that end upon which we have commented — the creation of supernal beauty. It may be, indeed, that this august aim is here even partially or imperfectly attained, *in fact*. The *elements* of that beauty which is felt in sound, *may be* the mutual or common heritage of Earth and Heaven. In the soul's struggles at combination it is thus not impossible that a harp may strike notes not unfamiliar to the angels. And in this view the wonder may well be less that all attempts at defining the character or sentiment of the deeper musical impressions, have been found absolutely futile. Contenting ourselves, therefore, with the firm conviction, that music (in its modifications of rhythm and rhyme) is of so vast a moment in Poesy, as *never* to be neglected by him who is truly poetical — is of so mighty a force in furthering the great aim intended that he is mad who rejects its assistance — content with this idea we shall not pause to maintain its absolute essentiality, for the mere sake of rounding a definition. We will but add, at this point, that the highest possible development of the Poetical Sentiment is to be found in the union of song with music, in its popular sense. The old Bards and Minnesingers possessed, in the fullest perfection, the finest and truest elements of Poesy; and Thomas Moore, singing his own ballads, is but putting the final touch to their completion as poems.

To recapitulate, then, we would define in brief the Poetry of words as the *Rhythmical Creation of Beauty*. Beyond the limits of Beauty its province does not extend. Its sole arbiter is Taste. With the Intellect or with the Conscience it has only collateral relations. It has no dependence, unless incidentally, upon either Duty or *Truth*. That our definition will necessarily exclude much of what, through a supine toleration, has been hitherto ranked as poetical, is a matter which affords us not even momentary concern. We address but the thoughtful, and heed only their approval — with our own. If our suggestions are truthful, then "after many days" shall they be understood as truth, even though found in contradiction of *all* that has been hitherto so understood. If false shall we not be the first to bid them die?

We would reject, of course, all such matters as "Armstrong on Health," a revolting production; Pope's "Essay on Man," which may well be content with the title of an "Essay in Rhyme;" "Hudibras" and other merely humorous pieces. We do not gainsay the peculiar merits of either of these latter compositions — but deny them the position held. In a notice, month before last, of Brainard's Poems, we took occasion to show that the common use of a certain instrument, (rhythm) had tended, more than aught else, to confound humorous verse with poetry. The observation is now recalled to corroborate what we have just said in respect to the vast effect or force of melody in itself — an effect which could elevate into even momentary confusion with the highest efforts of mind, compositions such as are the greater number of satires or burlesques.

Of the poets who have appeared most fully instinct with the principles now developed, we may mention *Keats* as the most remarkable. He is the sole British poet who has never erred in his themes. Beauty is always his aim.

We have thus shown our ground of objection to the general *themes* of Professor Longfellow. In common with all who claim the sacred title of poet, he should limit his endeavors to the creation of novel moods of beauty, in form, in color, in sound, in sentiment; for over all this wide range has the poetry of words dominion. To what the world terms *prose* may be safely and properly left all else. The artist who doubts of his thesis, may always resolve his doubt by the single question — "might not this matter be as well or better handled in *prose?*" If it *may*, then is it no subject for the Muse. In the general acceptation of the term *Beauty* we are content to rest; being careful only to suggest that, in our peculiar views, it must be understood as inclusive of *the sublime.*

Of the pieces which constitute the present volume, there are not more than one or two thoroughly fulfilling the idea above proposed; although the volume as a whole is by no means so chargeable with didacticism as Mr. Longfellow's previous book. We would mention as poems *nearly true*, "The Village Blacksmith;" "The Wreck of the Hesperus" and especially "The Skeleton in Armor." In the first-mentioned we have the *beauty* of simple-mindedness as a genuine thesis; and this thesis is inimitably handled until the concluding stanza, where the spirit of legitimate poesy is aggrieved in the pointed antithetical deduction of a *moral* from what has gone before. In "The Wreck of the Hesperus" we have the *beauty* of childlike confidence and innocence, with that of the father's stern courage and affection. But, with slight exception, those particulars of the storm here detailed are not poetic subjects. Their thrilling *horror* belongs to prose, in which it could be far more effectively discussed, as Professor Longfellow may assure himself at any moment by experiment. There *are* points of a tempest which afford the loftiest and truest poetical themes — points in which pure beauty is found, or, better still, beauty heightened into the sublime, by terror. But when we read, among other similar things, that

> The salt sea was frozen on her breast,
> The salt tears in her eyes,

we feel, if not positive disgust, at least a chilling sense of the inappropriate. In the "Skeleton in Armor" we find a pure and perfect thesis artistically treated. We find the beauty of bold courage and self-confidence, of love and maiden devotion, of reckless adventure, and finally of life-contemning grief. Combined with all this we have numerous *points* of beauty apparently insulated, but all aiding the main effect or impression. The heart is stirred, and the mind does not lament its mal-instruction. The metre is simple, sonorous, well-balanced and fully adapted to the subject. Upon the whole, there are few truer poems than this. It has but one defect — an important one. The prose remarks prefacing the narrative are really *necessary*. But every work of art should contain within itself all that is requisite for its own comprehension. And this remark is especially true of the ballad. In poems of magnitude the mind of the reader is not, at all times, enabled to include, in one comprehensive survey, the proportions and proper adjustment of the whole. He is pleased, if at all, with particular passages; and the sum of his pleasure is compounded of the sums of the pleasurable sentiments inspired by these individual passages in the progress of perusal. But, in pieces of less extent, the pleasure is *unique*, in the proper acceptation of this term — the understanding is employed, without difficulty, in the contemplation of the picture *as a whole;* and thus its effect will depend, in great measure, upon the perfection of its finish, upon the nice adaptation of its constituent parts, and especially, upon what is rightly termed by Schlegel *the unity or totality of interest.* But the practice of prefixing explanatory passages is utterly at variance with such unity. By the prefix, we are either put in possession of the subject of the poem; or some hint, historic fact, or suggestion, is thereby afforded, not included in the body of the piece, which, without the hint, is incomprehensible. In the latter case, while perusing the poem, the reader must revert, in mind at least, to the prefix, for the necessary explanation. In the former, the poem being a mere paraphrase of the prefix, the interest is divided between the prefix and the paraphrase. In either instance the totality of effect is destroyed.

Of the other original poems in the volume before us, there is none in which the aim of instruction, or *truth*, has not been too obviously substituted for the legitimate aim, *beauty*. In our last number, we took occasion to say that a didactic moral might be happily made the *under-current* of a poetical theme, and, in "Burton's Magazine," some two years since, we treated this point at length, in a review of Moore's "Alciphron"; but the moral thus conveyed is invariably an ill effect when obtruding beyond the upper current of the thesis itself. Perhaps the worst specimen of this obtrusion is given us by our poet in "Blind Bartimeus" and the "Goblet of Life," where, it will be observed that the *sole* interest of the upper current of meaning depends upon its relation or reference to the under. What we read upon the surface would be *vox et prœterea nihil* in default of the moral beneath. The Greek *finales* of "Blind Bartimeus" are an affectation altogether inexcusable. What the small, second-hand, Gibbon-ish pedantry of Byron introduced, is unworthy the imitation of Longfellow.

Of the translations we scarcely think it necessary to speak at all. We regret that our poet will persist in busying himself about such matters. *His* time might be better employed in original conception. Most of these versions are marked with the error upon which we have commented. This error is in fact, essentially Germanic. "The Luck of Edenhall," however, is a truly beautiful poem; and we say this with all that deference which the opinion of the "Democratic Review" demands. This composition appears to us *one of the very finest.* It has all the free, hearty, *obvious* movement of the true ballad-legend. The greatest force of language is combined in it with the richest imagination, acting in its most legitimate province. Upon the whole, we prefer it even to the "Sword-Song" of Körner. The pointed moral with which it terminates is so exceedingly natural — so perfectly fluent from the incidents — that we have hardly heart to pronounce it in ill taste. We may observe of this ballad, in conclusion, that its subject is more *physical* than is usual in Germany. Its images are rich rather in physical than in moral beauty. And this tendency, in Song, is the true one. It is chiefly, if we are not mistaken — it is chiefly amid forms of physical loveliness (we use the word *forms* in its widest sense as embracing modifications of sound and color) that the soul seeks the realization of its dreams of BEAUTY. It is to her demand in this sense especially, that the poet, who is wise, will most frequently and most earnestly respond.

"The Children of the Lord's Supper" is, beyond

doubt, a true and most beautiful poem in great part, while, in some particulars, it is too metaphysical to have any pretension to the name. In our last number, we objected, briefly, to its metre—the ordinary Latin or Greek Hexameter—dactyls and spondees at random, with a spondee in conclusion. We maintain that the Hexameter can never be introduced into our language, from the nature of that language itself. This rhythm demands, *for English ears*, a preponderance of natural spondees. Our tongue has few. Not only does the Latin and Greek, with the Swedish, and some others, abound in them; but the Greek and Roman ear had become reconciled (why or how is unknown) to the reception of artificial spondees—that is to say, spondaic words formed partly of one word and partly of another, or from an excised part of one word. In short the ancients were content to read *as they scanned*, or nearly so. It may be safely prophesied that we shall never do this; and thus we shall never admit English Hexameters. The attempt to introduce them, after the repeated failures of Sir Philip Sidney, and others, is, perhaps, somewhat discreditable to the scholarship of Professor Longfellow. The "Democratic Review," in saying that he has triumphed over difficulties in this rhythm, has been deceived, it is evident, by the facility with which some of these verses may be read. In glancing over the poem, we do not observe a single verse which can be read, *to English ears, as a Greek Hexameter*. There are many, however, which can be well read as mere English dactylic verses; such, for example, as the well-known lines of Byron, commencing

Know ye the | land where the | cypress and | myrtle.

These lines (although full of irregularities) are, in their perfection, formed of three dactyls and a cæsura — just as if we should cut short the initial verse of the Bucolics thus —

Tityre | tu patu | læ recu | bans —

The "myrtle," at the close of Byron's line, is a double rhyme, and must be understood as one syllable.

Now a great number of Professor Longfellow's Hexameters are merely these dactylic lines, *continued for two feet*. For example —

Whispered the | race of the | flowers and | merry on |
balancing | branches.

In this example, also, "branches," which is a double ending, must be regarded as the cæsura, or one syllable, of which alone it has the force.

As we have already alluded, in one or two regards, to a notice of these poems which appeared in the "Democratic Review," we may as well here proceed with some few further comments upon the article in question — with whose general tenor we are happy to agree.

The Review speaks of "Maidenhood" as a poem, "not to be understood but at the expense of more time and trouble than a song can justly claim." We are scarcely less surprised at this opinion from Mr. Langtree than we were at the condemnation of "The Luck of Edenhall."

"Maidenhood" is faulty, it appears to us, only on the score of its theme, which is somewhat didactic. Its *meaning* seems simplicity itself. A maiden on the verge of womanhood, hesitating to enjoy life (for which she has a strong appetite) through a false idea of duty, is bidden to fear nothing, having purity of heart as her lion of Una.

What Mr. Langtree styles "an unfortunate peculiaarity" in Mr. Longfellow, resulting from "adherence to a false system" has really been always regarded by us as one of his idiosyncratic merits. "In each poem," says the critic, "he has but *one* idea which, in the progress of his song is gradually unfolded, and at last reaches its full development in the concluding lines; this singleness of thought might lead a harsh critic to suspect intellectual barrenness." It leads *us*, individually, only to a full sense of the artistical power and knowledge of the poet. We confess that now, for the first time, we hear unity of conception objected to as a defect. But Mr. Langtree seams to have fallen into the singular error of supposing the poet to have absolutely *but one idea* in each of his ballads. Yet how "one idea" can be "gradually unfolded" without other ideas, is, to us, a mystery of mysteries. Mr. Longfellow, very properly, has but one *leading* idea which forms the basis of his poem; but to the aid and development of this one there are innumerable others, of which the rare excellence is, that all are in keeping, that none could be well omitted, that each tends to the one general effect. It is unnecessary to say another word upon this topic.

In speaking of "Excelsior," Mr. Langtree (are we wrong in attributing the notice to his very forcible pen?) seems to labor under some similar misconception. "It carries along with it," says he, "a false moral which greatly diminishes its merit in our eyes. The great merit of a picture, whether made with the pencil or pen, is its *truth;* and this merit does not belong to Mr. Longfellow's sketch. Men of genius may and probably do, meet with greater difficulties in their struggles with the world than their fellow-men who are less highly gifted; but their power of overcoming obstacles is proportionably greater, and the result of their laborious suffering is not death but immortality."

That the chief merit of a picture is its *truth,* is an assertion deplorably erroneous. Even in Painting, which is, more essentially than Poetry, a mimetic art, the proposition cannot be sustained. Truth is not even *the aim.* Indeed it is curious to observe how very slight a degree of truth is sufficient to satisfy the mind, which acquiesces in the absence of numerous essentials in the thing depicted. An outline frequently stirs the spirit more pleasantly than the most elaborate picture. We need only refer to the compositions of Flaxman and of Retzsch. Here all details are omitted — nothing can be farther from *truth.* Without even color the most thrilling effects are produced. In statues we are rather pleased than disgusted with *the want of the eyeball.* The hair of the Venus de Medici *was gilded.* Truth indeed! The grapes of Zeuxis as well as the curtain of Parrhasius were received as indisputable evidence of the truthful ability of these artists — but they are not even *classed among their pictures.* If truth is the highest aim of either Painting or Poesy, then Jan Steen was a greater artist than Angelo, and Crabbe is a more noble poet than Milton.

But we have not quoted the observation of Mr. Langtree to deny its philosophy; our design was simply to show that he has misunderstood the poet. "Excelsior" has not even a remote tendency to the interpretation assigned it by the critic. It depicts the *earnest upward impulse of the soul* — an impulse not to be subdued even in Death. Despising danger, resisting pleasure, the youth, bearing the banner inscribed "*Excelsior!*" (higher still!) struggles through all difficulties to an Alpine summit. Warned to be content with the elevation attained, his cry is still "*Excelsior!*" And, even in falling dead on the highest pinnacle, his cry is *still* "*Excelsior!*" There is yet an immortal height to be surmounted — an ascent in Eternity. The poet holds in view the idea of never-ending *progress*. That he is misunderstood is rather the misfortune of Mr. Langtree than the fault of Mr. Longfellow. There is an old adage about the difficulty of one's furnishing an auditor both with matter to be comprehended and brains for its comprehension.

Hawthorne's Twice-Told Tales

We said a few hurried words about Mr. Hawthorne in our last number, with the design of speaking more fully in the present. We are still, however, pressed for room, and must necessarily discuss his volumes more briefly and more at random than their high merits deserve.

The book professes to be a collection of *tales*, yet is, in two respects, misnamed. These pieces are now in their third republication, and, of course, are thrice-told. Moreover, they are by no means *all* tales, either in the ordinary or in the legitimate understanding of the term. Many of them are pure essays; for example, "Sights from a Steeple," "Sunday at Home," "Little Annie's Ramble," "A Rill from the Town Pump," "The Toll-Gatherer's Day," "The Haunted Mind," "The Sister Years," "Snow-Flakes," "Night Sketches," and "Foot-Prints on the Sea-Shore." We mention these matters chiefly on account of their discrepancy with that marked precision and finish by which the body of the work is distinguished.

Of the Essays just named, we must be content to speak in brief. They are each and all beautiful, without being characterized by the polish and adaptation so visible in the tales proper. A painter would at once note their leading or predominant feature, and style it *repose*. There is no attempt at effect. All is quiet, thoughtful, subdued. Yet this repose may exist simultaneously with high originality of thought; and Mr. Hawthorne has demonstrated the fact. At every turn we meet with novel combinations; yet these combinations never surpass the limits of the quiet. We are soothed as we read; and withal is a calm astonishment that ideas so apparently obvious have never occurred or been presented to us before. Herein our author differs materially from Lamb or Hunt or Hazlitt — who, with vivid originality of manner and expression, have less of the true novelty of thought than is generally supposed, and whose originality, at best, has an uneasy and meretricious quaintness, replete with startling effects unfounded in nature, and inducing trains of reflection which lead to no satisfactory result. The Essays of Hawthorne have much of the character of Irving, with more of originality, and less of finish; while, compared with the Spectator, they have a vast superiority at all points. The Spectator, Mr. Irving, and Mr. Hawthorne have in common that tranquil and subdued manner which we have chosen to denominate *repose;* but, in the case of the two former, this repose is attained rather by the absence of novel combination, or of originality, than otherwise, and consists chiefly in the calm, quiet, unostentatious expression of commonplace thoughts, in an unambitious unadulterated Saxon. In them, by strong effort, we are made to conceive the absence of all. In the essays before us the absence of effort is too obvious to be mistaken, and a strong under-current of *suggestion* runs continuously beneath the upper stream of the tranquil thesis. In short, these effusions of Mr. Hawthorne are the product of a truly imaginative intellect, restrained, and in some measure repressed, by fastidiousness of taste, by constitutional melancholy and by indolence.

But it is of his tales that we desire principally to speak. The tale proper, in our opinion, affords unquestionably the fairest field for the exercise of the loftiest talent, which can be afforded by the wide domains of mere prose. Were we bidden to say how the highest genius could be most advantageously employed for the best display of its own powers, we should answer, without hesitation — in the composition of a rhymed poem, not to exceed in length what might be perused in an hour. Within this limit alone can the highest order of true poetry exist. We need only here say, upon this topic, that, in almost all classes of composition, the unity of effect or impression is a point of the greatest importance. It is clear, moreover, that this unity cannot be thoroughly preserved in productions whose perusal cannot be completed at one sitting. We may continue the reading of a prose composition, from the very nature of prose itself, much longer than we can persevere, to any good purpose, in the perusal of a poem. This latter, if truly fulfilling the demands of the poetic sentiment, induces an exaltation of the soul which cannot be long sustained. All high excitements are necessarily transient. Thus a long poem is a paradox. And, without unity of impression, the deepest effects cannot be brought about. Epics were the offspring of an imperfect sense of Art, and their reign is no more. A poem *too* brief may produce a vivid, but never an intense or enduring impression. Without a certain continuity of effort — without a certain duration or repetition of purpose — the soul is never deeply moved. There must be the dropping of the water upon the rock. De Béranger has wrought brilliant things—pungent and spirit-stirring—but, like all immassive bodies, they lack *momentum*, and thus fail to satisfy the Poetic Sentiment. They sparkle and excite, but, from want of continuity, fail deeply to impress. Extreme brevity will degenerate into epigrammatism; but the sin of extreme length is even more unpardonable. *In medio tutissimus ibis.*

Were we called upon, however, to designate that class of composition which, next to such a poem as we have suggested, should best fulfil the demands of high genius—should offer it the most advantageous field of exertion—we should unhesitatingly speak of the prose tale, as Mr. Hawthorne has here exemplified it. We allude to the short prose narrative, requiring from a half-hour to one or two hours in its perusal. The ordinary novel is objectionable, from its length, for reasons already stated in substance. As it cannot be read at one sitting, it deprives itself, of course, of the immense force derivable from *totality*. Worldly interests intervening during the pauses of perusal, modify, annul, or counteract, in a greater or less degree, the impressions of the book. But simple cessation in reading, would, of itself, be sufficient to destroy the true unity. In the brief tale, however, the author is enabled to carry out the fulness of his intention, be it what it may. During the hour of perusal the soul of the reader is at the writer's control. There are no external or extrinsic influences—resulting from weariness or interruption.

A skilful literary artist has constructed a tale. If wise,

he has not fashioned his thoughts to accommodate his incidents; but having conceived, with deliberate care, a certain unique or single *effect* to be wrought out, he then invents such incidents — he then combines such events as may best aid him in establishing this preconceived effect. If his very initial sentence tend not to the outbringing of this effect, then he has failed in his first step. In the whole composition there should be no word written, of which the tendency, direct or indirect, is not to the one pre-established design. And by such means, with such care and skill, a picture is at length painted which leaves in the mind of him who contemplates it with a kindred art, a sense of the fullest satisfaction. The idea of the tale has been presented unblemished, because undisturbed; and this is an end unattainable by the novel. Undue brevity is just as exceptionable here as in the poem; but undue length is yet more to be avoided.

We have said that the tale has a point of superiority even over the poem. In fact, while the *rhythm* of this latter is an essential aid in the development of the poem's highest idea — the idea of the Beautiful — the artificialities of this rhythm are an inseparable bar to the development of all points of thought or expression which have their basis in *Truth*. But Truth is often, and in very great degree, the aim of the tale. Some of the finest tales are tales of ratiocination. Thus the field of this species of composition, if not in so elevated a region on the mountain of Mind, is a table-land of far vaster extent than the domain of the mere poem. Its products are never so rich, but infinitely more numerous, and more appreciable by the mass of mankind. The writer of the prose tale, in short, may bring to his theme a vast variety of modes or inflections of thought and expression — (the ratiocinative, for example, the sarcastic or the humorous) which are not only antagonistical to the nature of the poem, but absolutely forbidden by one of its most peculiar and indispensable adjuncts; we allude, of course, to rhythm. It may be added, here, *par parenthèse,* that the author who aims at the purely beautiful in a prose tale is laboring at great disadvantage. For Beauty can be better treated in the poem. Not so with terror, or passion, or horror, or a multitude of such other points. And here it will be seen how full of prejudice are the usual animadversions against those *tales of effect,* many fine examples of which were found in the earlier numbers of Blackwood. The impressions produced were wrought in a legitimate sphere of action, and constituted a legitimate although sometimes an exaggerated interest. They were relished by every man of genius: although there were found many men of genius who condemned them without just ground. The true critic will but demand that the design intended be accomplished, to the fullest extent, by the means most advantageously applicable.

We have very few American tales of real merit — we may say, indeed, none, with the exception of "The Tales of a Traveller" of Washington Irving, and these "Twice-Told Tales" of Mr. Hawthorne. Some of the pieces of Mr. John Neal abound in vigor and originality; but in general, his compositions of this class are excessively diffuse, extravagant, and indicative of an imperfect sentiment of Art. Articles at random are, now and then, met with in our periodicals which might be advantageously compared with the best effusions of the British Magazines; but, upon the whole, we are far behind our progenitors in this department of literature.

Of Mr. Hawthorne's Tales we would say, emphatically, that they belong to the highest region of Art — an Art subservient to genius of a very lofty order. We had supposed, with good reason for so supposing, that he had been thrust into his present position by one of the impudent *cliques* which beset our literature, and whose pretensions it is our full purpose to expose at the earliest opportunity; but we have been most agreeably mistaken. We know of few compositions which the critic can more honestly commend than these "Twice-Told Tales." As Americans, we feel proud of the book.

Mr. Hawthorne's distinctive trait is invention, creation, imagination, originality — a trait which, in the literature of fiction, is positively worth all the rest. But the nature of originality, so far as regards its manifestation in letters, is but imperfectly understood. The inventive or original mind as frequently displays itself in novelty of *tone* as in novelty of matter. Mr. Hawthorne is original at *all* points.

It would be a matter of some difficulty to designate the best of these tales; we repeat that, without exception, they are beautiful. "Wakefield" is remarkable for the skill with which an old idea — a well-known incident — is worked up or discussed. A man of whims conceives the purpose of quitting his wife and residing *incognito*, for twenty years, in her immediate neighborhood. Something of this kind actually happened in London. The force of Mr. Hawthorne's tale lies in the analysis of the motives which must or might have impelled the husband to such folly, in the first instance, with the possible causes of his perseverance. Upon this thesis a sketch of singular power has been constructed.

"The Wedding Knell" is full of the boldest imagination — an imagination fully controlled by taste. The most captious critic could find no flaw in this production.

"The Minister's Black Veil" is a masterly composition of which the sole defect is that to the rabble its exquisite skill will be *caviare.* The *obvious* meaning of this article will be found to smother its insinuated one. The *moral* put into the mouth of the dying minister will be supposed to convey the *true* import of the narrative; and that a crime of dark dye, (having reference to the "young lady") has been committed, is a point which only minds congenial with that of the author will perceive.

"Mr. Higginbotham's Catastrophe" is vividly original and managed most dexterously.

"Dr. Heidegger's Experiment" is exceedingly well imagined, and executed with surpassing ability. The artist breathes in every line of it.

"The White Old Maid" is objectionable, even more than the "Minister's Black Veil," on the score of its mysticism. Even with the thoughtful and analytic, there will be much trouble in penetrating its entire import.

"The Hollow of the Three Hills" we would quote in full, had we space; — not as evincing higher talent than any of the other pieces, but as affording an excellent example of the author's peculiar ability. The subject is commonplace. A witch subjects the Distant and the

Past to the view of a mourner. It has been the fashion to describe, in such cases, a mirror in which the images of the absent appear; or a cloud of smoke is made to arise, and thence the figures are gradually unfolded. Mr. Hawthorne has wonderfully heightened his effect by making the ear, in place of the eye, the medium by which the fantasy is conveyed. The head of the mourner is enveloped in the cloak of the witch, and within its magic folds there arise sounds which have an all-sufficient intelligence. Throughout this article also, the artist is conspicuous — not more in positive than in negative merits. Not only is all done that should be done, but (what perhaps is an end with more difficulty attained) there is nothing done which should not be. Every word *tells*, and there is not a word which does *not* tell.

In "Howe's Masquerade" we observe something which resembles a plagiarism — but which *may be* a very flattering coincidence of thought. We quote the passage in question.

> "*With a dark flush of wrath* upon his brow they saw the general *draw his sword* and *advance to meet* the figure *in the cloak* before the latter had stepped one pace upon the floor.
>
> "'Villain, *unmuffle yourself*,' cried he, 'you pass no farther!'
>
> "The figure, without blanching a hair's breadth from the sword which was pointed at his breast, made a solemn pause, and lowered the cape of the cloak from his face, yet not sufficiently for the spectators to catch a glimpse of it. But Sir William Howe had evidently seen enough. The sternness of his countenance gave place to a look of wild amazement, if not horror, while he recoiled several steps from the figure, *and let fall his sword* upon the floor."

The idea here is, that the figure in the cloak is the

phantom or reduplication of Sir William Howe; but in an article called "William Wilson," one of the "Tales of the Grotesque and Arabesque," we have not only the same idea, but the same idea similarly presented in several respects. We quote two paragraphs, which our readers may compare with what has been already given. We have italicized, above, the immediate particulars of resemblance.

> "The brief moment in which I averted my eyes had been sufficient to produce, apparently, a material change in the arrangement at the upper or farther end of the room. A large mirror, it appeared to me, now stood where none had been perceptible before: and as I stepped up to it in extremity of terror, mine own image, but with features all pale and dabbled in blood, *advanced* with a feeble and tottering gait to meet me.
>
> "Thus it appeared I say, but was not. It was Wilson, who then stood before me in the agonies of dissolution. Not a line in all the marked and singular lineaments of that face which was not even identically mine own. *His mask and cloak lay where he had thrown them, upon the floor.*"

Here it will be observed that, not only are the two general conceptions identical, but there are various *points* of similarity. In each case the figure seen is the wraith or duplication of the beholder. In each case the scene is a masquerade. In each case the figure is cloaked. In each, there is a quarrel — that is to say, angry words pass between the parties. In each the beholder is enraged. In each the cloak and sword fall upon the floor. The "villain, unmuffle yourself," of Mr. H. is precisely paralleled by a passage at page 56 of "William Wilson."

In the way of objection we have scarcely a word to say

of these tales. There is, perhaps, a somewhat too general or prevalent *tone* — a tone of melancholy and mysticism. The subjects are insufficiently varied. There is not so much of *versatility* evinced as we might well be warranted in expecting from the high powers of Mr. Hawthorne. But beyond these trivial exceptions we have really none to make. The style is purity itself. Force abounds. High imagination gleams from every page. Mr. Hawthorne is a man of the truest genius. We only regret that the limits of our Magazine will not permit us to pay him that full tribute of commendation, which, under other circumstances, we should be so eager to pay.

N. P. Willis

In his poetry, and in the *matter* of his prose, the author of "Melanie" and of the "Inklings of Adventure" has, beyond doubt, innumerable merits: — still, they are merits which he shares with other writers — which he possesses in common with Proctor, with Heber, and with Halleck — in common with Neal, with Hunt, with Lamb, and with Irving; his *prose style*, however, is not only a genus *per se*, but it is his own property "in fee simple impartite," and no man living has ever yet set foot upon it except himself.

Now, if any style has been long distinct — has been long markedly and universally peculiar — we must, of course, seek the source of the peculiarity not, as some persons are prone to suppose, in any physical habitude or mannerism — not in any quipping and quibbling of phrase — not in any twisting of antique conventionalities of expression — not, (to be brief,) in any mere sleight-of-pen trickeries which, at all times, may be more dexterously performed by an observant imitator than by the original quack — but in some mental idiosyncrasy, which, unimitated itself because inimitable, preserves the style which is its medium and its exponent from all danger of imitation.

In the style of Mr. Willis we easily detect this idiosyncrasy. We have no trouble in tracing it home — and when we reach it and look it fairly in the face, we recognize it on the instant. It is Fancy.

To be sure there is quite a tribe of Fancies — although one half of them never suspected themselves to be such until so told by the metaphysicians — but the one of which we speak has never yet been accredited among men, and we beg pardon of Mr. Willis for the liberty we take in employing the topic of his *style*, as the best possible vehicle and opportunity for the introduction of this, our protégé, to the consideration of the literary world.

"Fancy," says the author of "Aids to Reflection," (who aided Reflection to much better purpose in his "Genevieve") — "Fancy combines — Imagination creates." This was intended and has been received, as a distinction; but it is a distinction without a difference — without even a difference of degree. The Fancy as nearly creates as the imagination, and neither at all. Novel conceptions are merely unusual combinations. The mind of man can imagine nothing which does not exist: — if it could, it would create not only ideally, but substantially — as do the thoughts of God. It may be said — "We imagine a griffin, yet a griffin does not exist." Not the griffin certainly, but its component parts. It is no more than a collation of known limbs — features — qualities. Thus with all which claims to be new — which appears to be a *creation* of the intellect: — it is resoluble into the old. The wildest effort of the mind cannot stand the test of the analysis.

We might make a distinction *of degree* between the fancy and the imagination, in calling the latter the former loftily employed. But experience would prove this distinction to be unsatisfactory What we *feel* to be fancy, will be found still fanciful, whatever be the theme which engages it. No *subject* exalts it into imagination. When Moore is termed a fanciful poet, the epithet is precisely applied; he *is*. He is fanciful in "Lalla Rookh," and had he written the "Inferno," there he would have been fanciful still: for not only is he essentially fanciful, but he has no ability to be anything more, unless at rare intervals — by snatches — and with effort. What we say of him at this point, moreover, is equally true of all little frisky men, personally considered.

The fact seems to be that Imagination, Fancy, Fantasy, and Humor have in common the elements Combination and Novelty. The Imagination is the artist of the four. From novel arrangements of old forms which present themselves to it, it selects only such as are harmonious; — the result, of course, is *beauty* itself — using the term in its most extended sense, and as inclusive of the sublime. The pure Imagination chooses, *from either beauty or deformity*, only the most combinable things hitherto uncombined; — the compound as a general rule, partaking (in character) of sublimity or beauty, in the ratio of the respective sublimity or beauty of the things combined — which are themselves still to be considered as atomic — that is to say, as previous combinations. But, as often analogously happens in physical chemistry, so not unfrequently does it occur in this chemistry of the intellect, that the admixture of two elements will result in a something that shall have nothing of the quality of one of them — or even nothing of the qualities of either. The range of Imagination is therefore, unlimited. Its materials extend throughout the Universe. Even out of deformities it fabricates that *Beauty* which is at once its sole object and its inevitable test. But, in general, the richness or force of the matters combined — the facility of discovering combinable novelties worth combining — and the absolute "chemical combination" and proportion of the completed mass — are the particulars to be regarded in our estimate of Imagination. It is this thorough harmony of an imaginative work which so often causes it to be undervalued by the undiscriminating, through the character of *obviousness* which is superinduced. We are apt to find ourselves asking "*why is it* that these combinations have never been imagined before?"

Now, when this question *does not occur* — when the harmony of the combination is comparatively neglected, and when in addition to the element of novelty, there is introduced the sub-element of *unexpectedness* — when, for example, matters are brought into combination which not only have never been combined, but whose combination strikes us *as a difficulty happily overcome* — the result then appertains to the FANCY — and is, to the majority of mankind more grateful than the purely harmonious one — although, absolutely, it is less beautiful (or grand) for the reason that *it is* less harmonious.

Carrying its errors into excess — for, however enticing, they *are* errors still, or Nature lies, — Fancy is at length found impinging upon the province of *Fantasy*. The votaries of this latter delight not only in novelty and unexpectedness of combination, but in the *avoidance* of proportion. The result is therefore abnormal, and to a healthy mind affords less of pleasure through its novelty, than of pain through its incoherence. When, proceeding a step farther, however, Fantasy seeks not merely disproportionate but incongruous or antagonistical elements, the effect is rendered more pleasurable from its greater positiveness; — there is a merry effort of Truth to shake from her that which is no property of hers: — and we laugh outright in recognizing *Humor.*

The four faculties in question appear to me all of their class; — but when either Fancy or Humor is expressed to gain an end — is pointed at a purpose — whenever either becomes objective in place of subjective — then it becomes, also, pure Wit or Sarcasm, just as the purpose is well-intentioned or malevolent.

Having thus comfortably defined our position, we shall be the more readily understood when we repeat that the marked idiosyncrasy of the *prose style* of Mr. Willis — that the charm which has wrought for it so vast and so well-merited a popularity — is traceable, in the last result, to the brilliant FANCY with which it perpetually scintillates or glows — a fancy possessed *not* as in the case of Moore, to the exclusion of qualities more noble — but possessed, certainly, to an extent *altogether unparalleled,* and of a kind both relatively and intrinsically the most valuable, because at once the most radiant and the most rare.

The American Drama

A BIOGRAPHIST of Berryer calls him "*l'homme qui, dans sa description, demande la plus grande quantité possible d'antithèse*" — but that ever recurring topic, the decline of the drama, seems to have consumed, of late, more of the material in question than would have sufficed for a dozen prime ministers — even admitting them to be French. Every trick of thought and every harlequinade of phrase have been put in operation for the purpose "*de nier ce qui est, et d'expliquer ce qui n'est pas.*"

Ce qui n'est pas : — for the drama has *not declined.* The facts and the philosophy of the case seem to be these. The great opponent to Progress is Conservatism. In other words — the great adversary of Invention is Imitation : — the propositions are in spirit identical. Just as an art is imitative, is it stationary. The most imitative arts are the most prone to repose — and the converse. Upon the utilitarian — upon the business arts, where necessity impels, Invention, Necessity's well-understood offspring, is ever in attendance. And the less we see of the mother the less we behold of the child. No one complains of the decline of the art of Engineering. Here the Reason, which never retrogrades, or reposes, is called into play. But let us glance at Sculpture. We are not *worse,* here, than the ancients, let pedantry say what it may (the Venus of Canova is worth at any time two of that of Cleomenes), but it is equally certain that we have made, in general, no advances; and Sculpture, properly considered, is perhaps the *most* imitative of all arts which have a right to the title of Art at all. Looking next at Painting, we find that we have to boast of progress only in the ratio of the inferior imitativeness of Painting when compared with Sculpture. As far indeed as we have any means of judging, our improvement has been exceedingly little, and did we know anything of ancient Art in this department, we might be astonished at discovering that we had advanced even far less than we suppose. As regards Architecture, whatever progress we have made, has been precisely in those particulars which have no reference to imitation: — that is to say we have improved the utilitarian and not the ornamental provinces of the art. Where Reason predominated, we advanced; where mere Feeling or Taste was the guide, we remained as we were.

Coming to the Drama, we shall see that in its mechanisms we have made progress, while in its spirituality we have done little or nothing for centuries certainly — and, perhaps, little or nothing for thousands of years. And this is because what we term the spirituality of the drama is precisely its imitative portion — is exactly that portion which distinguishes it as one of the principal of the imitative arts.

Sculptors, painters, dramatists, are, from the very nature of their material, — their spiritual material — imitators — conservatists — prone to repose in old Feeling and in antique Taste. For this reason — and for this reason only — the arts of Sculpture, Painting and the Drama have not advanced — or have advanced feebly, and inversely in the ratio of their imitativeness.

But it by no means follows that either has *declined.* All *seem* to have declined, because they have remained stationary while the multitudinous other arts (of reason) have flitted so rapidly by them. In the same manner the traveller by railroad can imagine that the trees by the wayside are retrograding. The trees in this case are absolutely stationary — but the Drama has not been altogether so, although its progress has been so slight as not to interfere with the general effect — that of seeming retrogradation or decline.

This seeming retrogradation, however, is to all practical intents an absolute one. Whether the drama has declined, or whether it has merely remained stationary, is a point of no importance, so far as concerns the public encouragement of the drama. It is unsupported, in either case, because it does not deserve support.

But if this stagnation, or deterioration, grows out of the very idiosyncrasy of the drama itself, as one of the principal of the imitative arts, how is it possible that a remedy shall be applied — since it is clearly impossible to alter the nature of the art, and yet leave it the art which it now is?

We have already spoken of the improvements effected, in Architecture, in all its utilitarian departments, and in the Drama, at all the points of its mechanism. "Wherever Reason predominates we advance; where mere Feeling or Taste is the guide, we remain as we are." We wish now to suggest that, by the engrafting of Reason upon

Feeling and Taste, we shall be able, and thus alone shall be able, to force the modern Drama into the production of any profitable fruit.

At present, what is it we do? We are content if, with Feeling and Taste, a dramatist does *as other dramatists have done*. The most successful of the more immediately modern playwrights has been Sheridan Knowles and to play Sheridan Knowles seems to be the highest ambition of our writers for the stage. Now the author of "The Hunchback," possesses what we are weak enough to term the true "dramatic feeling," and this true dramatic feeling he has manifested in the most preposterous series of imitations of the Elizabethan drama, by which ever mankind were insulted and begulled. Not only did he adhere to the old plots, the old characters, the old stage conventionalities throughout; but, he went even so far as to persist in the obsolete phraseologies of the Elizabethan period — and just in proportion to his obstinacy and absurdity at all points, did we pretend to like him the better, and pretend to consider him a great dramatist.

Pretend — for every particle of it was pretence. Never was enthusiasm more utterly false than that which so many "respectable audiences" endeavored to get up for these plays — endeavored to get up, first, because there was a general desire to see the drama revive, and secondly, because we had been all along entertaining the fancy that "the decline of the drama" meant little, if anything, else than its deviation from the Elizabethan routine — and that, consequently, the return to the Elizabethan routine was, and of necessity must be, the revival of the drama.

But if the principles we have been at some trouble in explaining, are true — and most profoundly do we feel them to be so — if the spirit of imitation is, in fact, the real source of the drama's stagnation — and if it is so because of the tendency in all imitation to render Reason subservient to Feeling and to Taste — it is clear that only by deliberate counteracting of the spirit, and of the tendency of the spirit, we can hope to succeed in the drama's revival.

The first thing necessary is to burn or bury the "old models," and to forget, as quickly as possible, that ever a play has been penned. The second thing is to consider *de novo* what are the *capabilities* of the drama — not merely what hitherto have been its conventional purposes. The third and last point has reference to the composition of a play (showing to the fullest extent these capabilities), conceived and constructed with Feeling and with Taste, but with Feeling and Taste guided and controlled in every particular by the details of Reason — of Common Sense — in a word, of a Natural Art.

It is obvious, in the meantime, that towards the good end in view, much may be affected by discriminative criticism on what has already been done. The field, thus stated, is of course, practically illimitable — and to Americans the American drama is the special point of interest. We propose therefore, in a series of papers, to take a somewhat deliberate survey of some few of the most noticeable American plays. We shall do this without reference either to the date of the composition, or its adaptation for the closet or the stage. We shall speak with absolute frankness both of merits and defects — our principal object being understood not as that of mere commentary on the individual play — but on the drama in general, and on the American drama in especial, of which each individual play is a constituent part. We will commence at once with

Tortesa, the Usurer.

This is the third dramatic attempt of Mr. Willis, and may be regarded as particularly successful, since it has received, both on the stage and in the closet, no stinted measure of commendation. This success, as well as the high reputation of the author, will justify us in a more extended notice of the play than might, under other circumstances, be desirable.

The story runs thus:—Tortesa, an usurer of Florence, and whose character is a mingled web of good and evil feeling, gets into his possession the palace and lands of a certain Count Falcone. The usurer would wed the daughter (Isabella) of Falcone — not through love, but, in his own words,

> "To please a devil that inhabits him"—

in fact to mortify the pride of the nobility, and avenge himself of their scorn. He therefore bargains with Falcone (a narrow-souled villain) for the hand of Isabella. The deed of the Falcone property is restored to the Count, upon an agreement that the lady shall marry the usurer — this contract being invalid should Falcone change his mind in regard to the marriage, or should the maiden demur — but valid should the wedding be prevented through any fault of Tortesa, or through any accident not springing from the will of the father or child. The first Scene makes us aware of this bargain, and introduces us to Zippa, a glover's daughter, who resolves, with a view of befriending Isabella, to feign a love for Tortesa, (which, in fact, she partially feels) hoping thus to break off the match.

The second Scene makes us acquainted with a young painter, (Angelo) poor, but of high talents and ambition, and with his servant, (Tomaso) an old bottle-loving rascal, entertaining no very exalted opinion of his master's abilities. Tomaso does some injury to a picture, and Angelo is about to run him through the body, when he is interrupted by a sudden visit from the Duke of Florence, attended by Falcone. The Duke is enraged at the murderous attempt, but admires the paintings in the studio. Finding that the rage of the great man will prevent his patronage if he knows the aggressor as the artist, Angelo passes off Tomaso as himself, (Angelo) making an exchange of names. This is a point of some importance, as it introduces the true Angelo to a job which he had long coveted — the painting of the portrait of Isabella, of whose beauty he had become enamoured through report. The Duke wishes the portrait painted. Falcone, however, on account of a promise to Tortesa, would have objected to admit to his daughter's presence the handsome Angelo, but in regard to Tomaso, has no scruple. Supposing Tomaso to be Angelo and the artist, the Count writes a note to Isabella, requiring her "to admit the painter Angelo." The real Angelo is thus admitted. He and the lady love at first sight, (much in the manner of Romeo and Juliet,) each ignorant of the other's attachment.

The third Scene of the second Act is occupied with a conversation between Falcone and Tortesa, during which a letter arrives from the Duke, who, having heard of the intended sacrifice of Isabella, offers to redeem the Count's lands and palace, and desires him to preserve his daughter for a certain Count Julian. But Isabella, — who, before seeing Angelo, had been willing to sacrifice herself for her father's sake, and who, since seeing him, had entertained hopes of escaping the hateful match through means of a plot entered into by herself and Zippa — Isabella, we say, is now in despair. To gain time, she at once feigns a love for the usurer, and indignantly rejects the proposal of the Duke. The hour for the wedding draws near. The lady has prepared a sleeping potion, whose effects resemble those of death. (Romeo and Juliet.) She swallows it — knowing that her supposed corpse would lie at night, pursuant to an old custom, in the sanctuary of the cathedral; and believing that Angelo — whose love for herself she has elicited, by a stratagem, from his own lips — will watch by the body, in the strength of his devotion. Her ultimate design (we may suppose, for it is not told) is to confess all to her lover, on her revival, and throw herself upon his protection — their marriage being concealed, and herself regarded as dead by the world. Zippa, who *really* loves Angelo — (her love for Tortesa, it must be understood, is a very equivocal feeling, for the fact cannot be denied that Mr. Willis makes her love both at the same time) — Zippa, who really loves Angelo — who has discovered his passion for Isabella — and who, as well as that lady, believes that the painter will watch the corpse in the cathedral, — determines, through jealousy, to prevent his so doing, and with this view informs Tortesa that she has learned it to be Angelo's design to steal the body, *for artistical purposes*, — in short as a model to be used in his studio. The usurer, in consequence, sets a guard at the doors of the cathedral. This guard does, in fact, prevent the lover from watching the corpse, but, it appears, does *not* prevent the lady, on her revival and disappointment in not seeing the one she sought, from passing unperceived from the church. Weakened by her long sleep, she wanders aimlessly through the streets, and at length finds herself, when just sinking with exhaustion, at the door of her father. She has no resource but to knock. The Count — who here, we must say, acts very much as Thimble of old — the knight, we mean, of the "scolding wife" — maintains that she is dead, and shuts the door in her face. In other words, he supposes it to be the ghost of his daughter who speaks; and so the lady is left to perish on the steps. Meantime Angelo is absent from home, attempting to get access to the cathedral; and his servant, Tomaso, takes the opportunity of absenting himself also, and of indulging his bibulous propensities while perambulating the town. He finds Isabella as we left her; and, through motives which we will leave Mr. Willis to explain, conducts her unresistingly to Angelo's residence, and — *deposits her in Angelo's bed.* The artist now returns — Tomaso is kicked out of doors — and we are not told, but left to presume, that a full explanation and perfect understanding are brought about between the lady and her lover.

We find them, next morning, in the studio, where stands, leaning against an easel, the portrait (a full length) of Isabella, with curtains adjusted before it. The stage directions, moreover, inform us that "the back wall of the room is such as to form a natural ground for the picture." While Angelo is occupied in retouching it, he is interrupted by the arrival of Tortesa with a guard, and is accused of having stolen the corpse from the sanctuary — the lady, meanwhile, having stepped behind the curtain. The usurer insists upon seeing the painting, with a view of ascertaining whether any new touches had been put upon it, which would argue an examination, *post mortem*, of those charms of neck and bosom which the living Isabella would not have unveiled. Resistance is vain — the curtain is torn down; but, to the surprise of Angelo, the lady herself is discovered, "with her hands crossed on her breast, and her eyes fixed on the ground, standing motionless in the frame which had contained the picture." The *tableau*, we are to believe, deceives Tortesa, who steps back to contemplate what he supposes to be the portrait of his betrothed. In the meantime the guards, having searched the house, find the veil which had been thrown over the imagined corpse in the sanctuary; and, upon this evidence, the artist is carried before the Duke. Here he is accused, not only of sacrilege, but of the murder of Isabella, and is about to be condemned to death, when his mistress comes forward in person; thus resigning herself to the usurer to save the life of her lover. But the nobler nature of Tortesa now breaks forth; and, smitten with admiration of the lady's conduct, as well as convinced that her love for himself was feigned, he resigns her to Angelo — although now feeling and acknowledging for the first time that a fervent love has, in his own bosom, assumed the place of that misanthropic ambition which, hitherto, had alone actuated him in seeking her hand. Moreover, he endows Isabella with the lands of her father Falcone. The lovers are thus made happy. The usurer weds Zippa; and the curtain drops upon the promise of the Duke to honor the double nuptials with his presence.

This story, as we have given it, hangs better together (Mr. Willis will pardon our modesty) and is altogether more easily comprehended, than in the words of the play itself. We have really put the best face upon the matter, and presented the whole in the simplest and clearest light in our power. We mean to say that "Tortesa" (partaking largely, in this respect, of the drama of Cervantes and Calderon) is over-clouded — rendered misty — by a world of unnecessary and impertinent *intrigue*. This folly was adopted by the Spanish comedy, and is imitated by us, with the idea of imparting "action," "business," "vivacity." But vivacity, however desirable, can be attained in many other ways, and is dearly purchased, indeed, when the price is intelligibility.

The truth is that *cant* has never attained a more owl-like dignity than in the discussion of dramatic principle. A modern stage critic is nothing, if not a lofty contemner of all things simple and direct. He delights in mystery — revels in mystification — has transcendental notions concerning P. S. and O. P., and talks about "stage business and stage effect," as if he were discussing the differential calculus. For much of all this, we are indebted to the somewhat over-profound criticisms of Augustus William Schlegel.

But the *dicta* of common sense are of universal application, and, touching this matter of *intrigue*, if, from its superabundance, we are compelled, even in the quiet and critical *perusal* of a play, to pause frequently and reflect long — to reread passages over and over again, for the purpose of gathering their bearing upon the whole — of maintaining in our mind a general connexion — what but fatigue can result from the exertion? How then when we come to the representation? — when these passages — trifling, perhaps, in themselves, but important when considered in relation to the plot — are hurried and blurred over in the stuttering enunciation of some miserable rantipole, or omitted altogether through the constitutional lapse of memory so peculiar to those lights of the age and stage, bedight (from being of no conceivable use) supernumeraries? For it must be borne in mind that these bits of *intrigue* (we use the term in the sense of the German critics) appertain generally, indeed altogether, to the after-thoughts of the drama — to the underplots — are met with, consequently, in the mouth of the lacquies and chamber-maids — and are thus consigned to the tender mercies of the *stellæ minores*. Of course we get but an imperfect idea of what is going on before our eyes. Action after action ensues whose mystery we cannot unlock without the little key which these barbarians have thrown away and lost. Our weariness increases in proportion to the number of these embarrassments, and if the play escape damnation at all, it escapes *in spite* of that intrigue to which, in nine cases out of ten, the author attributes his success, and which he *will* persist in valuing exactly in proportion to the misapplied labor it has cost him.

But dramas of this kind are said, in our customary parlance, to "abound in *plot*." We have never yet met any one, however, who could tell us what precise ideas he connected with the phrase. A mere succession of incidents, even the most spirited, will no more constitute a plot, than a multiplication of zeros, even the most infinite, will result in the production of a unit. This all will admit — but few trouble themselves to think farther. The common notion seems to be in favor of mere *complexity;* but a plot, properly understood, is perfect only inasmuch as we shall find ourselves unable to detach from it *or disarrange* any single incident involved, without *destruction* to the mass. This we say is the point of perfection — a point never yet attained, but not on that account unattainable. Practically, we may consider a plot as of high excellence, when no one of its component parts shall be susceptible of *removal* without *detriment* to the whole. Here, indeed, is a vast lowering of the demand — and with less than this no writer of refined taste should content himself.

As this subject is not only in itself of great importance, but will have at all points a bearing upon what we shall say hereafter, in the examination of various plays, we shall be pardoned for quoting from the "Democratic Review" some passages (of our own) which enter more particularly into the rationale of the subject:

"All the Bridgewater treatises have failed in noticing the *great* idiosyncrasy in the Divine system of adaptation: — that idiosyncrasy which stamps the adaptation as divine, in distinction from that which is the work of merely human constructiveness. I speak of the complete *mutuality* of adaptation. For example: — in human constructions, a particular cause has a particular effect — a particular purpose brings about a particular object; but we see no reciprocity. The effect does not react upon the cause — the object does not change relations with the purpose. In Divine constructions, the object is either object or purpose as we choose to regard it, while the purpose is either purpose or object; so that we can never (abstractly — without concretion — without reference to facts of the moment) decide which is which.

"For secondary example: — In polar climates, the human frame, to maintain its animal heat, requires, for combustion in the capillary system, an abundant supply of highly azotized food, such as train oil. Again: — in polar climates nearly the sole food afforded man is the oil of abundant seals and whales. Now whether is oil at hand because imperatively demanded? or whether is it the only thing demanded because the only thing to be obtained? It is impossible to say: — there is an absolute reciprocity of adaptation for which we seek in vain among the works of man.

"The Bridgewater tractists may have avoided this point, on account of its apparent tendency to overthrow the idea of *cause* in general — consequently of a First Cause — of God. But it is more probable that they have failed to perceive what no one preceding them has, to my knowledge, perceived.

"The pleasure which we derive from any exertion of human ingenuity, is in the direct ratio of the *approach* to this species of reciprocity between cause and effect. In the construction of *plot*, for example, in fictitious literature, we should aim at so arranging the points, or incidents, that we cannot distinctly see, in respect to any one of them, whether that one depends from any one other or upholds it. In this sense, of course, perfection of plot is unattainable *in fact* — because Man is the constructor. The plots of God are perfect. The Universe is a plot of God."

The pleasure derived from the contemplation of the unity resulting from plot, is far more intense than is ordinarily supposed, and, as in Nature we meet with no such combination of *incident*, appertains to a very lofty region of the ideal. In speaking thus we have not said that plot is more than an adjunct to the drama — more than a perfectly distinct and separable source of pleasure. It is *not* an essential. In its intense artificiality it may even be conceived injurious in a certain degree (unless constructed with consummate skill) to that real *life-likeness* which is the soul of the drama of character. Good dramas have been written with very little plot — capital dramas might be written with none at all. Some plays of high merit, having plot, abound in irrelevant incident — in incident, we mean, which could be displaced or removed altogether without effect upon the plot itself, and yet are by no means objectionable as dramas; and for this reason — that the incidents are *evidently* irrelevant — *obviously* episodical. Of their digressive nature the spectator is so immediately aware, that he views them, as they arise, in the simple light of interlude, and does not fatigue his attention by attempting to establish for them a connexion, or more than an illustrative connexion, with the great interests of the subject. Such are the plays of Shakespeare. But all this is very different from *that* irrelevancy of intrigue which disfigures and very usually damns the work of the unskilful artist. With him the great error lies in *inconsequence*. Underplot is piled upon underplot (the very word is a paradox), and all to no purpose — *to no end*. The interposed incidents have no ultimate effect upon the main ones. They may hang upon the mass — they may even coalesce with it, or, as in some intricate cases, they may be so intimately blended as to be lost amid the chaos which they have been instrumental in bringing about — but still they have no portion in the plot, which exists, if at all, independently of their influence. Yet the *attempt* is made by the author to establish and demonstrate a dependence — an identity; and it is the *obviousness of this attempt* which is the cause of weariness in the spectator, who, of course, cannot at once see that his attention is challenged to no purpose — that intrigues so obtrusively forced upon it, are to be found, in the end, without effect upon the leading interests of the play.

"Tortesa" will afford us plentiful examples of this irrelevancy of intrigue — of this misconception of the nature and of the capacities of plot. We have said that our digest of the story is more easy of comprehension than the detail of Mr. Willis. If so, it is because we have forborne to give such portions as had no influence upon the whole. These served but to embarrass the narrative and fatigue the attention. How much was irrelevant is shown by the brevity of the space in which we have recorded, somewhat at length, all the influential incidents of a drama of five acts. There is scarcely a scene in which is not to be found the germ of an underplot — a germ, however, which seldom proceeds beyond the condition of a bud, or, if so fortunate as to swell into a flower, arrives, in no single instance, at the dignity of fruit. Zippa, a lady altogether without character (dramatic) is the most pertinacious of all conceivable concoctors of plans never to be matured — of vast designs that terminate in nothing — of *cul-de-sac* machinations. She plots in one page and counterplots in the next. She schemes her way from P. S. to O. P., and intrigues perseveringly from the footlights to the slips. A very singular instance of the inconsequence of her manœuvres is found towards the conclusion of the play. The whole of the second scene, (occupying five pages,) in the fifth act, is obviously introduced for the purpose of giving her information, through Tomaso's means of Angelo's arrest for the murder of Isabella. Upon learning his danger she rushes from the stage, to be present at the trial, exclaiming that her evidence can save his life. We, the audience, of course applaud, and now look with interest to her movements in the scene of the judgment hall. She, Zippa, we think, is somebody after all; she will be the means of Angelo's salvation; she will thus be the chief unraveller of the plot. All eyes are bent, therefore, upon Zippa — but alas, upon the point at issue, Zippa does not so much as open her mouth. It is scarcely too much to say that not a single action of this impertinent little busybody has any real influence upon the play: — yet she appears upon every occasion — appearing only to perplex.

Similar things abound; we should not have space even to allude to them all. The whole conclusion of the play is supererogatory. The immensity of pure *fuss* with which it is overloaded, forces us to the reflection that all of it might have been avoided by one word of explanation to the duke — an amiable man who admires the talents of Angelo, and who, *to prevent Isabella's marrying against her will*, had *previously* offered to free Falcone of his bonds to the usurer. That he would free him *now*, and thus set all matters straight, the spectator cannot doubt for an instant, and he can conceive no better reason why explanations are *not* made, than that Mr. Willis does not think proper they should be. In fact, the whole drama is exceedingly ill *motivirt.*

We have already mentioned an inadvertence, in the fourth Act, where Isabella is made to escape from the sanctuary through the midst of guards who prevented the ingress of Angelo. Another occurs where Falcone's conscience is made to reprove him, upon the appearance of his daughter's supposed ghost, for having occasioned her death by forcing her to marry against her will. The author had forgotten that Falcone submitted to the wedding, after the Duke's interposition, only upon Isabella's assurance *that she really loved the usurer.* In the third Scene, too, of the first Act, the imagination of the spectator is no doubt a little taxed, when he finds Angelo, in the first moment of his introduction to the palace of Isabella, commencing her portrait by laying on color after color, before he has made any attempt at an outline. In the last Act, moreover, Tortesa gives to Isabella a deed

> "Of the Falcone palaces and lands,
> And all the money forfeit by Falcone."

This is a terrible blunder, and the more important as upon this act of the usurer depends the development of his new-born sentiments of honor and virtue — depends, in fact, the most salient *point* of the play. Tortesa, we say, gives to Isabella the lands forfeited by Falcone; but Tortesa was surely not very generous in giving what, clearly, was not his own to give. Falcone had *not for-*

feited the deed, which had been restored to him by the usurer, and which was then in his (Falcone's) possession. Hear Tortesa :

> "He put it in the bond,
> *That if, by any humor of my own,*
> Or accident that came not from himself,
> Or from his daughter's will, the match were marred,
> *His tenure stood intact.*"

Now Falcone is still resolute for the match ; but this new generous "humor" of Tortesa induces him (Tortesa) to decline it. Falcone's tenure is then intact ; he retains the deed ; the usurer is giving away property not his own.

As a drama of character, "Tortesa" is by no means open to so many objections as when we view it in the light of its plot ; but it is still faulty. The merits are so exceedingly negative, that it is difficult to say anything about them. The Duke is nobody ; Falcone, nothing ; Zippa, less than nothing. Angelo may be regarded simply as the medium through which Mr. Willis conveys to the reader his own glowing feelings — his own refined and delicate fancy — (delicate, yet bold) — his own rich voluptuousness of sentiment — a voluptuousness which would offend in almost any other language than that in which it is so skilfully apparelled. Isabella is — the heroine of the Hunchback. The revolution in the character of Tortesa — or rather the final triumph of his innate virtue — is a dramatic point far older than the hills. It may be observed, too, that although the representation of no human character should be quarrelled with for its inconsistency, we yet require that the inconsistencies be not absolute antagonisms to the extent of neutralization: they may be permitted to be oils and waters, but they must not be alkalies and acids. When, in the course of the *dénouement*, the usurer bursts forth into an eloquence virtue-inspired, we cannot sympathize very heartily in his fine speeches, since they proceed from the mouth of the self-same egotist who, urged by a disgusting vanity, uttered so many sotticisms (about his fine legs, &c.) in the earlier passages of the play. Tomaso is, upon the whole, the best personage. We recognize some originality in his conception, and conception was seldom more admirably carried out.

One or two observations at random. In the third Scene of the fifth Act, Tomaso, the buffoon, is made to assume paternal authority over Isabella, (as usual, without sufficient purpose,) by virtue of a law which Tortesa thus expounds:

> "My gracious liege, there is a law in Florence,
> That if a father, for no guilt or shame,
> Disown and shut his door upon his daughter,
> She is the child of him who succors her,
> Who, by the shelter of a single night,
> Becomes endowed with the authority
> Lost by the other."

No one, of course, can be made to believe that any such stupid law as this ever existed either in Florence or Timbuctoo; but, on the ground *que le vrai n'est pas toujours le vraisemblable*, we say that even its real existence would be no justification of Mr. Willis. It has an air of the far-fetched — of the desperate — which a fine taste will avoid as a pestilence. Very much of the same nature is the attempt of Tortesa to extort a second bond from Falcone. The evidence which convicts Angelo of murder is ridiculously frail. The idea of Isabella's assuming the place of the portrait, and so deceiving the usurer, is not only glaringly improbable, but seems adopted from the "Winter's Tale." But in this latter play, the deception is at least possible, for the human figure but imitates a statue. What, however, are we to make of Mr. W.'s stage direction about the back wall's being "so arranged as to form a natural ground for the picture?" Of course, the very slightest movement of Tortesa (and he makes many) would have annihilated the illusion by disarranging the perspective; and in no manner could this latter have been arranged at all for more than one particular point of view — in other words, for more than one particular person in the whole audience. The "asides," moreover, are unjustifiably frequent. The prevalence of this folly (of speaking aside) detracts as much from the acting merit of our drama generally, as any other inartisticality. It utterly destroys verisimilitude. People are not in the habit of soliloquizing aloud — at least, not to any positive extent; and why should an author have to be told, what the slightest reflection would teach him, that an audience, by dint of no imagination, can or will conceive that what is sonorous in their own ears at the distance of fifty feet, cannot be heard by an actor at the distance of one or two?

Having spoken thus of "Tortesa" — in terms of nearly unmitigated censure — our readers may be surprised to hear us say that we think highly of the drama as a whole — and have little hesitation in ranking it before most of the dramas of Sheridan Knowles. Its leading faults are those of the modern drama generally — they are not peculiar to itself — while its great merits *are*. If in support of our opinion, we do not cite points of commendation, it is because those form the mass of the work. And were we to speak of fine passages, we should speak of the entire play. Nor by "fine passages" do we mean passages of merely fine language, embodying fine sentiment, but such as are replete with truthfulness, and teem with the loftiest qualities of the dramatic art. *Points* — capital points abound; and these have far more to do with the general excellence of a play, than a too speculative criticism has been willing to admit. Upon the whole we are proud of "Tortesa" — and here again, for the fiftieth time at least, record our warm admiration of the abilities of Mr. Willis.

We proceed now to Mr. Longfellow's

SPANISH STUDENT.

The reputation of its author as a poet, and as a graceful writer of prose, is, of course, long and deservedly established — but as a dramatist he was unknown before the publication of this play. Upon its original appearance, in "Graham's Magazine," the general opinion was greatly in favor — if not exactly of "The Spanish Student" — at all events of the writer of Outre-Mer. But this general opinion is the most equivocal thing in the world. It is never self-formed. It has very seldom indeed an original development. In regard to the work of an already famous or infamous author it decides, to be sure, with a laudable promptitude; making up all the mind that it has, by reference to the reception of the author's immediately previous publication; — making up thus the ghost of a mind *pro tem.*—a species of critical shadow, that fully answers, nevertheless, all the purposes of a substance itself, until the substance itself shall be forthcoming. But, beyond this point, the general opinion can only be considered that of the public, as a man may call a book *his*, having bought it. When a *new* writer arises, the shop of the true, thoughtful, or critical opinion, is not simultaneously thrown open — is not immediately set up. Some weeks elapse; and, during this interval, the public, at a loss where to procure an opinion of the *débutant*, have necessarily no opinion of him at all, for the nonce.

The popular voice, then, which ran so much in favor of "The Spanish Student," upon its original issue, should be looked upon as merely the ghost *pro tem.* — as based upon critical decisions respecting the previous works of the author — as having reference in no manner to "The Spanish Student" itself — and thus as utterly meaningless and valueless *per se*.

The few — by which we mean those who think, in contradistinction from the many who think they think — the few who think at first hand, and thus twice before speaking at all — these received the play with a commendation somewhat less *prononcée* — somewhat more guardedly qualified — than Professor Longfellow might have desired, or may have been taught to expect. Still the composition was approved upon the whole. The few words of censure were very far, indeed, from amounting to condemnation. The chief defect insisted upon, was the feebleness of the *dénouement*, and, generally, of the concluding scenes, as compared with the opening passages. We are not sure, however, that anything like detailed criticism has been attempted in the case — nor do we propose now to attempt it. Nevertheless, the work has interest, not only within itself, but as the first dramatic effort of an author who has remarkably succeeded in almost every other department of light literature than that of the drama. It may be as well, therefore, to speak of it, if not analytically, at least somewhat in detail; and we cannot, perhaps, more suitably commence than by a quotation, without comment, of some of the finer passages:

"And, though she is a virgin outwardly,
Within she is a sinner; like those panels
Of doors and altar-pieces the old monks
Painted in convents, with the Virgin Mary
On the outside, and on the inside Venus."

"I believe
That woman, in her deepest degradation,
Holds something sacred, something undefiled,
Some pledge and keepsake of her higher nature,
And, like the diamond in the dark, retains
Some quenchless gleam of the celestial light."

"And we shall sit together unmolested,
And words of true love pass from tongue to tongue,
As singing birds from one bough to another."

"Our feelings and our thoughts
Tend ever on and rest not in the Present.
As drops of rain fall into some dark well,
And from below comes a scarce audible sound,
So fall our thoughts into the dark Hereafter,
And their mysterious echo reaches us."

"Her tender limbs are still, and, on her breast,
The cross she prayed to, ere she fell asleep,
Rises or falls with the soft tide of dreams,
Like a light barge safe moored."

"Hark! how the large and ponderous mace of Time
Knocks at the golden portals of the day!"

"The lady Violante, bathed in tears
Of love and anger, like the maid of Colchis,
Whom thou, another faithless Argonaut,
Having won that golden fleece, a woman's love,
Desertest for this Glaucé."

"I read or sit in reverie and watch
The changing color of the waves that break
Upon the idle sea-shore of the mind."

"I will forget her. All dear recollections
Pressed in my heart, like flowers within a book,
Shall be torn out and scattered to the winds."

"O yes! I see it now —
Yet rather with my heart than with mine eyes,
So faint it is. And all my thoughts sail thither,
Freighted with prayers and hopes, and forward urged
Against all stress of accident, as, in
The Eastern Tale, against the wind and tide
Great ships were drawn to the Magnetic Mountains."

"But there are brighter dreams than those of Fame,
Which are the dreams of Love! Out of the heart
Rises the bright ideal of these dreams,
As from some woodland fount a spirit rises
And sinks again into its silent deeps,
Ere the enamoured knight can touch her robe!
'Tis this ideal that the soul of Man,
Like the enamoured knight beside the fountain,
Waits for upon the margin of Life's stream;
Waits to behold her rise from the dark waters,
Clad in a mortal shape! Alas, how many
Must wait in vain! The stream flows evermore,
But from its silent deeps no spirit rises!
Yet I, born under a propitious star,
Have found the bright ideal of my dreams."

"Yes; by the Darro's side
My childhood passed. I can remember still
The river, and the mountains capped with snow;
The villages where, yet a little child,
I told the traveller's fortune in the street;
The smuggler's horse; the brigand and the shepherd;
The march across the moor; the halt at noon;
The red fire of the evening camp, that lighted
The forest where we slept; and, farther back,
As in a dream, or in some former life,
Gardens and palace walls."

"This path will lead us to it,
Over the wheat-fields, where the shadows sail
Across the running sea, now green, now blue,
And, like an idle mariner on the ocean,
Whistles the quail."

These extracts will be universally admired. They are graceful, well expressed, imaginative, and altogether replete with the true poetic feeling. We quote them *now*, at the beginning of our review, by way of justice to the poet, and because, in what follows, we are not sure that we have more than a very few words of what may be termed commendation to bestow.

The "Spanish Student" has an unfortunate beginning, in a most unpardonable, and yet, to render the matter worse, in a most indispensable "Preface":

"The subject of the following play," says Mr. L., "is taken in part from the beautiful play of Cervantes, *La Gitanilla.* To this source, however, I am indebted for the main incident only, the love of a Spanish student for a Gypsy girl, and the name of the heroine, Preciosa. I have not followed the story in any of its details. In Spain this subject has been twice handled dramatically; first by Juan Perez de Montalvan, in *La Gitanilla*, and afterwards by Antonio de Solis y Rivadeneira in *La Gitanilla de Madrid.* The same subject has also been made use of by Thomas Middleton, an English dramatist of the seventeenth century. His play is called *The Spanish Gypsy.* The main plot is the same as in the Spanish pieces; but there runs through it a tragic underplot of the loves of Rodrigo and Doña Clara, which is taken from another tale of Cervantes, *La Fuerza de la Sangre.* The reader who is acquainted with *La Gitanilla* of Cervantes, and the plays of Montalvan, Solis, and Middleton, will perceive that my treatment of the subject differs entirely from theirs."

Now the autorial originality, properly considered, is threefold. There is, first, the originality of the general thesis; secondly, that of the several incidents, or thoughts, by which the thesis is developed; and, thirdly, that of manner, or *tone*, by which means alone, an old subject, even when developed through hackneyed incidents, or thoughts, may be made to produce a fully original *effect* — which, after all, is the end truly in view.

But originality, as it is one of the highest, is also one of the rarest of merits. In America it is especially, and very remarkably rare: — this through causes sufficiently well understood. We are content perforce, therefore, as a general thing, with either of the lower branches of originality mentioned above, and would regard with high favor indeed any author who should supply the great *desideratum* in combining the three. Still the three *should* be combined; and from whom, if not from such men as Professor Longfellow — if not from those who occupy the chief niches in our Literary Temple — shall we expect the combination? But in the present instance, what has Professor Longfellow accomplished? Is he original at any one point? Is he original in respect to the first and most important of our three divisions? "The *subject* of the following play," he says himself, "is taken *in part* from the beautiful play of Cervantes, La Gitanilla." "To this source, however, I am indebted for *the main incident only*, the love of the Spanish student for a Gipsy girl, and the name of the heroine, Preciosa."

The Italics are our own, and the words italicized involve an obvious contradiction. We cannot understand how "the love of the Spanish student for the Gipsy girl" can be called an "incident," or even a "main incident," at all. In fact, this love — this discordant and therefore eventful or incidentful love — is the true *thesis* of the drama of Cervantes. It is this anomalous "love" which originates the incidents by means of which, itself, this "love," the thesis, is developed. Having based his play, then, upon this "love," we cannot admit his claim to originality upon our first count; nor has he any right to say that he has adopted his "subject" "in part." It is clear that he has adopted it altogether. Nor would he have been entitled to claim originality of subject, even had he based his story upon *any variety* of love arising between parties naturally separated by prejudices of *caste* — such, for example, as those which divide the Brahmin from the Pariah, the Ammonite from the African, or even the Christian from the Jew. For here in its ultimate analysis, is the real thesis of the Spaniard. But when the drama is founded, not merely upon this general thesis, but upon this general thesis in the identical application given it by Cervantes — that is to say, upon the prejudice of *caste* exemplified in the case of a Catholic, and this Catholic a Spaniard, and this Spaniard a student, and this student loving a Gipsy, and this Gipsy a dancing-girl, and this dancing-girl bearing the name Preciosa — we are not altogether prepared to be informed by Professor Longfellow that he is indebted for an "incident only" to the "beautiful Gitanilla of Cervantes."

Whether our author is original upon our second and third points — in the true incidents of his story, or in the manner and *tone* of their handling — will be more distinctly seen as we proceed.

It is to be regretted that "The Spanish Student" was not sub-entitled "A Dramatic Poem," rather than "A

Play." The former title would have more fully conveyed the intention of the poet; for, of course, we shall not do Mr. Longfellow the injustice to suppose that his design has been, in any respect, *a play*, in the ordinary acceptation of the term. Whatever may be its merits in a merely poetical view, "The Spanish Student" could not be endured upon the stage.

Its plot runs thus: — Preciosa, the daughter of a Spanish gentleman, is stolen, while an infant, by Gipsies; brought up as his own daughter, and as a dancing-girl, by a Gipsy leader, Crusado; and by him betrothed to a young Gipsy, Bartolomé. At Madrid, Preciosa loves and is beloved by Victorian, a student of Alcalá, who resolves to marry her, notwithstanding her *caste*, rumors involving her purity, the dissuasions of his friends, and his betrothal to an heiress of Madrid. Preciosa is also sought by the Count of Lara, a *roué*. She rejects him. He forces his way into her chamber, and is there seen by Victorian, who, misinterpreting some words overheard, doubts the fidelity of his mistress, and leaves her in anger, after challenging the Count of Lara. In the duel, the Count receives his life at the hands of Victorian; declares his ignorance of the understanding between Victorian and Preciosa; boasts of favors received from the latter; and, to make good his words, produces a ring which she gave him, he asserts, as a pledge of her love. This ring is a duplicate of one previously given the girl by Victorian, and known to have been so given, by the Count. Victorian mistakes it for his own, believes all that has been said, and abandons the field to his rival, who, immediately afterwards, while attempting to procure access to the Gipsy, is assassinated by Bartolomé. Meanwhile, Victorian, wandering through the country, reaches Guadarrama. Here he receives a letter from Madrid, disclosing the treachery practised by Lara, and telling that Preciosa, rejecting his addresses, had been, through his instrumentality, hissed from the stage, and now again roamed with the Gipsies. He goes in search of her; finds her in a wood near Guadarrama; approaches her, disguising his voice; she recognizes him, pretending she does not, and unaware that he knows her innocence; a conversation of *équivoques* ensues; he sees his ring upon her finger; offers to purchase it; she refuses to part with it; a full *éclaircissement* takes place; at this juncture, a servant of Victorian's arrives with "news from court," giving the first intimation of the true parentage of Preciosa. The lovers set out, forthwith, for Madrid, to see the newly-discovered father. On the route, Bartolomé dogs their steps; fires at Preciosa; misses her; the shot is returned; he falls; and "The Spanish Student" is concluded.

This plot, however, like that of "Tortesa," looks better in our naked digest than amidst the details which develop only to disfigure it. The reader of the play itself will be astonished, when he remembers the name of the author, at the inconsequence of the incidents — at the utter want of skill — of art — manifested in their conception and introduction. In dramatic writing, no principle is more clear than that nothing should be said or done which has not a tendency to develop the catastrophe, or the characters. But Mr. Longfellow's play abounds in events and conversations that have no ostensible purpose, and certainly answer no end. In what light, for example, since we cannot suppose this drama intended for the stage, are we to regard the second scene of the second act, where a long dialogue between an Archbishop and a Cardinal is wound up by a dance from Preciosa? The Pope thinks of abolishing public dances in Spain, and the priests in question have been delegated to examine, personally, the proprieties or improprieties of such exhibitions. With this view, Preciosa is summoned and required to give a specimen of her skill. Now this, in a mere spectacle, would do very well; for here all that is demanded is an occasion or an excuse for a dance; but what business has it in a pure drama? or in what regard does it further the end of a dramatic poem, intended only to be read? In the same manner, the whole of Scene the eighth, in the same act, is occupied with six lines of stage directions, as follows:

The Theatre. The orchestra plays the Cachuca. Sound of castanets behind the scenes. The curtain rises and discovers Preciosa in the attitude of commencing the dance. The Cachuca. Tumult. Hisses. Cries of Brava! and Afuera! She falters and pauses. The music stops. General confusion. Preciosa faints.

But the *inconsequence* of which we complain will be best exemplified by an entire scene. We take Scene the Fourth, Act the First:

An inn on the road to Alcalá. BALTASAR *asleep on a bench. Enter* CHISPA.

Chispa. And here we are, half way to Alcalá, between cocks and midnight. Body o' me! what an inn this is! The light out and the landlord asleep! Holá! ancient Baltasar!

Baltasar [*waking*]. Here I am.

Chispa. Yes, there you are, like a one-eyed alcalde in a town without inhabitants. Bring a light, and let me have supper.

Baltasar. Where is your master?

Chispa. Do not trouble yourself about him. We have stopped a moment to breathe our horses; and if he chooses to walk up and down in the open air, looking into the sky as one who hears it rain, that does not satisfy my hunger, you know. But be quick, for I am in a hurry, and every one stretches his legs according to the length of his coverlet. What have we here?

Baltasar [*setting a light on the table*]. Stewed rabbit.

Chispa [*eating*]. Conscience of Portalegre! stewed kitten, you mean!

Baltasar. And a pitcher of Pedro Ximenes, with a roasted pear in it.

Chispa [*drinking*]. Ancient Baltasar, amigo! you know how to cry wine and sell vinegar. I tell you this is nothing but vino tinto of La Mancha, with a tang of the swine-skin.

Baltasar. I swear to you by Saint Simon and Judas, it is all as I say.

Chispa. And I swear to you by Saint Peter and Saint Paul, that it is no such thing. Moreover, your supper is like the hidalgo's dinner — very little meat and a great deal of table-cloth.

Baltasar. Ha! ha! ha!

Chispa. And more noise than nuts.

Baltasar. Ha! ha! ha! You must have your joke, Master Chispa. But shall I not ask Don Victorian in to take a draught of the Pedro Ximenes?

Chispa. No; you might as well say, "Don't you want some?" to a dead man.

Baltasar. Why does he go so often to Madrid?

Chispa. For the same reason that he eats no supper. He is in love. Were you ever in love, Baltasar?

Baltasar. I was never out of it, good Chispa. It has been the torment of my life.

Chispa. What! are you on fire, too, old hay-stack? Why, we shall never be able to put you out.

Victorian [*without*]. Chispa!

Chispa. Go to bed, Pero Grullo, for the cocks are crowing.

Victorian. Ea! Chispa! Chispa!

Chispa. Ea! Señor. Come with me, ancient Baltasar, and bring water for the horses. I will pay for the supper to-morrow.

[*Exeunt.*]

Now here the question occurs — what is accomplished? — how has the subject been forwarded? We did not need to learn that Victorian was in love — that was known before; and all that we glean is that a stupid imitation of Sancho Panza drinks, in the course of two minutes, (the time occupied in the perusal of the scene,) a bottle of vino tinto, by way of Pedro Ximenes, and devours a stewed kitten in place of a rabbit.

In the beginning of the play this Chispa is the valet of Victorian; subsequently we find him the servant of another; and near the *dénouement*, he returns to his original master. No cause is assigned, and not even the shadow of an object is attained; the whole tergiversation being but another instance of the gross inconsequence which abounds in the play.

The author's deficiency of skill is especially evinced in the scene of the *éclaircissement* between Victorian and Preciosa. The former having been enlightened respecting the true character of the latter, by means *of a letter* received at Guadarrama, from a friend at Madrid, (how wofully inartistical is this!) resolves to go in search of her forthwith, and forthwith, also, discovers her in a wood close at hand. Whereupon he approaches, disguising *his voice*: — yes, we are required to believe that a lover may so disguise his voice from his mistress, as even to render his person in full view, irrecognizable! He approaches, and each knowing the other, a conversation ensues under the hypothesis that each to the other is unknown — a very unoriginal and of course, a very silly source of *équivoque*, fit only for the gum-elastic imagination of an infant. But what we especially complain of here, is that our poet should have taken so many and so obvious pains to bring about this position of *équivoque*, when it was impossible that it could have served any other purpose than that of injuring his intended effect! Read, for example, this passage:

Victorian. I never loved a maid;
For she I loved was then a maid no more.
Preciosa. How know you that?
Victorian. A little bird in the air
Whispered the secret.
Preciosa. There take back your gold!
Your hand is cold like a deceiver's hand!
There is no blessing in its charity!
Make her your wife, for you have been abused;
And you shall mend your fortunes mending hers.
Victorian. How like an angel's speaks the tongue of woman,
When pleading in another's cause her own!

Now here it is clear that if we understood Preciosa to be really ignorant of Victorian's identity, the "pleading in another's cause her own," would create a favorable impression upon the reader, or spectator. But the advice, — " Make her your wife," &c., takes an interested and selfish turn when we remember that she knows to whom she speaks.

Again, when Victorian says,

> That is a pretty ring upon your finger.
> Pray give it me!

And when she replies:

> No, never from my hand
> Shall that be taken,

we are inclined to think her only an artful coquette, knowing, as we do, the extent of her knowledge; on the other hand, we should have applauded her constancy (as the author intended) had she been represented ignorant of Victorian's presence. The effect upon the audience, in a word, would be pleasant in place of disagreeable were the case altered as we suggest, while the effect upon Victorian would remain altogether untouched.

A still more remarkable instance of deficiency in the dramatic *tact* is to be found in the mode of bringing about the discovery of Preciosa's parentage. In the very moment of the *éclaircissement* between the lovers, Chispa arrives almost as a matter of course, and settles the point in a sentence:

> Good news from Court; Good news! Beltran Cruzado,
> The Count of the Calés is not your father,
> But your true father has returned to Spain
> Laden with wealth. You are no more a Gipsy.

Now here are three points:—first, the extreme baldness, platitude, and *independence* of the incident narrated by Chispa. The *opportune* return of the father (we are tempted to say the *excessively* opportune) stands by itself—has no relation to any other event in the play—does not appear to arise, in the way of *result*, from any incident or incidents that have arisen before. It has the air of a happy chance, of a God-send, of an ultra-accident, invented by the playwright by way of compromise for his lack of invention. *Nec Deus intersit*, &c. — but here the God has interposed, and the knot is laughably unworthy of the God.

The second point concerns the return of the father "laden with wealth." The lover has abandoned his mistress in her poverty, and, while yet the words of his proffered reconciliation hang upon his lips, comes his own servant with the news that the mistress' father has returned "laden with wealth." Now, so far as regards the audience, who are behind the scenes and know the fidelity of the lover — so far as regards the audience, all is right; but the poet had no business to place his heroine in the sad predicament of being forced, provided she is not a fool, to suspect both the ignorance and the disinterestedness of the hero.

The third point has reference to the words — "You are now no more a Gipsy." The thesis of this drama, as we have already said, is love disregarding the prejudices of *caste*, and in the development of this thesis, the powers of the dramatist have been engaged, or should have been engaged, during the whole of the three Acts of the play. The interest excited lies in our admiration of the sacrifice, and of the love that could make it; but this interest immediately and disagreeably subsides when we find that the sacrifice has been made to no purpose. "You are no more a Gipsy" dissolves the charm, and obliterates the whole impression which the author has been at so much labor to convey. Our romantic sense of the hero's chivalry declines into a complacent satisfaction with his fate. We drop our enthusiasm, with the enthusiast, and jovially shake by the hand the mere man of good luck. But is not the latter feeling the more comfortable of the two? Perhaps so; but "comfortable" is not exactly the word Mr. Longfellow might wish applied to the end of his drama, and then why be at the trouble of building up an effect through a hundred and eighty pages, merely to knock it down at the end of the hundred and eighty-first?

We have already given, at some length, our conceptions of the nature of *plot* — and of that of "The Spanish Student," it seems almost superfluous to speak at all. It has nothing of construction about it. Indeed there is scarcely a single incident which has any necessary dependence upon any one other. Not only might we take away two-thirds of the whole without ruin — but without detriment — indeed with a positive benefit to the mass. And, even as regards the mere order of arrangement, we might with a very decided *chance* of improvement, put the scenes in a bag, give them a shake or two by way of shuffle, and tumble them out. The whole mode of collocation — not to speak of the feebleness of the incidents in themselves — evinces, on the part of the author, an utter and radical want of the adapting or constructive power which the drama so imperatively demands.

Of the unoriginality of the thesis we have already spoken; and now, to the unoriginality of the events by which the thesis is developed, we need do little more than allude. What, indeed, *could* we say of such incidents as the child stolen by gipsies — as her education as a *danseuse*

— as her betrothal to a Gipsy — as her preference for a gentleman — as the rumors against her purity — as her persecution by a *roué* — as the inruption of the *roué* into her chamber — as the consequent misunderstanding between her and her lover — as the duel — as the defeat of the *roué* — as the receipt of his life from the hero — as his boasts of success with the girl — as the *ruse* of the duplicate ring — as the field, in consequence, abandoned by the lover — as the assassination of Lara while scaling the girl's bed-chamber — as the disconsolate peregrination of Victorian — as the *équivoque* scene with Preciosa — as the offering to purchase the ring and the refusal to part with it — as the "news from court" telling of the Gipsy's true parentage — what *could* we say of all these ridiculous things, except that we have met them, each and all, some two or three hundred times before, and that they have formed, in a greater or less degree, the staple material of every Hop O' My Thumb tragedy since the flood? There is not an incident, from the first page of "The Spanish Student" to the last and most satisfactory, which we would not undertake to find bodily, at ten minutes' notice, in some one of the thousand and one comedies of intrigue attributed to Calderon and Lope de Vega.

But if our poet is grossly unoriginal in his subject, and in the events which evolve it, may he not be original in his handling or *tone*? We really grieve to say that he is not, unless, indeed, we grant him the meed of originality for the peculiar manner in which he has jumbled together the quaint and stilted tone of the old English dramatists with the *dégagée* air of Cervantes. But this is a point upon which, through want of space, we must necessarily permit the reader to judge altogether for himself. We quote, however, a passage from the Second Scene of the First Act, by way of showing how very easy a matter it is to make a man discourse Sancho Panza:

Chispa. Abernuncio Satanas! and a plague upon all lovers who ramble about at night, drinking the elements, instead of sleeping quietly in their beds. Every dead man to his cemetery, say I; and every friar to his monastery. Now, here's my master Victorian, yesterday a cow-keeper and to-day a gentleman; yesterday a student and to-day a lover; and I must be up later than the nightingale, for as the abbot sings so must the sacristan respond. God grant he may soon be married, for then shall all this serenading cease. Ay, marry, marry, marry! Mother, what does marry mean? It means to spin, to bear children, and to weep, my daughter! And, of a truth, there is something more in matrimony than the wedding-ring. And now, gentlemen, Pax vobiscum! as the ass said to the cabbages!

And, we might add, as an ass *only* should say.

In fact throughout "The Spanish Student," as well as throughout other compositions of its author, there runs a very obvious vein of *imitation.* We are perpetually reminded of something we have seen before — some old acquaintance in manner or matter; and even where the similarity cannot be said to amount to plagiarism, it is still injurious to the poet in the good opinion of him who reads.

Among the minor defects of the play, we may mention the frequent allusion to book incidents not generally known, and requiring each a *Note* by way of explanation. The drama demands that everything be so instantaneously evident that he who runs may read; and the only impression effected by these *Notes* to a play is that the author is desirous of showing his reading.

We may mention, also, occasional tautologies—such as:

> "Never did I behold thee so *attired*
> And *garmented* in beauty as to-night!"

Or,

> "What we need
> Is the celestial fire to change the fruit
> Into *transparent* crystal, *bright and clear!*"

We may speak, too, of more than occasional errors of grammar. For example, p. 23:

> "Did no one see thee? None, my love, but *thou*."

Here "but" is not a conjunction, but a preposition, and governs *thee* in the objective. "None but *thee*" would be right; meaning none *except* thee, *saving* thee.

At page 27, "mayst" is somewhat incorrectly written "may'st."

At page 34 we have:

> "I have no other saint than *thou* to pray to."

Here authority and analogy are both against Mr. Longfellow. "Than" also is here a preposition governing the objective, and meaning *save*, or *except*. "I have none other God than thee," &c. See Horne Tooke. The Latin "*quam te*" is exactly equivalent. At page 80 we read:

> "*Like thee* I am a captive, and, *like thee*,
> I have a gentle gaoler."

Here "like thee" (although grammatical of course) does not convey the idea. Mr. L. does not mean that the speaker is *like* the bird itself, but that his *condition* resembles it. The true reading would thus be:

> *As thou* I am a captive, and, *as thou*,
> I have a gentle gaoler:

That is to say, *as thou art*, and *as thou hast*.

Upon the whole, we regret that Professor Longfellow has written this work, and feel especially vexed that he has committed himself by its republication. Only when regarded as a mere poem, can it be said to have merit of any kind. For, in fact, it is only when we separate the poem from the drama, that the passages we have commended as beautiful can be understood to have beauty. We are not too sure, indeed, that a "dramatic poem" is not a flat contradiction in terms. At all events a man of true genius, (and such Mr. L. unquestionably is,) has no business with these hybrid and paradoxical compositions. Let a poem be a poem only; let a play be a play and nothing more. As for "The Spanish Student," its thesis is unoriginal; its incidents are antique; its plot is no plot; its characters have no character: in short, it is little better than a play upon words, to style it "A Play" at all.

Preface to the Poems
(1845)

THESE trifles are collected and republished chiefly with a view to their redemption from the many improvements to which they have been subjected while going "the rounds of the press." I am naturally anxious that if what I have written is to circulate at all, it should circulate as I wrote it. In defence of my own taste, nevertheless, it is incumbent on me to say that I think nothing in this volume of much value to the public, or very creditable to myself. Events not to be controlled have prevented me from making, at any time, any serious effort in what, under happier circumstances, would have been the field of my choice. With me poetry has been not a purpose, but a passion; and the passions should be held in reverence; they must not—they cannot at will be excited with an eye to the paltry compensations, or the more paltry commendations, of mankind.

E. A. P.

The Philosophy of Composition

CHARLES DICKENS, in a note now lying before me, alluding to an examination I once made of the mechanism of "Barnaby Rudge," says—"By the way, are you aware that Godwin wrote his 'Caleb Williams' backwards? He first involved his hero in a web of difficulties, forming the second volume, and then, for the first, cast about him for some mode of accounting for what had been done."

I cannot think this the *precise* mode of procedure on the part of Godwin—and indeed what he himself acknowledges, is not altogether in accordance with Mr. Dickens' idea—but the author of "Caleb Williams" was too good an artist not to perceive the advantage derivable from at least a somewhat similar process. Nothing is more clear than that every plot, worth the name, must be elaborated to its *dénouement* before anything be attempted with the pen. It is only with the *dénouement* constantly in view that we can give a plot its indispensable air of consequence, or causation, by making the incidents, and especially the tone at all points, tend to the development of the intention.

There is a radical error, I think, in the usual mode of constructing a story. Either history affords a thesis—or one is suggested by an incident of the day—or, at best, the author sets himself to work in the combination of striking events to form merely the basis of his narrative—designing, generally, to fill in with description, dialogue, or autorial comment, whatever crevices of fact, or action, may, from page to page, render themselves apparent.

I prefer commencing with the consideration of an *effect*. Keeping originality *always* in view — for he is false to himself who ventures to dispense with so obvious and so easily attainable a source of interest — I say to myself, in the first place, "Of the innumerable effects, or impressions, of which the heart, the intellect, or (more generally) the soul is susceptible, what one shall I, on the present occasion, select?" Having chosen a novel, first, and secondly a vivid effect, I consider whether it can be best wrought by incident or tone — whether by ordinary incidents and peculiar tone, or the converse, or by peculiarity both of incident and tone — afterward looking about me (or rather within) for such combinations of event, or tone, as shall best aid me in the construction of the effect.

I have often thought how interesting a magazine paper might be written by any author who would — that is to say, who could — detail, step by step, the processes by which any one of his compositions attained its ultimate point of completion. Why such a paper has never been given to the world, I am much at a loss to say — but, perhaps, the autorial vanity has had more to do with the omission than any one other cause. Most writers — poets in especial — prefer having it understood that they compose by a species of fine frenzy — an ecstatic intuition — and would positively shudder at letting the public take a peep behind the scenes, at the elaborate and vacillating crudities of thought — at the true purposes seized only at the last moment — at the innumerable glimpses of idea that arrived not at the maturity of full view — at the fully matured fancies discarded in despair as unmanageable — at the cautious selections and rejections — at the painful erasures and interpolations — in a word, at the wheels and pinions — the tackle for scene-shifting — the step-ladders and demon-traps — the cock's feathers, the red paint and the black patches, which, in ninety-nine cases out of the hundred, constitute the properties of the literary *histrio.*

I am aware, on the other hand, that the case is by no means common, in which an author is at all in condition to retrace the steps by which his conclusions have been attained. In general, suggestions, having arisen pell-mell, are pursued and forgotten in a similar manner.

For my own part, I have neither sympathy with the repugnance alluded to, nor, at any time, the least difficulty in recalling to mind the progressive steps of any of my compositions; and, since the interest of an analysis, or reconstruction, such as I have considered a *desideratum*, is quite independent of any real or fancied interest in the thing analyzed, it will not be regarded as a breach of decorum on my part to show the *modus operandi* by which some one of my own works was put together. I select "The Raven," as the most generally known. It is my design to render it manifest that no one point in its composition is referable either to accident or intuition — that the work proceeded, step by step, to its completion with the precision and rigid consequence of a mathematical problem.

Let us dismiss, as irrelevant to the poem, *per se*, the

circumstance — or say the necessity — which, in the first place, gave rise to the intention of composing *a* poem that should suit at once the popular and the critical taste.

We commence, then, with this intention.

The initial consideration was that of extent. If any literary work is too long to be read at one sitting, we must be content to dispense with the immensely important effect derivable from unity of impression — for, if two sittings be required, the affairs of the world interfere, and everything like totality is at once destroyed. But since, *ceteris paribus*, no poet can afford to dispense with *anything* that may advance his design, it but remains to be seen whether there is, in extent, any advantage to counterbalance the loss of unity which attends it. Here I say no, at once. What we term a long poem is, in fact, merely a succession of brief ones — that is to say, of brief poetical effects. It is needless to demonstrate that a poem is such, only inasmuch as it intensely excites, by elevating, the soul; and all intense excitements are, through a psychal necessity, brief. For this reason, at least one half of the "Paradise Lost" is essentially prose — a succession of poetical excitements interspersed, *inevitably*, with corresponding depressions — the whole being deprived, through the extremeness of its length, of the vastly important artistic element, totality, or unity, of effect.

It appears evident, then, that there is a distinct limit, as regards length, to all works of literary art — the limit of a single sitting — and that, although in certain classes of prose composition, such as "Robinson Crusoe," (demanding no unity,) this limit may be advantageously overpassed, it can never properly be overpassed in a poem. Within this limit, the extent of a poem may be made to bear mathematical relation to its merit — in other words, to the excitement or elevation — again in other words, to the degree of the true poetical effect which it is capable of inducing; for it is clear that the brevity must be in direct ratio of the intensity of the intended effect: — this, with one proviso — that a certain degree of duration is absolutely requisite for the production of any effect at all.

Holding in view these considerations, as well as that degree of excitement which I deemed not above the popular, while not below the critical, taste, I reached at once what I conceived the proper *length* for my intended poem — a length of about one hundred lines. It is, in fact, a hundred and eight.

My next thought concerned the choice of an impression, or effect, to be conveyed: and here I may as well observe that, throughout the construction, I kept steadily in view the design of rendering the work *universally* appreciable. I should be carried too far out of my immediate topic were I to demonstrate a point upon which I have repeatedly insisted, and which, with the poetical, stands not in the slightest need of demonstration — the point, I mean, that Beauty is the sole legitimate province of the poem. A few words, however, in elucidation of my real meaning, which some of my friends have evinced a disposition to misrepresent. That pleasure which is at once the most intense, the most elevating, and the most pure, is, I believe, found in the contemplation of the beautiful. When, indeed, men speak of Beauty, they mean, precisely, not a quality, as is supposed, but an effect — they refer, in short, just to that intense and pure elevation of *soul* — *not* of intellect, or of heart — upon which I have commented, and which is experienced in consequence of contemplating "the beautiful." Now I designate Beauty as the province of the poem, merely because it is an obvious rule of Art that effects should be made to spring from direct causes — that objects should be attained through means best adapted for their attainment — no one as yet having been weak enough to deny that the peculiar elevation alluded to is *most readily* attained in the poem. Now the object, Truth, or the satisfaction of the intellect, and the object Passion, or the excitement of the heart, are, although attainable, to a certain extent, in poetry, far more readily attainable in prose. Truth, in fact, demands a precision, and Passion, a *homeliness* (the truly passionate will comprehend me) which are absolutely antagonistic to that Beauty which, I maintain, is the excitement, or pleasurable elevation, of the soul. It by no means follows from anything here said, that passion, or even truth, may not be introduced, and even profitably introduced, into a poem — for they may serve in elucidation, or aid the general effect, as do discords in music, by contrast — but the true artist will always contrive, first, to tone them into proper subservience to the predominant aim, and, secondly, to enveil them, as far as possible, in that Beauty which is the atmosphere and the essence of the poem.

Regarding, then, Beauty as my province, my next question referred to the *tone* of its highest manifestation

— and all experience has shown that this tone is one of *sadness.* Beauty of whatever kind, in its supreme development, invariably excites the sensitive soul to tears. Melancholy is thus the most legitimate of all the poetical tones.

The length, the province, and the tone, being thus determined, I betook myself to ordinary induction, with the view of obtaining some artistic piquancy which might serve me as a key-note in the construction of the poem — some pivot upon which the whole structure might turn. In carefully thinking over all the usual artistic effects — or more properly *points,* in the theatrical sense — I did not fail to perceive immediately that no one had been so universally employed as that of the *refrain.* The universality of its employment sufficed to assure me of its intrinsic value, and spared me the necessity of submitting it to analysis. I considered it, however, with regard to its susceptibility of improvement, and soon saw it to be in a primitive condition. As commonly used, the *refrain,* or burden, not only is limited to lyric verse, but depends for its impression upon the force of monotone — both in sound and thought. The pleasure is deduced solely from the sense of identity — of repetition. I resolved to diversify, and so vastly heighten, the effect, by adhering, in general, to the monotone of sound, while I continually varied that of thought: that is to say, I determined to produce continuously novel effects, by the variation *of the application* of the *refrain* — the *refrain* itself remaining, for the most part, unvaried.

These points being settled, I next bethought me of the *nature* of my *refrain.* Since its application was to be repeatedly varied, it was clear that the *refrain* itself must be brief, for there would have been an insurmountable difficulty in frequent variations of application in any sentence of length. In proportion to the brevity of the sentence, would, of course, be the facility of the variation. This led me at once to a single word as the best *refrain*.

The question now arose as to the *character* of the word. Having made up my mind to a *refrain*, the division of the poem into stanzas was, of course, a corollary: the *refrain* forming the close to each stanza. That such a close, to have force, must be sonorous and susceptible of protracted emphasis, admitted no doubt: and these considerations inevitably led me to the long *o* as the most sonorous vowel, in connection with *r* as the most producible consonant.

The sound of the *refrain* being thus determined, it became necessary to select a word embodying this sound, and at the same time in the fullest possible keeping with that melancholy which I had predetermined as the tone of the poem. In such a search it would have been absolutely impossible to overlook the word "Nevermore." In fact, it was the very first which presented itself.

The next *desideratum* was a pretext for the continuous use of the one word "nevermore." In observing the difficulty which I at once found in inventing a sufficiently plausible reason for its continuous repetition, I did not fail to perceive that this difficulty arose solely from the pre-assumption that the word was to be so continuously or monotonously spoken by *a human* being — I did not fail to perceive, in short, that the difficulty lay in the reconciliation of this monotony with the exercise of reason on the part of the creature repeating the word. Here, then, immediately arose the idea of a *non*-reasoning creature capable of speech; and, very naturally, a parrot, in the first instance, suggested itself, but was superseded forthwith by a Raven, as equally capable of speech, and infinitely more in keeping with the intended *tone*.

I had now gone so far as the conception of a Raven — the bird of ill omen — monotonously repeating the one word, "Nevermore," at the conclusion of each stanza, in a poem of melancholy tone, and in length about one hundred lines. Now, never losing sight of the object *supremeness*, or perfection, at all points, I asked myself — "Of all melancholy topics, what, according to the *universal* understanding of mankind, is the *most* melancholy?" Death — was the obvious reply. "And when," I said, "is this most melancholy of topics most poetical?" From what I have already explained at some length, the answer, here also, is obvious — "When it most closely allies itself to *Beauty*: the death, then, of a beautiful woman is, unquestionably, the most poetical topic in the world — and equally is it beyond doubt that the lips best suited for such topic are those of a bereaved lover."

I had now to combine the two ideas, of a lover lamenting his deceased mistress and a Raven continuously repeating the word "Nevermore" — I had to combine these, bearing in mind my design of varying, at every turn, the *application* of the word repeated; but the only intelligible mode of such combination is that of imagining the Raven employing the word in answer to the queries of the lover. And here it was that I saw at once the opportunity afforded for the effect on which I had been depending — that is to say, the effect of the *variation of application.* I saw that I could make the first query propounded by the lover — the first query to which the Raven should reply "Nevermore" — that I could make this first query a commonplace one — the second less so — the third still less, and so on — until at length the lover, startled from his original *nonchalance* by the melancholy character of the word itself — by its frequent repetition — and by a consideration of the ominous reputation of the fowl that uttered it — is at length excited to superstition, and wildly propounds queries of a far different character — queries whose solution he has passionately at heart — propounds them half in superstition and half in that species of despair which delights in self-torture — propounds them not altogether because he believes in the prophetic or demoniac character of the bird (which, reason assures him, is merely repeating a lesson learned by rote) but because he experiences a phrenzied pleasure in so modeling his questions as to receive from the *expected* "Nevermore" the most delicious because the most intolerable of sorrow. Perceiving the opportunity thus afforded me — or, more strictly, thus forced upon me in the progress of the construction — I first established in mind the climax, or concluding query — that to which "Nevermore" should be in the last place an answer — that in reply to which this word "Nevermore" should involve the utmost conceivable amount of sorrow and despair.

Here then the poem may be said to have its beginning

— at the end, where all works of art should begin — for it was here, at this point of my preconsiderations, that I first put pen to paper in the composition of the stanza:

"Prophet," said I, "thing of evil! prophet still if bird or devil!
By that heaven that bends above us — by that God we both adore,
Tell this soul with sorrow laden, if within the distant Aidenn,
It shall clasp a sainted maiden whom the angels name Lenore —
Clasp a rare and radiant maiden whom the angels name Lenore."
Quoth the raven "Nevermore."

I composed this stanza, at this point, first that, by establishing the climax, I might the better vary and graduate, as regards seriousness and importance, the preceding queries of the lover — and, secondly, that I might definitely settle the rhythm, the metre, and the length and general arrangement of the stanza — as well as graduate the stanzas which were to precede, so that none of them might surpass this in rhythmical effect. Had I been able, in the subsequent composition, to construct more vigorous stanzas, I should, without scruple, have purposely enfeebled them, so as not to interfere with the climacteric effect.

And here I may as well say a few words of the versification. My first object (as usual) was originality. The extent to which this has been neglected, in versification, is one of the most unaccountable things in the world. Admitting that there is little possibility of variety in mere *rhythm*, it is still clear that the possible varieties of metre and stanza are absolutely infinite — and yet, *for centuries, no man, in verse, has ever done, or ever seemed to think of doing, an original thing*. The fact is, originality (unless in minds of very unusual force) is by no means a matter, as some suppose, of impulse or intuition. In general, to be found, it must be elaborately sought, and although a positive merit of the highest class, demands in its attainment less of invention than negation.

Of course, I pretend to no originality in either the rhythm or metre of the "Raven." The former is trochaic — the latter is octameter acatalectic, alternating with heptameter catalectic repeated in the *refrain* of the fifth verse, and terminating with tetrameter catalectic. Less pedantically — the feet employed throughout (trochees) consist of a long syllable followed by a short: the first line of the stanza consists of eight of these feet — the second of seven and a half (in effect two-thirds) — the third of eight — the fourth of seven and a half — the fifth the same — the sixth three and a half. Now, each of these lines, taken individually, has been employed before, and what originality the "Raven" has, is in their *combination into stanza;* nothing even remotely approaching this combination has ever been attempted. The effect of this originality of combination is aided by other unusual, and some altogether novel effects, arising from an extension of the application of the principles of rhyme and alliteration.

The next point to be considered was the mode of bringing together the lover and the Raven — and the first branch of this consideration was the *locale*. For this the most natural suggestion might seem to be a forest, or the fields — but it has always appeared to me that a close *circumscription of space* is absolutely necessary to the effect of insulated incident; — it has the force of a frame to a picture. It has an indisputable moral power in keeping concentrated the attention, and, of course, must not be confounded with mere unity of place.

I determined, then, to place the lover in his chamber — in a chamber rendered sacred to him by memories of her who had frequented it. The room is represented as richly furnished — this in mere pursuance of the ideas I have already explained on the subject of Beauty, as the sole true poetical thesis.

The *locale* being thus determined, I had now to introduce the bird — and the thought of introducing him through the window, was inevitable. The idea of making the lover suppose, in the first instance, that the flapping of the wings of the bird against the shutter, is a "tapping" at the door, originated in a wish to increase, by prolonging, the reader's curiosity, and in a desire to admit the incidental effect arising from the lover's throwing open the door, finding all dark, and thence adopting the half-fancy that it was the spirit of his mistress that knocked.

I made the night tempestuous, first, to account for the Raven's seeking admission, and secondly, for the effect of contrast with the (physical) serenity within the chamber.

I made the bird alight on the bust of Pallas, also for the effect of contrast between the marble and the plumage — it being understood that the bust was absolutely *suggested* by the bird — the bust of *Pallas* being chosen, first, as most in keeping with the scholarship of the lover, and, secondly, for the sonorousness of the word, Pallas, itself.

About the middle of the poem, also, I have availed myself of the force of contrast, with a view of deepening the ultimate impression. For example, an air of the fantastic — approaching as nearly to the ludicrous as was admissible — is given to the Raven's entrance. He comes in "with many a flirt and flutter."

Not the *least obeisance made he* — not a moment stopped or stayed he,
But with mien of lord or lady, perched above my chamber door.

In the two stanzas which follow, the design is more obviously carried out: —

Then this ebony bird beguiling my sad fancy into smiling
By the *grave and stern decorum of the countenance it wore*,
"Though thy *crest be shorn and shaven* thou," I said, "art sure no craven,
Ghastly grim and ancient Raven wandering from the nightly shore —
Tell me what thy lordly name is on the Night's Plutonian shore!"
Quoth the Raven "Nevermore."

Much I marvelled *this ungainly fowl* to hear discourse so plainly,
Though its answer little meaning — little relevancy bore;
For we cannot help agreeing that no living human being
Ever yet was blessed with seeing bird above his chamber door —
Bird or beast upon the sculptured bust above his chamber door,
With such name as "Nevermore."

The effect of the *dénouement* being thus provided for, I immediately drop the fantastic for a tone of the most profound seriousness: — this tone commencing in the stanza directly following the one last quoted, with the line,

But the Raven, sitting lonely on that placid bust, spoke only, etc

From this epoch the lover no longer jests — no longer

sees anything even of the fantastic in the Raven's demeanor. He speaks of him as a "grim, ungainly, ghastly, gaunt, and ominous bird of yore," and feels the "fiery eyes" burning into his "bosom's core." This revolution of thought, or fancy, on the lover's part, is intended to induce a similar one on the part of the reader — to bring the mind into a proper frame for the *dénouement* — which is now brought about as rapidly and as *directly* as possible.

With the *dénouement* proper — with the Raven's reply, "Nevermore," to the lover's final demand if he shall meet his mistress in another world — the poem, in its obvious phase, that of a simple narrative, may be said to have its completion. So far, everything is within the limits of the accountable — of the real. A raven, having learned by rote the single word "Nevermore," and having escaped from the custody of its owner, is driven at midnight, through the violence of a storm, to seek admission at a window from which a light still gleams — the chamber-window of a student, occupied half in poring over a volume, half in dreaming of a beloved mistress deceased. The casement being thrown open at the fluttering of the bird's wings, the bird itself perches on the most convenient seat out of the immediate reach of the student, who, amused by the incident and the oddity of the visitor's demeanor, demands of it, in jest and without looking for a reply, its name. The raven addressed, answers with its customary word, "Nevermore" — a word which finds immediate echo in the melancholy heart of the student, who, giving utterance aloud to certain thoughts suggested by the occasion, is again startled by the fowl's repetition of "Nevermore." The student now guesses the state of the case, but is impelled, as I have before explained, by the human thirst for self-torture, and in part by superstition, to propound such queries to the bird as will bring him, the lover, the most of the luxury of sorrow, through the anticipated answer "Nevermore." With the indulgence, to the utmost extreme, of this self-torture, the narration, in what I have termed its first or obvious phase, has a natural termination, and so far there has been no overstepping of the limits of the real.

But in subjects so handled, however skilfully, or with however vivid an array of incident, there is always a certain hardness or nakedness, which repels the artistical eye. Two things are invariably required — first, some amount of complexity, or more properly, adaptation; and, secondly, some amount of suggestiveness — some under current, however indefinite, of meaning. It is this latter, in especial, which imparts to a work of art so much of that *richness* (to borrow from colloquy a forcible term) which we are too fond of confounding with *the ideal.* It is the *excess* of the suggested meaning — it is the rendering this the upper instead of the undercurrent of the theme — which turns into prose (and that of the very flattest kind) the so called poetry of the so called transcendentalists.

Holding these opinions, I added the two concluding stanzas of the poem — their suggestiveness being thus made to pervade all the narrative which has preceded them. The undercurrent of meaning is rendered first apparent in the lines —

"Take thy beak from out *my heart*, and take thy form from off my door!"
Quoth the Raven "Nevermore!"

It will be observed that the words, "from out my heart," involve the first metaphorical expression in the poem. They, with the answer, "Nevermore," dispose the mind to seek a moral in all that has been previously narrated. The reader begins now to regard the Raven as emblematical — but it is not until the very last line of the very last stanza, that the intention of making him emblematical of *Mournful and Never-ending Remembrance* is permitted distinctly to be seen:

And the Raven, never flitting, still is sitting, still is sitting,
On the pallid bust of Pallas just above my chamber door;
And his eyes have all the seeming of a demon's that is dreaming,
And the lamplight o'er him streaming throws his shadow on the floor;
And my soul *from out that shadow* that lies floating on the floor
Shall be lifted — nevermore.

The Rationale of Verse

The word "Verse" is here used not in its strict or primitive sense, but as the term most convenient for expressing generally and without pedantry all that is involved in the consideration of rhythm, rhyme, metre, and versification.

There is, perhaps, no topic in polite literature which has been more pertinaciously discussed, and there is certainly not one about which so much inaccuracy, confusion, misconception, misrepresentation, mystification, and downright ignorance on all sides, can be fairly said to exist. Were the topic really difficult, or did it lie, even, in the cloudland of metaphysics, where the doubt-vapors may be made to assume any and every shape at the will or at the fancy of the gazer, we should have less reason to wonder at all this contradiction and perplexity; but in fact the subject is exceedingly simple; one tenth of it, possibly, may be called ethical; nine tenths, however, appertain to the mathematics; and the whole is included within the limits of the commonest common sense.

"But, if this is the case, how," it will be asked, "can so much misunderstanding have arisen? Is it conceivable that a thousand profound scholars, investigating so very simple a matter for centuries, have not been able to place it in the fullest light, at least, of which it is susceptible?" These queries, I confess, are not easily answered: — at all events a satisfactory reply to them might cost more trouble than would, if properly considered, the whole *vexata quæstio* to which they have reference. Nevertheless, there is little difficulty or danger in suggesting that the "thousand profound scholars" *may* have failed, first, because they were scholars, secondly, because they were profound, and thirdly because they were a thousand — the impotency of the scholarship and profundity having been thus multiplied a thousand fold. I am serious in these suggestions; for, first again, there is something in "scholarship" which seduces us into blind worship of Bacon's Idol of the Theatre — into irrational deference to antiquity; secondly, the proper "profundity" is rarely profound — it is the nature of Truth in general, as of some ores in particular, to be richest when most superficial; thirdly, the clearest subject may be overclouded by mere superabundance of talk. In chemistry, the best way of separating two bodies is to add a third; in speculation, fact often agrees with fact and argument with argument, until an additional well-meaning fact or argument sets everything by the ears. In one case out of a hundred a point is excessively discussed because it is obscure; in the ninety-nine remaining it is obscure because excessively discussed. When a topic is thus circumstanced, the readiest mode of investigating it is to forget that any previous investigation has been attempted.

But, in fact, while much has been written on the Greek and Latin rhythms, and even on the Hebrew, little effort has been made at examining that of any of the modern tongues. As regards the English, comparatively nothing has been done. It may be said, indeed, that we are without a treatise on our own verse. In our ordinary grammars and in our works on rhetoric or prosody in general, may be found occasional chapters, it is true, which have the heading, "Versification," but these are, in all instances, exceedingly meagre. They pretend to no analysis; they propose nothing like system; they make no attempt at even rule; everything depends upon "authority." They are confined, in fact, to mere exemplification of the supposed varieties of English feet and English lines; — although in no work with which I am acquainted are these feet correctly given or these lines detailed in anything like their full extent. Yet what has been mentioned is all — if we except the occasional introduction of some pedagogue-ism, such as this, borrowed from the Greek Prosodies: — "When a syllable is wanting, the verse is said to be catalectic; when the measure is exact, the line is acatalectic; when there is a redundant syllable it forms hypermeter." Now whether a line be termed catalectic or acatalectic is, perhaps, a point of no vital importance; — it is even possible that the student may be able to decide, promptly, when the *a* should be employed and when omitted, yet be incognizant, at the same time, of *all* that is worth knowing in regard to the structure of verse.

A leading defect in each of our treatises, (if treatises they can be called,) is the confining the subject to mere *Versification*, while *Verse* in general, with the understanding given to the term in the heading of this paper, is the real question at issue. Nor am I aware of even one of our Grammars which so much as properly defines the word versification itself. "Versification," says a work now before me, of which the accuracy is far more than usual — the "English Grammar" of Goold Brown — "Versification is the art of arranging words into lines of correspondent length, so as to produce harmony by the regular alternation of syllables differing in quantity." The commencement of this definition might apply, indeed, to the *art* of versification, but not versification itself. Versification is not the art of arranging, &c., but the actual arranging — a distinction too obvious to need comment. The error here is identical with one which has been too long permitted to disgrace the initial page of every one of our school grammars. I allude to the definitions of English Grammar itself. "English Grammar," it is said, "is the art of speaking and writing the English language correctly." This phraseology, or something essentially similar, is employed, I believe, by Bacon, Miller, Fisk, Greenleaf, Ingersoll, Kirkland, Cooper, Flint, Pue, Comly, and many others. These gentlemen, it is presumed, adopted it without examination from Murray, who derived it from Lily, (whose work was "*quam solam Regia Majestas in omnibus scholis docendam præcipit,*") and who appropriated it without acknowledgment, but with some unimportant modification, from the Latin Grammar of Leonicenus. It may be shown, however, that this definition, so complacently received, is not, and cannot be, a proper definition of English Grammar. A definition is that which so describes its object as to distinguish it from all others: — it is no definition of any one thing if its terms are applicable to any one other.

But if it be asked—"What is the design—the end—the aim of English Grammar?" our obvious answer is, "The art of speaking and writing the English language correctly:"—that is to say, we must use the precise words employed as the definition of English Grammar itself. But the object to be obtained by any means is, assuredly, not the means. English Grammar and the end contemplated by English Grammar, are two matters sufficiently distinct; nor can the one be more reasonably regarded as the other than a fishing-hook as a fish. The definition, therefore, which is applicable in the latter instance, *cannot*, in the former, be true. Grammar in general is the analysis of language; English Grammar of the English.

But to return to Versification as defined in our extract above. "It is the art," says the extract, "of arranging words into lines *of correspondent length*." Not so:—a correspondence in the length of lines is by no means essential. Pindaric odes are, surely, instances of versification, yet these compositions are noted for extreme diversity in the length of their lines.

The arrangement is moreover said to be for the purpose of producing "*harmony* by the regular alternation," &c. But *harmony* is not the sôle aim—not even the principal one. In the construction of verse, *melody* should never be left out of view; yet this is a point which all our Prosodies have most unaccountably forborne to touch. Reasoned rules on this topic should form a portion of all systems of rhythm.

"So as to produce harmony," says the definition, "by the *regular alternation*," &c. A *regular* alternation, as described, forms no part of any principle of versification. The arrangement of spondees and dactyls, for example, in the Greek hexameter, is an arrangement which may be termed *at random.* At least it is arbitrary. Without interference with the line as a whole, a dactyl may be substituted for a spondee, or the converse, at any point other than the ultimate and penultimate feet, of which the former is always a spondee, the latter nearly always a dactyl. Here, it is clear, we have no "*regular* alternation of syllables differing in quantity."

"So as to produce harmony," proceeds the definition, "by the regular alternation of *syllables differing in quantity,*"—in other words by the alternation of long and short syllables; for in rhythm all syllables are necessarily either short or long. But not only do I deny the necessity of any *regularity* in the succession of feet and, by consequence, of syllables, but dispute the essentiality of any *alternation,* regular or irregular, of syllables long and short. Our author, observe, is now engaged in a definition of versification in general, not of English versification in particular. But the Greek and Latin metres abound in the spondee and pyrrhic—the former consisting of two long syllables; the latter of two short; and there are innumerable instances of the immediate succession of many spondees and many pyrrhics.

Here is a passage from Silius Italicus:

> Fallit te mensas inter quod credis inermem.
> Tot bellis quæsita viro, tot cædibus armat
> Majestas æterna ducem: si admoveris ora,
> Cannas et Trebiam ante oculos Trasymenaque busta,
> Et Pauli stare ingentem miraberis umbram.

Making the elisions demanded by the classic Prosodies, we should scan these Hexameters thus:

Fāllīt | tē mēn | sās īn | tēr qūod | crēdĭs ĭn | ērmēm |
Tōt bēl | līs qūæ | sītă vī | rō tōt | cædĭbŭs | ārmăt |
Mājēs | tās ǣ ¦ tērnă dŭ | cēm s'ād | mōvĕrĭs | ōrā |
Cānnās | ēt Trĕbĭ' | ānt'ŏcŭ | lōs Trăsy | mēnăqŭe | būstā
Ēt Pāu | lī stā | r'īngēn | tēm mī | rābĕrĭs | ūmbrām |

It will be seen that, in the first and last of these lines, we have only two short syllables in thirteen, with an uninterrupted succession of no less than *nine* long syllables. But how are we to reconcile all this with a definition of versification which describes it as "the art of arranging words into lines of correspondent length so as to produce harmony by the *regular alternation of syllables differing in quantity?*"

It may be urged, however, that our prosodist's *intention* was to speak of the English metres alone, and that, by omitting all mention of the spondee and pyrrhic, he has virtually avowed their exclusion from our rhythms. A grammarian is never excusable on the ground of good intentions. We demand from him, if from any one, rigorous precision of style. But grant the design. Let us admit that our author, following the example of all authors on English Prosody, has, in defining versification at large, intended a definition merely of the English. All these prosodists, we will say, reject the spondee and pyrrhic. Still all admit the iambus, which consists of a short syllable followed by a long; the trochee, which is the converse of the iambus; the dactyl, formed of one long syllable followed by two short; and the anapæst—

two short succeeded by a long. The spondee is improperly rejected, as I shall presently show. The pyrrhic is rightfully dismissed. Its existence in either ancient or modern rhythm is purely chimerical, and the insisting on so perplexing a nonentity as a foot of *two short* syllables, affords, perhaps, the best evidence of the gross irrationality and subservience to authority which characterize our Prosody. In the meantime the acknowledged dactyl and anapæst are enough to sustain my proposition about the "alternation," &c., without reference to feet which are assumed to exist in the Greek and Latin metres alone: for an anapæst and a dactyl may meet in the same line: when of course we shall have an uninterrupted succession of four short syllables. The meeting of these two feet, to be sure, is an accident not contemplated in the definition now discussed; for this definition, in demanding a "regular alternation of syllables differing in quantity," insists on a regular succession of similar *feet*. But here is an example:

Sīng tŏ mĕ | Isăbēlle

This is the opening line of a little ballad now before me, which proceeds in the same rhythm—a peculiarly beautiful one. More than all this:—English lines are often well composed, entirely, of a regular succession of syllables *all of the same quantity*:—the first lines, for instance, of the following quatrain by Arthur C. Coxe:

March! March! March!
Making sounds as they tread,
Ho! ho! how they step,
Going down to the dead!

The line italicized is formed of three cæsuras. The cæsura, of which I have much to say hereafter, is rejected by the English Prosodies and grossly misrepresented in the classic. It is a perfect foot—the most important in all verse—and consists of a single *long syllable; but the length of this syllable varies.*

It has thus been made evident that there is *not one* point of the definition in question which does not involve an error. And for anything more satisfactory or more intelligible we shall look in vain to any published treatise on the topic.

So general and so total a failure can be referred only to radical misconception. In fact the English Prosodists have blindly followed the pedants. These latter, like *les moutons de Panurge*, have been occupied in incessant tumbling into ditches, for the excellent reason that their leaders have so tumbled before. The Iliad, being taken as a starting-point, was made to stand instead of Nature and common sense. Upon this poem, in place of facts and deduction from fact, or from natural law, were built systems of feet, metres, rhythms, rules, — rules that contradict each other every five minutes, and for nearly all of which there may be found twice as many exceptions as examples. If any one has a fancy to be thoroughly confounded — to see how far the infatuation of what is termed "classical scholarship" can lead a bookworm in the manufacture of darkness out of sunshine, let him turn over, for a few moments, any of the German Greek Prosodies. The only thing clearly made out in them is a very magnificent contempt for Leibnitz's principle of "a sufficient reason."

To divert attention from the real matter in hand by any farther reference to these works, is unnecessary, and would be weak. I cannot call to mind, at this moment, one essential particular of information that is to be gleaned from them; and I will drop them here with merely this one observation: that, employing from among the numerous "*ancient*" feet the spondee, the trochee, the iambus, the anapæst, the dactyl, and the cæsura alone, I will engage to scan *correctly* any of the Horatian rhythms, or any true rhythm that human ingenuity can conceive. And this excess of chimerical feet is, perhaps, the very least of the scholastic supererogations. *Ex uno disce omnia.* The fact is that *Quantity* is a point in whose investigation the lumber of mere learning may be dispensed with, if ever in any. Its appreciation is universal. It appertains to no region, nor race, nor æra in especial. To melody and to harmony the Greeks hearkened with ears precisely similar to those which we employ for similar purposes at present; and I should not be condemned for heresy in asserting that a pendulum at Athens would have vibrated much after the same fashion as does a pendulum in the city of Penn.

Verse originates in the human enjoyment of equality, fitness. To this enjoyment, also, all the moods of verse — rhythm, metre, stanza, rhyme, alliteration, the *refrain*, and other analogous effects — are to be referred. As there are some readers who habitually confound rhythm and metre, it may be as well here to say that the former concerns the *character* of feet (that is, the arrangements of syllables) while the latter has to do with the *number* of these feet. Thus by "a dactylic *rhythm*" we express a sequence of dactyls. By "a dactylic hexa*meter*" we imply a line or measure consisting of six of these dactyls.

To return to *equality*. Its idea embraces those of similarity, proportion, identity, repetition, and adaptation or fitness. It might not be very difficult to go even behind the idea of equality, and show both how and why it is that the human nature takes pleasure in it, but such an investigation would, for any purpose now in view, be supererogatory. It is sufficient that the *fact* is undeniable — the fact that man derives enjoyment from his perception of equality. Let us examine a crystal. We are at once interested by the equality between the sides and between the angles of one of its faces: the equality of the sides pleases us; that of the angles doubles the pleasure. On bringing to view a second face in all respects similar to the first, this pleasure seems to be squared; on bringing to view a third it appears to be cubed, and so on. I have no doubt, indeed, that the delight experienced, if measurable, would be found to have exact mathematical relations such as I suggest; that is to say, as far as a certain point, beyond which there would be a decrease in similar relations.

The perception of pleasure in the equality of *sounds* is the principle of *Music*. Unpractised ears can appreciate only simple equalities, such as are found in ballad airs. While comparing one simple sound with another they are too much occupied to be capable of comparing the equality subsisting between these two simple sounds, taken conjointly, and two other similar simple sounds taken conjointly. Practised ears, on the other hand, appreciate both equalities at the same instant — although it is absurd to suppose that both are *heard* at the same instant. One is heard and appreciated from itself: the other is heard by the memory; and the instant glides into and is confounded with the secondary, appreciation. Highly cultivated musical taste in this manner enjoys not only these double equalities, all appreciated at once, but takes pleasurable cognizance, through memory, of equalities the members of which occur at intervals so great that the uncultivated taste loses them altogether. That this latter can properly estimate or decide on the merits of what is called scientific music, is of course impossible. But scientific music has no claim to intrinsic excellence — it is fit for scientific ears alone. In its excess it is the triumph of the *physique* over the *morale* of music. The sentiment is overwhelmed by the sense. On the whole, the advocates of the simpler melody and harmony have infinitely the best of the argument; — although there has been very little of real argument on the subject.

In *verse*, which cannot be better designated than as an inferior or less capable Music, there is, happily, little chance for complexity. Its rigidly simple character not even Science — not even Pedantry can greatly pervert.

The rudiment of verse may, possibly, be found in the *spondee*. The very germ of a thought seeking satisfaction in equality of sound, would result in the construction of words of two syllables, equally accented. In corroboration of this idea we find that spondees most abound in the most ancient tongues. The second step we can easily suppose to be the comparison, that is to say, the collocation, of two spondees — of two words composed each of a spondee. The third step would be the juxtaposition of three of these words. By this time the perception of monotone would induce farther consideration: and thus arises what Leigh Hunt so flounders in discussing under the title of "The *Principle* of Variety in Uniformity." Of course there is no principle in the case — nor in maintaining it. The "Uniformity" is the principle: — the "Variety" is but the principle's natural safeguard from self-destruction by excess of self. "Uniformity," besides, is the very worst word that could have been chosen for the expression of the *general* idea at which it aims.

The perception of monotone having given rise to an attempt at its relief, the first thought in this new direction would be that of collating two or more words formed each of two syllables differently accented (that is to say, short and long) but having the same order in each word: — in other terms, of collating two or more iambuses, or two or more trochees. And here let me pause to assert that more pitiable nonsense has been written on the topic of *long* and *short* syllables than on any other subject under the sun. In general, a syllable is long or short, just as it is difficult or easy of enunciation. The *natural* long syllables are those encumbered — the *natural* short syllables are those *un*encumbered, with consonants; all the rest is mere artificiality and jargon. The Latin Prosodies have a rule that "a vowel before two consonants is long." This rule is deduced from "authority" — that is, from the observation that vowels so circumstanced, in the ancient poems, are always in syllables long by the laws of scansion. The philosophy of the rule is untouched, and lies simply in the physical difficulty of giving voice to such syllables — of performing the lingual evolutions necessary for their utterance. Of course, it is not the *vowel* that is long, (although the rule says so) but the syllable of which the vowel is a part. It will be seen that the length of a syllable, depending on the facility or difficulty of its enunciation, must have great variation in various syllables; but for the purposes of verse we suppose a long syllable equal to two short ones: — and the natural deviation from this relativeness we correct in perusal. The more closely our long syllables approach this relation with our short ones, the better, *ceteris paribus*, will be our verse: but if the relation does not exist of itself, we force it by emphasis, which can, of course, make any syllable as long as desired; — or, by an effort we can pronounce with unnatural brevity a syllable that is naturally too long. *Accented* syllables are of course always long — but, where *un*encumbered with consonants, must be classed among the *unnaturally* long. Mere custom has declared that we shall accent them — that is to say, dwell upon them; but no inevitable lingual difficulty forces us to do so. In fine, every long syllable must of its own accord occupy in its utterance, or must be *made* to occupy, precisely the time demanded for two short ones. The only exception to this rule is found in the cæsura — of which more anon.

The success of the experiment with the trochees or iambuses (the one would have suggested the other) must have led to a trial of dactyls or anapæsts — natural dactyls or anapæsts — dactylic or anapæstic *words*. And now some degree of complexity has been attained. There is an appreciation, first, of the equality between the several dactyls, or anapæsts, and, secondly, of that between the long syllable and the two short conjointly. But here it may be said, that step after step would have been taken, in continuation of this routine, until all the feet of the Greek Prosodies became exhausted. Not so: — these remaining feet have no existence except in the brains of the scholiasts. It is needless to imagine men inventing these things, and folly to explain how and why they invented them, until it shall be first shown that they are actually invented. All other "feet" than those which I have specified, are, if not impossible at first view, merely combinations of the specified; and, although this assertion is rigidly true, I will, to avoid misunderstanding, put it in a somewhat different shape. I will say, then, that at present I am aware of no *rhythm* — nor do I believe that any one can be constructed — which, in its last analysis, will not be found to consist altogether of the feet I have mentioned, either existing in their individual and obvious condition, or interwoven with each other in accordance with simple natural laws which I will endeavor to point out hereafter.

We have now gone so far as to suppose men constructing indefinite sequences of spondaic, iambic, trochaic, dactylic, or anapæstic words. In *extending* these sequences, they would be again arrested by the sense of monotone. A succession of spondees would *immediately* have displeased; one of iambuses or of trochees, on account of the variety included within the foot itself, would have taken longer to displease; one of dactyls or anapæsts, still longer: but even the last, if extended very far, must have become wearisome. The idea, first, of curtailing, and, secondly, of defining the length of, a sequence, would thus at once have arisen. Here then is the *line*, or verse proper.[1] The principle of equality being constantly at the bottom of the whole process, lines would naturally be made, in the first instance, equal in the number of their feet; in the second instance there would be variation in the mere number; one line would be twice as long as another; then one would be some less obvious multiple of another; then still less obvious proportions would be adopted: — nevertheless there would be *proportion*, that is to say, a phase of equality, still.

Lines being once introduced, the necessity of distinctly defining these lines *to the ear*, (as yet written verse does not exist,) would lead to a scrutiny of their capabilities *at their terminations:* — and now would spring up the idea of equality in sound between the final syllables — in other words, of *rhyme*. First, it would be used only in the iambic, anapæstic, and spondaic rhythms, (granting that the latter had not been thrown aside, long since, on account of its tameness;) because in these rhythms the concluding syllable being long, could best sustain the necessary protraction of the voice. No great while could elapse, however, before the effect, found pleasant as well as useful, would be applied to the two remaining rhythms. But as the chief force of rhyme must lie in the accented syllable, the attempt to create rhyme

[1] Verse, from the Latin *vertere*, to turn, is so called on account of the turning or re-commencement of the series of feet. Thus a verse, strictly speaking, is a line. In this sense, however, I have preferred using the latter word alone; employing the former in the general acceptation given it in the heading of this paper.

at all in these two remaining rhythms, the trochaic and dactylic, would necessarily result in double and triple rhymes, such as *beauty* with *duty* (trochaic,) and *beautiful* with *dutiful* (dactylic).

It must be observed that in suggesting these processes, I assign them no date; nor do I even insist upon their order. Rhyme is supposed to be of modern origin, and were this proved, my positions remain untouched. I may say, however, in passing, that several instances of rhyme occur in the "Clouds" of Aristophanes, and that the Roman poets occasionally employ it. There is an effective species of ancient rhyming which has never descended to the moderns; that in which the ultimate and penultimate syllables rhyme with each other. For example:

> Parturiunt montes et nascitur ridicu*lus mus.*

and again —

> Litoreis ingens inventa sub ilicib*us sus.*

The terminations of Hebrew verse, (as far as understood,) show no signs of rhyme; but what thinking person can doubt that it did actually exist? That men have so obstinately and blindly insisted, *in general,* even up to the present day, in confining rhyme to the *ends* of lines, when its effect is even better applicable elsewhere, intimates, in my opinion, the sense of some *necessity* in the connection of the end with the rhyme — hints that the origin of rhyme lay in a necessity which connected it with the end — shows that neither mere accident nor mere fancy gave rise to the connection — points, in a word, at the very necessity which I have suggested, (that of some mode of defining lines *to the ear*,) as the true origin of rhyme. Admit this, and we throw the origin far back in the night of Time — beyond the origin of written verse.

But, to resume. The amount of complexity I have now supposed to be attained is very considerable. Various systems of equalization are appreciated at once (or nearly so) in their respective values and in the value of each system with reference to all the others. As our present *ultimatum* of complexity, we have arrived at triple-rhymed, natural-dactylic lines, existing proportionally as well as equally with regard to other triple-rhymed, natural-dactylic lines. For example:

> Virginal Lilian, rigidly, humblily dutiful;
> Saintlily, lowlily,
> Thrillingly, holily
> Beautiful!

Here we appreciate, first, the absolute equality between the long syllable of each dactyl and the two short conjointly; secondly, the absolute equality between each dactyl and any other dactyl — in other words, among all the dactyls; thirdly, the absolute equality between the two middle lines; fourthly, the absolute equality between the first line and the three others taken conjointly; fifthly, the absolute equality between the last two syllables of the respective words "dutiful" and "beautiful;" sixthly, the absolute equality between the two last syllables of the respective words "lowlily" and "holily;" seventhly, the proximate equality between the first syllable of "dutiful" and the first syllable of "beautiful;"

eighthly, the proximate equality between the first syllable of "lowlily" and that of "holily;" ninthly, the proportional equality (that of five to one,) between the first line and each of its members, the dactyls; tenthly, the proportional equality (that of two to one,) between each of the middle lines and its members, the dactyls; eleventhly, the proportional equality between the first line and each of the two middle — that of five to two; twelfthly, the proportional equality between the first line and the last — that of five to one; thirteenthly, the proportional equality between each of the middle lines and the last — that of two to one; lastly, the proportional equality, as concerns number, between all the lines, taken collectively and any individual line — that of four to one.

The consideration of this last equality would give birth immediately to the idea of *stanza*[1] — that is to say, the insulation of lines into equal or obviously proportional masses. In its primitive, (which was also its best,) form, the stanza would most probably have had absolute unity. In other words, the removal of any one of its lines would have rendered it imperfect; as in the case above, where, if the last line, for example, be taken away, there is left no rhyme to the "dutiful" of the first. Modern stanza is excessively loose — and where so, ineffective, as a matter of course.

Now, although in the deliberate written statement which I have here given of these various systems of equalities, there seems to be an infinity of complexity — so much that it is hard to conceive the mind taking cogni-

[1] A stanza is often vulgarly, and with gross impropriety, called a *verse*.

zance of them all in the brief period occupied by the perusal or recital of the stanza — yet the difficulty is in fact apparent only when we will it to become so. Any one fond of mental experiment may satisfy himself, by trial, that, in listening to the lines, he does actually, (although with a seeming unconsciousness, on account of the rapid evolutions of sensation,) recognize and instantaneously appreciate, (more or less intensely as his ear is cultivated,) each and all of the equalizations detailed. The pleasure received, or receivable, has very much such progressive increase, and in very nearly such mathematical relations, as those which I have suggested in the case of the crystal.

It will be observed that I speak of merely a proximate equality between the first syllable of "dutiful" and that of "beautiful;" and it may be asked why we cannot imagine the earliest rhymes to have had absolute instead of proximate equality of sound. But absolute equality would have involved the use of identical words; and it is the duplicate sameness or monotony — that of sense as well as that of sound — which would have caused these rhymes to be rejected in the very first instance.

The narrowness of the limits within which verse composed of natural feet alone, must necessarily have been confined, would have led, after a *very* brief interval, to the trial and immediate adoption of artificial feet — that is to say of feet *not* constituted each of a single word, but two or even three words; or of parts of words. These feet would be intermingled with natural ones. For example:

ă brēath | căn māke | thĕm ās | ă brēath | hăs māde.

This is an iambic line in which each iambus is formed of two words. Again:

Thĕ ūn | ĭmā | gīnā | blĕ mīght | ŏf Jōve. |

This is an iambic line in which the first foot is formed of a word and a part of a word; the second and third of parts taken from the body or interior of a word; the fourth of a part and a whole; the fifth of two complete words. There are no *natural* feet in either lines. Again:

Cān ĭt bĕ | fāncĭĕd thăt | Dēĭty | ēvĕr vĭn | dīctĭvely |
Māde ĭn hĭs | īmăge ă | mānnĭkĭn | mĕrely tŏ | māddĕn ĭt? |

These are two dactylic lines in which we find natural feet, ("Deity," "mannikin;") feet composed of two words ("fancied that," "image a," "merely to," "madden it;") feet composed of three words ("can it be," "made in his;") a foot composed of a part of a word ("dictively;") and a foot composed of a word and a part of a word ("ever vin.")

And now, in our supposititious progress, we have gone so far as to exhaust all the *essentialities* of verse. What follows may, strictly speaking, be regarded as embellishment merely — but even in this embellishment, the rudimental sense of *equality* would have been the never-ceasing impulse. It would, for example, be simply in seeking farther administration to this sense that men would come, in time, to think of the *refrain*, or burden, where, at the closes of the several stanzas of a poem, one word or phrase is *repeated;* and of alliteration, in whose simplest form a consonant is *repeated* in the commencements of various words. This effect would be extended so as to embrace repetitions both of vowels and of consonants, in the bodies as well as in the beginnings of words; and, at a later period, would be made to infringe on the province of rhyme, by the introduction of general similarity of sound between whole feet occurring in the body of a line: — all of which modifications I have exemplified in the line above,

> *M*ade in his i*m*age a *mannikin m*erely to *madden it.*

Farther cultivation would improve also the *refrain* by relieving its monotone in slightly varying the phrase at each repetition, or, (as I have attempted to do in "The Raven,") in retaining the phrase and varying its application — although this latter point is not strictly a rhythmical effect *alone*. Finally, poets when fairly wearied with following precedent — following it the more closely the less they perceived it in company with Reason — would adventure so far as to indulge in positive rhyme at other points than the ends of lines. First, they would put it in the middle of the line; then at some point where the multiple would be less obvious; then, alarmed at their own audacity, they would undo all their work by cutting these lines in two. And here is the fruitful source of the infinity of "short metre," by which modern poetry, if not distinguished, is at least disgraced. It would require a high degree, indeed, both of cultivation and of courage, on the part of any versifier, to enable him to place his rhymes — and let them remain — at unquestionably their best position, that of unusual and *unanticipated* intervals.

On account of the stupidity of some people, or, (if talent be a more respectable word,) on account of their talent for misconception — I think it necessary to add here, first, that I believe the "processes" above detailed to be nearly if not accurately those which *did* occur in the gradual creation of what we now call verse; secondly, that, although I so believe, I yet urge neither the assumed fact nor my belief in it, as a part of the true propositions of this paper; thirdly, that in regard to the aim of this paper, it is of no consequence whether these processes did occur either in the order I have assigned them, or at all; my design being simply, in presenting a general type of what such processes *might* have been and *must* have resembled, to help *them*, the "some people," to an easy understanding of what I have farther to say on the topic of Verse.

There is one point which, in my summary of the processes, I have purposely forborne to touch; because this point, being the most important of all, on account of the immensity of error usually involved in its consideration, would have led me into a series of detail inconsistent with the object of a summary.

Every reader of verse must have observed how seldom it happens that even any one line proceeds uniformly with a succession, such as I have supposed, of absolutely equal feet; that is to say, with a succession of iambuses only, or of trochees only, or of dactyls only, or of anapæsts only, or of spondees only. Even in the most musical lines we find the succession interrupted. The iambic pentameters of Pope, for example, will be found on examination, frequently varied by trochees in the beginning, or by (what seem to be) anapæsts in the body, of the line.

> Ŏh thōu | whătē | vĕr tī | tlĕ pleāse | thīne eār |
> Dĕan Drā | piĕr Bīck | ĕrstăff | ŏr Gūll | īvēr |
> Whēthĕr | thŏu choōse | Cĕrvān | tĕs' sē | rīoŭs āir |
> Ŏr laūgh | ănd shāke | īn Rāb | ĕlaīs' eā | sy chaīr. |

Were any one weak enough to refer to the Prosodies for the solution of the difficulty here, he would find it *solved* as usual by a *rule*, stating the fact, (or what it, the rule, supposes to be the fact,) but without the slightest attempt at the *rationale*. "By a *synæresis* of the two short syllables," say the books, "an anapæst may sometimes be employed for an iambus, or a dactyl for a trochee. . . . In the beginning of a line a trochee is often used for an iambus."

Blending is the plain English for *synæresis* — but there should be *no* blending; neither is an anapæst *ever* employed for an iambus, or a dactyl for a trochee. These feet differ in time; and *no* feet so differing can ever be legitimately used in the same line. An anapæst is equal to four short syllables — an iambus only to three. Dactyls and trochees hold the same relation. The principle of *equality*, in verse, admits, it is true, of variation at certain points, for the relief of monotone, as I have already shown, but the point of *time* is that point which, being the rudimental one, must never be tampered with at all.

To explain : — In farther efforts for the relief of monotone than those to which I have alluded in the summary, men soon came to see that there was no absolute necessity for adhering to the precise number of syllables, provided the time required for the whole foot was preserved inviolate. They saw, for instance, that in such a line as

ŏr lāugh | ănd shāke | ĭn Rāb | ĕlaĭs' ēa | sy chāir, |

the equalization of the three syllables *elais ea* with the two syllables composing any of the other feet, could be readily effected by pronouncing the two syllables *elais* in double quick time. By pronouncing each of the syllables *e* and *lais* twice as rapidly as the syllable *sy*, or the syllable *in*, or any other short syllable, they could bring the two of them, taken together, to the length, that is to say to the time, of any one short syllable. This consideration enabled them to effect the agreeable variation of three syllables in place of the uniform two. And variation was the object — variation to the ear. What sense is there, then, in supposing this object rendered null by the *blending* of the two syllables so as to render them, in absolute effect, one? Of course, there must be *no* blending. Each syllable must be pronounced as distinctly as possible, (or the variation is lost,) but with twice the rapidity in which the ordinary short syllable is enunciated. That the syllables *elais ea* do not compose an *anapæst* is evident, and the signs (ăăā) of their accentuation are erroneous. The foot might be written thus (a̯a̯a̱) the inverted crescents expressing double quick time; and might be called a bastard iambus.

Here is a trochaic line:

Sēe thĕ | dēlĭcāte | fōotĕd | rēin-deĕr. |

The prosodies — that is to say the most considerate of

them — would here decide that "*delicate*" is a dactyl used in place of a trochee, and would refer to what they call their "rule," for justification. Others, varying the stupidity, would insist upon a Procrustean adjustment thus (del'cate) — an adjustment recommended to all such words as *silvery*, *murmuring*, etc., which, it is said, should be not only pronounced, but written *silv'ry*, *murm'ring*, and so on, whenever they find themselves in trochaic predicament. I have only to say that "delicate," when circumstanced as above, is neither a dactyl nor a dactyl's equivalent; that I would suggest for it this (áa̯a̯ = inverted) accentuation; that I think it as well to call it a bastard trochee; and that all words, at all events, should be written and pronounced *in full*, and as nearly as possible as nature intended them.

About eleven years ago, there appeared in "The American Monthly Magazine," (then edited, I believe, by Mess. Hoffman and Benjamin,) a review of Mr. Willis' Poems; the critic putting forth his strength, or his weakness, in an endeavor to show that the poet was either absurdly affected, or grossly ignorant of the laws of verse; the accusation being based altogether on the fact that Mr. W. made occasional use of this very word "delicate" and other similar words, in "the Heroic measure which every one knew consisted of feet of two syllables." Mr. W. has often, for example, such lines as

> That binds him to a woman's *delicate* love —
> In the gay sunshine, *reverent* in the storm —
> With its *invisible* fingers my loose hair.

Here, of course, the feet *licate love*, *verent in*, and *sible fin*, are bastard iambuses; are *not* anapæsts; and are *not* improperly used. Their employment, on the contrary, by Mr. Willis, is but one of the innumerable instances he has given of keen sensibility in all those matters of taste which may be classed under the general head of *fanciful embellishment*.

It is also about eleven years ago, if I am not mistaken, since Mr. Horne, (of England,) the author of "Orion," one of the noblest epics in any language, thought it necessary to preface his "Chaucer Modernized" by a very long and evidently a very elaborate essay, of which the greater portion was occupied in a discussion of the seemingly anomalous foot of which we have been speaking. Mr. Horne upholds Chaucer in its frequent use; maintains his superiority, *on account* of his so frequently using it, over all English versifiers; and, indignantly repelling the common idea of those who make verse on their fingers — that the superfluous syllable is a roughness and an error — very chivalrously makes battle for it as "a grace." That a grace it *is*, there can be no doubt; and what I complain of is, that the author of the most happily versified long poem in existence, should have been under the necessity of discussing this grace merely *as* a grace, through forty or fifty vague pages, solely because of his inability to show *how* and *why* it is a grace — by which showing the question would have been settled in an instant.

About the trochee used for an iambus, as we see in the beginning of the line,

> Whĕthĕr thou choose Cervantes' serious air,

there is little that need be said. It brings me to the general proposition that, in all rhythms, the prevalent or distinctive feet may be varied at will, and nearly at random, by the *occasional* introduction of equivalent feet — that is to say, feet the sum of whose syllabic times is equal to the sum of the syllabic times of the distinctive feet. Thus the trochee, *whēthĕr*, is equal, in the sum of the times of its syllables, to the iambus, *thŏu choōse*, in the sum of the times of *its* syllables; each foot being, in time, equal to three short syllables. Good versifiers who happen to be, also, good poets, contrive to relieve the monotone of a series of feet, by the use of equivalent feet only at rare intervals, and at such points of their subject as seem in accordance with the *startling* character of the variation. Nothing of this care is seen in the line quoted above — although Pope has some fine instances of the duplicate effect. Where vehemence is to be strongly expressed, I am not sure that we should be wrong in venturing on *two consecutive* equivalent feet — although I cannot say that I have ever known the adventure made, except in the following passage, which occurs in "Al Aaraaf," a boyish poem, written by myself when a boy. I am referring to the sudden and rapid advent of a star.

> Dim was its little disk, and angel eyes
> Alone could see the phantom in the skies,
> Whĕn fīrst thĕ phāntŏm's cōurse wăs fōund tŏ bē
> *Hēadlŏng hīthĕr*ward o'er the starry sea.

In the "general proposition" above, I speak of the *occasional* introduction of equivalent feet. It sometimes happens that unskilful versifiers, without knowing what they do, or why they do it, introduce so many "variations" as to exceed in number the "distinctive" feet; when the ear becomes at once balked by the *bouleversement* of the rhythm. Too many trochees, for example, inserted in an iambic rhythm, would convert the latter to a trochaic. I may note here, that, in all cases, the rhythm designed should be commenced and continued, *without* variation, until the ear has had full time to comprehend what *is* the rhythm. In violation of a rule so obviously founded in common sense, many even of our best poets, do not scruple to begin an iambic rhythm with a trochee, or the converse; or a dactylic with an anapæst, or the converse; and so on.

A somewhat less objectionable error, although still a decided one, is that of commencing a rhythm, not with a different equivalent foot, but with a "bastard" foot of the rhythm intended. For example:

Mānў ă | thōūght wĭll | cōme tŏ | mēmŏry. |

Here *many a* is what I have explained to be a bastard trochee, and to be understood should be accented with inverted crescents. It is objectionable solely on account of its position as the *opening* foot of a trochaic rhythm. *Memory*, similarly accented, is also a bastard trochee, but *un*objectionable, although by no means demanded.

The farther illustration of this point will enable me to take an important step.

One of our finest poets, Mr. Christopher Pearse Cranch, begins a very beautiful poem thus:

Many are the thoughts that come to me
  In my lonely musing;
And they drift so strange and swift
  There's no time for choosing
Which to follow; for to leave
  Any, seems a losing.

"A losing" to Mr. Cranch, of course — but this *en passant.* It will be seen here that the intention is trochaic; — although we do *not* see this intention by the opening foot, as we should do — or even by the opening line. Reading the whole stanza, however, we perceive the trochaic rhythm as the general design, and so, after some reflection, we divide the first line thus:

Many are the | thōughts thăt | cōme tŏ | mē. |

Thus scanned, the line will seem musical. It *is* — highly so. And it is because there is no end to instances of just such lines of apparently incomprehensible music, that Coleridge thought proper to invent his nonsensical *system* of what he calls "scanning by accents" — as if "scanning by accents" were anything more than a phrase. Whenever "Christabel" is really *not rough,* it can be as readily scanned by the true *laws* (not the supposititious *rules*) of verse, as can the simplest pentameter of Pope; and where it *is* rough (*passim*) these same laws will enable any one of common sense to show *why* it is rough and to point out, instantaneously, the remedy for the roughness.

A reads and re-reads a certain line, and pronounces it false in rhythm — unmusical. *B*, however, reads it *to A*, and *A* is at once struck with the perfection of the rhythm, and wonders at his dulness in not "catching" it before. Henceforward he admits the line to be musical. *B*, triumphant, asserts, that, to be sure, the line is musical —for it is the work of Coleridge—and that it is *A* who is *not;* the fault being in *A's* false reading. Now here *A* is right and *B* wrong. *That* rhythm is erroneous, (at some point or other more or less obvious,) which *any* ordinary reader *can*, without design, read improperly. It is the business of the poet so to construct his line that the intention *must* be caught *at once.* Even when these men have precisely the same understanding of a sentence, they differ and often widely, in their modes of enunciating it. Any one who has taken the trouble to examine the topic of emphasis, (by which I here mean not *accent* of particular syllables, but the dwelling on entire words,) must have seen that men emphasize in the most singularly arbitrary manner. There are certain large classes of people, for example, who persist in emphasizing their monosyllables. Little uniformity of emphasis prevails; because the thing itself—the idea, emphasis,—is referable to no natural—at least, to no well comprehended and therefore uniform law. Beyond a very narrow and vague limit, the whole matter is conventionality. And if we differ in emphasis even when we agree in comprehension, how much more so in the former when in the latter too! Apart, however, from the consideration of natural disagreement, is it not clear that, by tripping here and mouthing there, any sequence of words may be twisted into any species of rhythm? But are we thence to deduce that all sequences of words are rhythmical in a rational understanding of the term?—for this is the deduction, precisely to which the *reductio ad absurdum* will, in the end, bring all the propositions of Coleridge. Out of a hundred readers of "Christabel," fifty will be able to make nothing of its rhythm, while forty-nine of the remaining fifty will, with some ado, fancy they comprehend it, after the fourth or fifth perusal. The one out of the whole hundred who shall both comprehend and admire it at first sight — must be an unaccountably clever person — and I am by far too modest to assume, for a moment, that that very clever person is myself.

In illustration of what is here advanced I cannot do better than quote a poem:

Pease porridge hot — pease porridge cold —
Pease porridge in the pot — nine days old.

Now those of my readers who have never *heard* this poem pronounced according to the nursery conventionality, will find its rhythm as obscure as an explanatory note; while those who *have* heard it, will divide it thus, declare it musical, and wonder how there can be any doubt about it.

Pease | porridge | hot | pease | porridge | cold |
Pease | porridge | in the | pot | nine | days | old. |

The chief thing in the way of this species of rhythm, is the necessity which it imposes upon the poet of travelling in constant company with his compositions, so as to be ready at a moment's notice, to avail himself of a well understood poetical license — that of reading aloud one's own doggerel.

In Mr. Cranch's line,

> Many are the | thoughts that | come to | me, |

the general error of which I speak is, of course, very partially exemplified, and the purpose for which, chiefly, I cite it, lies yet further on in our topic.

The two divisions (*thoughts that*) and (*come to*) are ordinary trochees. Of the last division (*me*) we will talk hereafter. The first division (*many are the*) would be thus accented by the Greek Prosodies (mānў ăre thĕ) and would be called by them ἀστρόλογος. The Latin books would style the foot *Pæon Primus*, and both Greek and Latin would swear that it was composed of a trochee and what they term a pyrrhic — that is to say, a foot of two *short* syllables — a thing that *cannot be*, as I shall presently show.

But now, there is an obvious difficulty. The *astrologos*, according to the Prosodies' own showing, is equal to *five* short syllables, and the trochee to *three* — yet, in the line quoted, these two feet are equal. They occupy *precisely* the same time. In fact, the whole music of the line depends upon their being *made* to occupy the same time. The Prosodies then, have demonstrated what all mathematicians have stupidly failed in demonstrating — that three and five are one and the same thing.

After what I have already said, however, about the bastard trochee and the bastard iambus, no one can have any trouble in understanding that *many are the* is of similar character. It is merely a bolder variation than usual from the routine of trochees, and introduces to the bastard trochee one additional syllable. But this syllable is not *short*. That is, it is not short in the sense of "*short*" as applied to the final syllable of the ordinary trochee, where the word means merely *the half of long*.

In this case (that of the additional syllable) "short," if used at all, must be used in the sense of *the sixth of long*. And all the three final syllables can be called *short* only with the same understanding of the term. The three together are equal only to the one short syllable (whose place they supply) of the ordinary trochee. It follows that there is no sense in thus (˘) accenting these syllables. We must devise for them some new character which shall denote the sixth of long. Let it be (c) — the crescent placed with the curve to the left. The whole foot (mā̄nẏ arė thė) might be called a *quick trochee*.

We come now to the final division (*me*) of Mr. Cranch's line. It is clear that this foot, short as it appears, is fully equal in time to each of the preceding. It is in fact the cæsura — the foot which, in the beginning of this paper, I called the most important in all verse. Its chief office is that of pause or termination; and here — at the end of a line — its use is easy, because there is no danger of misapprehending its value. We pause on it, by a seeming necessity, just so long as it has taken us to pronounce the preceding feet, whether iambuses, trochees, dactyls, or anapæsts. It is thus a *variable foot*, and, with some care, may be well introduced into the body of a line, as in a little poem of great beauty by Mrs. Welby:

I have | a lit | tle step | sŏ̄n | of on | ly three | years old. |

Here we dwell on the cæsura, *son*, just as long as it requires us to pronounce either of the preceding or succeeding iambuses. Its value, therefore, in this line, is that of three short syllables. In the following dactylic line its value is that of four short syllables.

Pale as a | lily was | Emily | Gray.

I have accented the cæsura with a (⌢⌣⌣⌣) by way of expressing this variability of value.

I observed, just now, that there could be no such foot as one of two short syllables. What we start from in the very beginning of all idea on the topic of verse, is quantity, *length.* Thus when we enunciate an independent syllable it is long, as a matter of course. If we enunciate two, dwelling on both equally, we express equality in the enumeration, or length, and have a right to call them two long syllables. If we dwell on one more than the other, we have also a right to call one short, because it is short in relation to the other. But if we dwell on both equally and with a tripping voice, saying to ourselves here are two short syllables, the query might well be asked of us — "In relation to what are they short?" Shortness is but the negation of length. To say, then, that two syllables, placed independently of any other syllable, are short, is merely to say that they have no positive length, or enunciation — in other words that they are no syllables — that they do not exist at all. And if, persisting, we add anything about their equality, we are merely floundering in the idea of an identical equation, where, x being equal to x, nothing is shown to be equal to zero. In a word, we can form no conception of a pyrrhic as of an independent foot. It is a mere chimera bred in the mad fancy of a pedant.

From what I have said about the equalization of the several feet of a *line*, it must not be deduced that any *necessity* for equality in time exists between the rhythm of *several* lines. A poem, or even a stanza, may begin with iambuses, in the first line, and proceed with anapæsts in the second, or even with the less accordant dactyls, as in the opening of quite a pretty specimen of verse by Miss Mary A. S. Aldrich:

> The wa | ter li | ly sleeps | in pride |
> Dōwn ĭn thĕ | dēpths ŏf thĕ | āzūre | lake. |

Here *azure* is a spondee, equivalent to a dactyl; *lake* a cæsura.

I shall now best proceed in quoting the initial lines of Byron's "Bride of Abydos:"

> Know ye the land where the cypress and myrtle
> Are emblems of deeds that are done in their clime —
> Where the rage of the vulture, the love of the turtle
> Now melt into softness, now madden to crime?
> Know ye the land of the cedar and vine,
> Where the flowers ever blossom, the beams ever shine,
> And the light wings of Zephyr, oppressed with perfume,
> Wax faint o'er the gardens of Gul in their bloom?
> Where the citron and olive are fairest of fruit
> And the voice of the nightingale never is mute —
>
> . . . .
>
> Where the virgins are soft as the roses they twine,
> And all save the spirit of man is divine?
> 'Tis the land of the East — 'tis the clime of the Sun —
> Can he smile on such deeds as his children have done?
> Oh, wild as the accents of lovers' farewell
> Are the hearts that they bear and the tales that they tell.

Now the flow of these lines, (as times go,) is very sweet and musical. They have been often admired, and justly — as times go — that is to say, it is a rare thing to find better versification of its kind. And where verse is pleasant to the ear, it is silly to find fault with it because it refuses to be scanned. Yet I have heard men, professing to be scholars, who made no scruple of abusing these lines of Byron's on the ground that they were musical in spite of *all law*. Other gentlemen, *not* scholars, abused "all law" for the same reason: — and it occurred neither to the one party nor to the other that the law about which they were disputing might possibly be no law at all — an ass of a law in the skin of a lion.

The Grammars said something about dactylic lines, and it was easily seen that *these* lines were at least meant for dactylic. The first one was, therefore, thus divided:

> Knōw yĕ thĕ | lānd whĕre thĕ | cyprĕss ănd | mȳrtlĕ. |

The concluding foot was a mystery; but the Prosodies said something about the dactylic "measure" calling now and then for a double rhyme; and the court of inquiry were content to rest in the double rhyme, without exactly perceiving what a double rhyme had to do with the question of an irregular foot. Quitting the first line, the second was thus scanned:

> Arē ĕmblĕms | ŏf deĕds thăt | āre dŏne ĭn | thēir clīme. |

It was immediately seen, however, that *this* would not do: — it was at war with the whole emphasis of the reading. It could not be supposed that Byron, or any one in his senses, intended to place stress upon such monosyllables as "are," "of," and "their," nor could "their clime," collated with "to crime," in the corresponding line below, be fairly twisted into anything like a "double rhyme," so as to bring everything within the category of the Grammars. But farther these Grammars spoke not. The inquirers, therefore, in spite of their sense of harmony in the lines, when considered without reference to scansion, fell back upon the idea that the "Are" was a blunder — an excess for which the poet should be sent to Coventry — and, striking it out, they scanned the remainder of the line as follows:

—— ēmblĕms ŏf | deēds thăt ăre | dōne ĭn thĕir | clīme. |

This answered pretty well; but the Grammars admitted no such foot as a foot of one syllable; and besides the rhythm was dactylic. In despair, the books are well searched, however, and at last the investigators are gratified by a full solution of the riddle in the profound "Observation" quoted in the beginning of this article: — "When a syllable is wanting, the verse is said to be catalectic; when the measure is exact, the line is acatalectic; when there is a redundant syllable it forms hypermeter." This is enough. The anomalous line is pronounced to be catalectic at the head and to form hypermeter at the tail: — and so on, and so on; it being soon discovered that nearly all the remaining lines are in a similar predicament, and that what flows so smoothly to the ear, although so roughly to the eye, is, after all, a mere jumble of catalecticism, acatalecticism, and hypermeter — not to say worse.

Now, had this court of inquiry been in possession of even the shadow of the *philosophy* of Verse, they would have had no trouble in reconciling this oil and water of the eye and ear, by merely scanning the passage without reference to lines, and, continuously, thus :

> Know ye the | land where the | cypress and | myrtle Are | emblems of | deeds that are | done in their | clime Where the | rage of the | vulture the | love of the | turtle Now | melt into | softness now | madden to | *crime* | Know ye the | land of the | cedar and | vine Where the | flowers ever | blossom the | beams ever | shine Where the | light wings of | Zephyr op | pressed by per | *fume Wax* | faint o'er the | gardens of | Gul in their | bloom Where the | citron and | olive are | fairest of | fruit And the | voice of the | nightingale | never is | mute Where the | virgins are | soft as the | roses they | *twine And* | all save the | spirit of | man is di | vine 'Tis the | land of the | East 'tis the | clime of the | Sun Can he | smile on such | deeds as his | children have | *done Oh* | wild as the | accents of | lovers' fare | well Are the | hearts that they | bear and the | tales that they | *tell.*

Here "crime" and "tell" (italicized) are cæsuras, each having the value of a dactyl, four short syllables; while "fume Wax," "twine and," and "done Oh," are spondees which, of course, being composed of two long syllables, are also equal to four short, and are the dactyl's natural equivalent. The nicety of Byron's ear has led him into a succession of feet which, with two trivial exceptions as regards melody, are absolutely accurate — a very rare occurrence this in dactylic or anapæstic rhythms. The exceptions are found in the spondee "*twine And,*" and the dactyl, "*smile on such.*" Both feet are false in point of melody. In "*twine And,*" to make out the rhythm, we must force "*And*" into a length which it will not naturally bear. We are called on to sacrifice either the proper length of the syllable as demanded by its position as a member of a spondee, or the customary accentuation of the word in conversation. There is no hesitation, and should be none. We at once give up the sound for the sense; and the rhythm is imperfect. In this instance it is *very* slightly so; — not one person in ten thousand could, by ear, detect the inaccuracy. But the *perfection* of verse, as regards melody, consists in its *never* demanding any such sacrifice as is here demanded. The rhythmical must agree, *thoroughly*, with the reading, flow. This perfection has in no instance been attained — but is unquestionably attainable. "*Smile on such*," the dactyl, is incorrect, because "*such*," from the character of the two consonants *ch*, cannot *easily* be enunciated in the ordinary time of a short syllable, which its position declares that it is. Almost every reader will be able to appreciate the slight difficulty here; and yet the error is by no means so important as that of the "*And*" in the spondee. By dexterity we *may* pronounce "*such*" in the true time; but the attempt to remedy the rhythmical deficiency of the *And* by drawing it out, merely aggravates the offence against natural enunciation, by directing attention to the offence.

My main object, however, in quoting these lines, is to show that, in spite of the Prosodies, the length of a line is entirely an arbitrary matter. We might divide the commencement of Byron's poem thus:

Know ye the | land where the. |

or thus:

Know ye the | land where the | cypress and. |

or thus:

Know ye the ↓ land where the | cypress and | myrtle are. |

or thus:

Know ye the | land where·the | cypress and | myrtle are | emblems of. |

In short, we may give it any division we please, and the lines will be good — provided we have at least *two* feet in a line. As in mathematics two units are required to form number, so rhythm, (from the Greek ἀριθμος, number,) demands for its formation at least two feet. Beyond doubt, we often see such lines as

Know ye the —
Land where the —

lines of one foot; and our Prosodies admit such; but with impropriety; for common sense would dictate that every so obvious division of a poem as is made by a line, should include within itself all that is necessary for its own comprehension; but in a line of one foot we can have no appreciation of *rhythm*, which depends upon the equality between *two* or more pulsations. The false lines, consisting sometimes of a single cæsura, which are seen in mock Pindaric odes, are of course "rhythmical" only in connection with some other line; and it is this want of independent rhythm which adapts them to the purposes of burlesque alone. Their effect is that of incongruity (the principle of mirth;) for they include the blankness of prose amid the harmony of verse.

My second object in quoting Byron's lines, was that of showing how absurd it often is to cite a single line from amid the body of a poem, for the purpose of instancing the perfection or imperfection of the line's rhythm. Were we to see by itself

> Know ye the land where the cypress and myrtle,

we might justly condemn it as defective in the final foot, which is equal to only three, instead of being equal to four, short syllables.

In the foot (*flowers ever*) we shall find a further exemplification of the principle of the bastard iambus, bastard trochee, and quick trochee, as I have been at some pains in describing these feet above. All the Prosodies on English verse would insist upon making an elision in "flowers," thus (flow'rs,) but this is nonsense. In the quick trochee (mānў ăre thĕ) occurring in Mr. Cranch's *trochaic* line, we had to equalize the time of the three syllables (*ny*, *are*, *the*,) to that of the one *short* syllable whose position they usurp. Accordingly each of these syllables is equal to the third of a short syllable, that is to say, the *sixth of a long*. But in Byron's *dactylic* rhythm, we have to equalize the time of the three syllables (*ers*, *ev*, *er*,) to that of the one *long* syllable whose position they usurp or, (which is the same thing,) of the *two short*. Therefore the value of each of the syllables (*ers*, *ev*, and *er*) is the *third of a long*. We enunciate them with only half the rapidity we employ in enunciating the three final syllables of the quick trochee —which latter is a rare foot. The "*flowers ever*," on the contrary, is as common in the dactylic rhythm as is the *bastard* trochee in the trochaic, or the bastard iambus in the iambic. We may as well accent it with the curve of the crescent to the right, and call it a *bastard dactyl.* A *bastard anapæst,* whose nature I now need be at no trouble in explaining, will of course occur, now and then, in an anapæstic rhythm.

In order to avoid any chance of that confusion which is apt to be introduced in an essay of this kind by too sudden and radical an alteration of the conventionalities to which the reader has been accustomed, I have thought it right to suggest for the accent marks of the bastard trochee, bastard iambus, etc., etc., certain characters which, in merely varying the direction of the ordinary short accent (˘) should imply, what is the fact, that the feet themselves are not *new* feet, in any proper sense, but simply modifications of the feet, respectively, from which they derive their names. Thus a bastard iambus is, in its essentiality, that is to say, in its time, an iambus. The variation lies only in the *distribution* of this time. The time, for example, occupied by the one short (or *half of long*) syllable, in the ordinary iambus, is, in the bastard, spread equally over two syllables, which are accordingly the *fourth of long.*

But this fact — the fact of the essentiality, or whole time, of the foot being unchanged, is now so fully before the reader, that I may venture to propose, finally, an accentuation which shall answer the real purpose — that is to say, what should be the real purpose of all accentuation — the purpose of expressing to the eye the exact relative value of every syllable employed in Verse.

I have already shown that enunciation, or *length,* is the point from which we start. In other words, we begin with a *long syllable.* This then is our unit; and there

will be no need of accenting it at all. An unaccented syllable, in a system of accentuation, is to be regarded always as a long syllable. Thus a spondee would be without accent. In an iambus, the first syllable being "short," or the *half* of long, should be accented with a small 2, placed *beneath* the syllable; the last syllable, being long, should be unaccented; — the whole would be thus (control.) In a trochee, these accents would be
2
merely conversed, thus (manly.) In a dactyl, each of
2
the two final syllables, being the half of long, should, also, be accented with a small 2 beneath the syllable; and, the first syllable left unaccented, the whole would be thus (happiness.) In an anapæst we should converse the
2 2
dactyl thus, (in the land.) In the bastard dactyl, each of
2 2
the three concluding syllables being the *third* of long, should be accented with a small 3 beneath the syllable and the whole foot would stand thus, (flowers ever.) In
3 3 3
the bastard anapæst we should converse the bastard dactyl thus, (in the rebound.) In the bastard iambus,
3 3 3
each of the two initial syllables, being the fourth of long, should be accented, below with a small 4; the whole foot would be thus, (in the rain.) In the bastard trochee,
4 4
we should converse the bastard iambus thus, (many a.)
4 4
In the quick trochee, each of the three concluding syllables, being the *sixth* of long, should be accented, below, with a small 6; the whole foot would be thus, (many are the.) The quick iambus is not yet created,
6 6 6
and most probably never will be, for it will be excessively

useless, awkward, and liable to misconception — as I have already shown that even the quick trochee is: — but, should it appear, we must accent it by conversing the quick trochee. The cæsura, being variable in length, but always *longer than "long,"* should be accented, *above*, with a number expressing the length, or value, of the distinctive foot of the rhythm in which it occurs. Thus a cæsura, occurring in a spondaic rhythm, would be accented with a small 2 above the syllable, or, rather, foot. Occurring in a dactylic or anapæstic rhythm, we also accent it with the 2, above the foot. Occurring in an iambic rhythm, however, it must be accented, above, with $1\frac{1}{2}$; for this is the relative value of the iambus. Occurring in the trochaic rhythm, we give it, of course, the same accentuation. For the complex $1\frac{1}{2}$, however, it would be advisable to substitute the simpler expression $\frac{3}{2}$ which amounts to the same thing.

In this system of accentuation Mr. Cranch's lines, quoted above, would thus be written:

$\frac{3}{2}$
Many are the | thoughts that | come to | me
6 6 6 2 2
In my | lonely | musing, |
2 2 2
$\frac{3}{2}$
And they | drift so | strange and | swift
2 2 2
There's no | time for | choosing |
2 2 2
$\frac{3}{2}$
Which to | follow | for to | leave
2 2 2
Any, | seems a | losing. |
2 2 2

In the ordinary system the accentuation would be thus:

Mānȳ arĕ thĕ | thōughts thăt | cōme tŏ | mē
  Īn mȳ | lōnelȳ | mūsĭng, |
Ānd thĕy | drĭft sŏ | strānge ănd | swĭft |
  Thēre's nŏ | tīme fŏr | choōsĭng |
Whĭch tŏ | fōllŏw, | fōr tŏ | lēave
  Ānȳ, | seēms ă | lōsĭng. |

It must be observed, here, that I do not grant this to be the "ordinary" *scansion.* On the contrary, I never yet met the man who had the faintest comprehension of the true scanning of these lines, or of such as these. But granting this to be the mode in which our Prosodies would divide the feet, they would accentuate the syllables as just above.

Now, let any reasonable person compare the two modes. The first advantage seen in my mode is that of simplicity—of time, labor, and ink saved. Counting the fractions as *two* accents, even, there will be found only *twenty-six* accents to the stanza. In the common accentuation there are *forty-one.* But admit that all this is a trifle, which it is *not*, and let us proceed to points of importance. Does the common accentuation express the truth, in particular, in general, or in any regard? Is it consistent with itself? Does it convey either to the ignorant or to the scholar a just conception of the rhythm of the lines? Each of these questions must be answered in the negative. The crescents, being precisely similar, must be understood as expressing, all of them, one and the same thing; and so all Prosodies have always understood them and wished them to be understood. They express, indeed, "short"—but this word has all kinds of meanings. It serves to represent (the reader is left to guess *when*) sometimes the half, sometimes the third, sometimes the fourth, sometimes the sixth, of "long" — while "long" itself, in the books, is left undefined and undescribed. On the other hand, the horizontal accent, it may be said, expresses sufficiently well, and unvaryingly, the syllables which are meant to be long. It does nothing of the kind. This horizontal accent is placed over the cæsura (wherever, as in the Latin Prosodies, the cæsura is recognized) as well as over the ordinary long syllable, and implies anything and everything, just as the crescent. But grant that it does express the ordinary long syllables, (leaving the cæsura out of question,) have I not given the identical expression, by not employing any expression at all? In a word, while the Prosodies, with a certain number of accents, express *precisely nothing whatever*, I, with scarcely half the number, have expressed everything which, in a system of accentuation, demands expression. In glancing at my mode in the lines of Mr. Cranch, it will be seen that it conveys not only the exact relation of the syllables and feet, among themselves, in those particular lines, but their precise value in relation to any other existing or conceivable feet or syllables, in any existing or conceivable system of rhythm.

The object of what we call *scansion* is the distinct marking of the rhythmical flow. Scansion with accents or perpendicular lines between the feet — that is to say scansion *by* the voice only — is scansion *to* the ear only; and all very good in its way. The written scansion addresses the ear through the eye. In either case the object is the distinct marking of the rhythmical, musical, or reading flow. There *can* be no other object and there is none. Of course, then, the scansion and the reading flow should go hand in hand. The former must agree with the latter. The former represents and expresses the latter; and is good or bad as it truly or falsely represents and expresses it. If by the written scansion of a line we are not enabled to perceive any rhythm or music in the line, then either the line is unrhythmical or the scansion false. Apply all this to the English lines which we have quoted, at various points, in the course of this article. It will be found that the scansion exactly conveys the rhythm, and thus thoroughly fulfills the only purpose for which scansion is required.

But let the scansion *of the schools* be applied to the Greek and Latin verse, and what result do we find?—that the verse is one thing and the scansion quite another. The ancient verse, *read* aloud, is in general musical, and occasionally *very* musical. *Scanned* by the Prosodial rules we can, for the most part, make nothing of it whatever. In the case of the English verse, the more emphatically we dwell on the divisions between the feet, the more distinct is our perception of the kind of rhythm intended. In the case of the Greek and Latin, the more we dwell the *less* distinct is this perception. To make this clear by an example:

> Mæcenas, atavis edite regibus,
> O, et præsidium et dulce decus meum,
> Sunt quos curriculo pulverem Olympicum
> Collegisse juvat, metaque fervidis
> Evitata rotis, palmaque nobilis
> Terrarum dominos evehit ad Deos.

Now in *reading* these lines, there is scarcely one person in a thousand who, if even ignorant of Latin, will not immediately feel and appreciate their flow — their music. A prosodist, however, informs the public that the *scansion* runs thus:

Mæce | nas ata | vis | edite | regibus |
O, et | præsidi' | et | dulce de | cus meum |
Sunt quos | curricu | lo | pulver' O | lympicum |
Colle | gisse ju | vat | metaque | fervidis |
Evi | tata ro | tis | palmaque | nobilis |
Terra | rum domi | nos | evehit | ad Deos. |

Now I do not deny that we get a *certain sort* of music from the lines if we read them according to this scansion, but I wish to call attention to the fact that this scansion and the certain sort of music which grows out of it, are entirely at war not only with the reading flow which any ordinary person would naturally give the lines, but with the reading flow universally given them, and never denied them, by even the most obstinate and stolid of scholars.

And now these questions are forced upon us — "Why exists this discrepancy between the modern verse with its scansion, and the ancient verse with its scansion?" — "Why, in the former case, are there agreement and representation, while in the latter there is neither the one or the other?" or, to come to the point, — "How are we to reconcile the ancient verse with the scholastic scansion of it?" This absolutely necessary conciliation — shall we bring it about by supposing the scholastic scansion wrong because the ancient verse is right, or by maintaining that the ancient verse is wrong because the scholastic scansion is not to be gainsaid?

Were we to adopt the latter mode of arranging the difficulty, we might, in some measure, at least simplify the expression of the arrangement by putting it thus — Because the pedants have no eyes, therefore the old poets had no ears.

"But," say the gentlemen without the eyes, "the scholastic scansion, although certainly not handed down to us in form from the old poets themselves (the gentlemen without the ears,) is nevertheless deduced from certain facts which are supplied us by careful observation of the old poems."

And let us illustrate this strong position by an example from an American poet — who must be a poet of some eminence, or he will not answer the purpose. Let us take Mr. Alfred B. Street. I remember these two lines of his:

His sinuous path, by blazes, wound
Among trunks grouped in myriads round.

With the *sense* of these lines I have nothing to do. When a poet is in a "fine phrenzy," he may as well imagine a large forest as a small one — and "by blazes!" is *not* intended for an oath. My concern is with the rhythm, which is iambic.

Now let us suppose that, a thousand years hence, when the "American language" is dead, a learned prosodist should be deducing from "careful observation" of our best poets, a system of scansion for our poetry. And let us suppose that this prosodist had so little dependence in the generality and immutability of the laws of Nature, as to assume in the outset, that, because we lived a thousand years before his time and made use of steam-engines instead of mesmeric balloons, we must therefore have had a *very* singular fashion of mouthing our vowels, and altogether of hudsonizing our verse. And let us suppose that with these and other fundamental propositions carefully put away in his brain, he should arrive at the line,—

Among | trunks grouped | in my | riads round.

Finding it an obviously iambic rhythm, he would divide it as above, and observing that "trunks" made the first member of an iambus, he would call it short, as Mr. Street intended it to be. Now farther: — if instead of admitting the possibility that Mr. Street, (who by that time would be called Street simply, just as we say Homer) — that Mr. Street might have been in the habit of writing carelessly, as the poets of the prosodist's own era did, and as all poets will do (on account of being geniuses) — instead of admitting this, suppose the learned scholar should make a "rule" and put it in a book, to the effect that, in the American verse, the vowel *u*, *when found imbedded among nine consonants* was *short*: what, under such circumstances, would the sensible people of the scholar's day have a right not only to think, but to say of that scholar? — why, that he was "a fool, — by blazes!"

I have put an extreme case, but it strikes at the root of the error. The "rules" are grounded in "authority" — and this "authority" — can any one tell us what it means? or can any one suggest anything that it may *not* mean? Is it not clear that the "scholar" above referred to, might as readily have deduced from authority a totally false system as a partially true one? To deduce from authority a consistent prosody of the ancient metres would indeed have been within the limits of the barest possibility; and the task has *not* been accomplished, for the reason that it demands a species of ratiocination altogether out of keeping with the brain of a bookworm. A rigid scrutiny will show that the very few "rules" which have not as many exceptions as examples, are those which have, by accident, their true bases not in authority, but in the omni-prevalent laws of syllabification; such, for example, as the rule which declares a vowel before two consonants to be long.

In a word, the gross confusion and antagonism of the scholastic prosody, as well as its marked inapplicability to the reading flow of the rhythms it pretends to illustrate, are attributable, first, to the utter absence of natural principle as a guide in the investigations which have been undertaken by inadequate men; and secondly, to the neglect of the obvious consideration that the ancient poems, which have been the *criteria* throughout, were the work of men who must have written as loosely, and with as little definitive system, as ourselves.

Were Horace alive to-day, he would divide for us his first Ode thus, and "make great eyes" when assured by the prosodists that he had no business to make any such division!

```
Mæcenas | atavis | edite | regibus |
    2 2       2 2     2 2      2   2
O et præ | sidium et | dulce de | cus meum |
  2    2          3  3  3       2   2        2 2
Sunt quos cur | riculo | pulverem O | lympicum |
         2     2        2 2       3   3   3        2    2
```

Collegisse | juvat | metaque | fervidis |
3 3 3 2 2 2 2
Evitata | rotis | palmaque | nobilis |
3 3 3 2 2 2 2
Terrarum | dominos | evehit | ad Deos. |
2 2 2 2 2 2 2 2

Read by this scansion, the flow is preserved; and the more we dwell on the divisions, the more the intended rhythm becomes apparent. Moreover, the feet have all the same time; while, in the scholastic scansion, trochees—admitted trochees—are absurdly employed as equivalents to spondees and dactyls. The books declare, for instance, that *Colle*, which begins the fourth line, is a trochee, and seem to be gloriously unconscious that to put a trochee in opposition with a longer foot, is to violate the inviolable principle of all music, *time.*

It will be said, however, by "some people," that I have no business to make a dactyl out of such obviously long syllables as *sunt*, *quos*, *cur*. Certainly I have no business to do so. I *never* do so. And Horace should not have done so. But he did. Mr. Bryant and Mr. Longfellow do the same thing every day. And merely because these gentlemen, now and then, forget themselves in this way, it would be hard if some future prosodist should insist upon twisting the "Thanatopsis," or the "Spanish Student," into a jumble of trochees, spondees, and dactyls.

It may be said, also, by some other people, that in the word *decus*, I have succeeded no better than the books, in making the scansional agree with the reading flow; and that *decus* was not pronounced de*cus*. I reply, that there can be no doubt of the word having been pronounced, in this case, de*cus*. It must be observed, that the Latin inflection, or variation of a word in its terminating syllables, caused the Romans — *must* have caused them, to pay greater attention to the termination of a word than to its commencement, or than we do to the terminations of our words. The end of the Latin word established that relation of the word with other words which we establish by prepositions or auxiliary verbs. Therefore, it would seem infinitely less odd to them than it does to us, to dwell at any time, for any slight purpose, abnormally, on a terminating syllable. In verse, this license — scarcely a license — would be frequently admitted. These ideas unlock the secret of such lines as the

> Litoreis ingens inventa sub ilici*bus sus*,

and the

> Parturiunt montes et nascitur ridicu*lus mus*,

which I quoted, some time ago, while speaking of rhyme.

As regards the prosodial elisions, such as that of *rem* before *O*, in *pulverem Olympicum*, it is really difficult to understand how so dismally silly a notion could have entered the brain even of a pedant. Were it demanded of me why the books cut off one *vowel* before another, I might say — it is, perhaps, because the books think that, since a bad reader is so apt to slide the one vowel into the other at any rate, it is just as well to print them *ready-slided*. But in the case of the terminating *m*, which is the most readily pronounced of all consonants, (as the infantile *mama* will testify,) and the most impossible to cheat the ear of by any system of sliding — in the case of the *m*, I should be driven to reply that, to the best of my belief, the prosodists did the thing, because they had a fancy for doing it, and wished to see how funny it would look after it was done. The thinking reader will perceive that, from the great facility with which *em* may be enunciated, it is admirably suited to form one of the rapid short syllables in the bastard dactyl (pulverem O;) but because the books had no

3 3 3

conception of a bastard dactyl, they knocked it in the head at once — by cutting off its tail!

Let me now give a specimen of the true scansion of another Horatian measure; embodying an instance of proper elision.

> Integer | vitæ | scelerisque | purus |
> 2 2 3 3 3
> Non eget | Mauri | jaculis ne | que arcu |
> 2 2 3 3 3
> Nec vene | natis | gravida sa | gittis,
> 2 2 3 3 3
> Fusce, pha | retrâ.
> 2 2

Here the regular recurrence of the bastard dactyl, gives great animation to the rhythm. The *e* before the *a* in *que arcu*, is, almost of sheer necessity, cut off — that is to say, run into the *a* so as to preserve the spondee. But even this license it would have been better not to take.

Had I space, nothing would afford me greater pleasure than to proceed with the scansion of *all* the ancient rhythms, and to show how easily, by the help of common sense, the intended music of each and all can be rendered instantaneously apparent. But I have already overstepped my limits, and must bring this paper to an end.

It will never do, however, to omit all mention of the heroic hexameter.

I began the "processes" by a suggestion of the spondee as the first step towards verse. But the innate monotony of the spondee has caused its disappearance, as the basis of rhythm, from all modern poetry. We *may* say, indeed, that the French heroic — the most wretchedly monotonous verse in existence — is, to all intents and purposes, spondaic. But it is not designedly spondaic — and if the French were ever to examine it at all, they would no doubt pronounce it iambic. It must be observed, that the French language is strangely peculiar in this point — *that it is without accentuation and consequently without verse.* The genius of the people, rather than the structure of the tongue, declares that their words are, for the most part, enunciated with an uniform dwelling on each syllable. For example — *we* say, "syl*la*bifi*ca*tion." A Frenchman would say, syl-la-bi-fi-ca-ti-on; dwelling on no one of the syllables with any noticeable particularity. Here again I put an extreme case, in order to be well understood; but the general fact is as I give it — that, comparatively, the French have *no* accentuation. And there can be nothing worth the name of verse, without. Therefore, the French have no verse worth the name — which is the fact, put in sufficiently plain terms. Their iambic rhythm so superabounds in absolute spondees as to warrant me in calling its basis spondaic; but French is the *only* modern tongue which has any rhythm with such basis; and even in the French, it is, as I have said, unintentional.

Admitting, however, the validity of my suggestion,

that the spondee was the first approach to verse, we should expect to find, first, natural spondees (words each forming just a spondee,) most abundant in the most ancient languages; and, secondly, we should expect to find spondees forming the basis of the most ancient rhythms. These expectations are in both cases confirmed.

Of the Greek hexameter, the intentional basis is spondaic. The dactyls are the *variation* of the theme. It will be observed that there is no absolute certainty about *their* points of interposition. The penultimate foot, it is true, is usually a dactyl; but not uniformly so; while the ultimate, on which the ear *lingers* is always a spondee. Even that the penultimate is usually a dactyl may be clearly referred to the necessity of winding up with the *distinctive* spondee. In corroboration of this idea, again, we should look to find the penultimate spondee most usual in the most ancient verse; and, accordingly, we find it more frequent in the Greek than in the Latin hexameter.

But besides all this, spondees are not only more prevalent in the heroic hexameter than dactyls, but occur to such an extent as is even unpleasant to modern ears, on account of monotony. What the modern chiefly appreciates and admires in the Greek hexameter, is the *melody of the abundant vowel sounds.* The Latin hexameters *really* please very few moderns — although so many pretend to fall into ecstasies about them. In the hexameters quoted, several pages ago, from Silius Italicus, the preponderance of the spondee is strikingly manifest. Besides the natural spondees of the Greek and Latin, numerous artificial ones arise in the verse of these tongues on account of the tendency which *case* has to throw full accentuation on terminal syllables; and the preponderance of the spondee is farther ensured by the comparative infrequency of the small prepositions which *we* have to serve us *instead* of case, and also the absence of the diminutive auxiliary verbs with which *we* have to eke out the expression of our primary ones. These are the monosyllables whose abundance serve to stamp the poetic genius of a language as tripping or dactylic.

Now paying no attention to these facts, Sir Philip Sidney, Professor Longfellow, and innumerable other persons more or less modern, have busied themselves in constructing what they supposed to be "English hexameters on the model of the Greek." The only difficulty was that (even leaving out of question the melodious masses of vowel,) these gentlemen never could get their English hexameters to *sound* Greek. Did they *look* Greek?—that should have been the query; and the reply might have led to a solution of the riddle. In placing a copy of ancient hexameters side by side with a copy (in similar type) of such hexameters as Professor Longfellow, or Professor Felton, or the Frogpondian Professors collectively, are in the shameful practice of composing "on the model of the Greek," it will be seen that the latter (hexameters, not professors) are about one third longer *to the eye*, on an average, than the former. The more abundant dactyls make the difference. And it is the greater number of spondees in the Greek than in the English—in the ancient than in the modern tongue—which has caused it to fall out that while these eminent scholars were groping about in the dark for a Greek hexameter, which is a spondaic rhythm varied now and then by dactyls, they merely stumbled, to the lasting scandal of scholarship, over something which, on account of its long-leggedness, we may as well term a Feltonian hexameter, and which is a dactylic rhythm, interrupted, rarely, by artificial spondees which are no spondees at all, and which are curiously thrown in by the heels at all kinds of improper and impertinent points.

Here is a specimen of the Longfellownian hexameter,

Also the | church with | in was a | dorned for | this was the | season |
In which the | young their | parents' | hope and the | loved ones of | Heaven |
Should at the | foot of the | altar re | new the | vows of their | baptism |
Therefore each | nook and | corner was | swept and | cleaned and the | dust was |
Blown from the | walls and | ceiling and | from the | oil-painted | benches. |

Mr. Longfellow is a man of imagination — but *can* he imagine that any individual, with a proper understanding of the danger of lockjaw, would make the attempt of twisting his mouth into the shape necessary for the emission of such spondees as "par*ents*," or such dactyls as "cleaned and the" and "loved ones of?" "Baptism" is by no means a bad spondee — perhaps because it happens to be a dactyl; — of all the rest, however, I am dreadfully ashamed.

But these feet — dactyls and spondees, all together, — should thus be put at once into their proper position:

"Also, the church within was adorned; for this was the season in which the young, their parents' hope, and the loved ones of Heaven, should, at the feet of the altar, renew the vows of their baptism. Therefore, each nook and corner was swept and cleaned; and the dust was blown from the walls and ceiling, and from the oil-painted benches."

There!—that is respectable prose; and it will incur no danger of ever getting its character ruined by anybody's mistaking it for verse.

But even when we let these modern hexameters go, as Greek, and merely hold them fast in their proper character of Longfellownian, or Feltonian, or Frogpondian, we must still condemn them as having been committed in a radical misconception of the philosophy of verse. The spondee, as I observed, is the *theme* of the Greek line. Most of the ancient hexameters *begin* with spondees, for the reason that the spondee *is* the theme; and the ear is filled with it as with a burden. Now the Feltonian dactylics have, in the same way, dactyls for the theme, and most of them begin with dactyls—which is all very proper if not very Greek—but, unhappily, the one point at which they *are* very Greek is that point, precisely, at which they should be nothing but Feltonian. They always *close* with what is meant for a spondee. To be consistently silly, they should die off in a dactyl.

That a truly Greek hexameter *cannot*, however, be readily composed in English, is a proposition which I am by no means inclined to admit. I think I could manage the point myself. For example:

Do tell! | when may we | hope to make | men of sense | out of
the | Pundits |
Born and brought | up with their | snouts deep | down in the | mud
of the | Frog-pond ?
Why ask ? | who ever | yet saw | money made | out of a | fat old |
Jew, or | downright | upright | nutmegs | out of a | pine-
knot ? |

The proper spondee predominance is here preserved. Some of the dactyls are not so good as I could wish — but, upon the whole, the rhythm is very decent — to say nothing of its excellent sense.

The Poetic Principle

IN speaking of the Poetic Principle, I have no design to be either thorough or profound. While discussing, very much at random, the essentiality of what we call Poetry, my principal purpose will be to cite for consideration, some few of those minor English or American poems which best suit my own taste, or which, upon my own fancy, have left the most definite impression. By "minor poems" I mean, of course, poems of little length. And here, in the beginning, permit me to say a few words in regard to a somewhat peculiar principle, which, whether rightfully or wrongfully, has always had its influence in my own critical estimate of the poem. I hold that a long poem does not exist. I maintain that the phrase, "a long poem," is simply a flat contradiction in terms.

I need scarcely observe that a poem deserves its title only inasmuch as it excites, by elevating the soul. The value of the poem is in the ratio of this elevating excitement. But all excitements are, through a psychal necessity, transient. That degree of excitement which would entitle a poem to be so called at all, cannot be sustained throughout a composition of any great length. After the lapse of half an hour, at the very utmost, it flags — fails — a revulsion ensues — and then the poem is, in effect, and in fact, no longer such.

There are, no doubt, many who have found difficulty in reconciling the critical dictum that the "Paradise

Lost" is to be devoutly admired throughout, with the absolute impossibility of maintaining for it, during perusal, the amount of enthusiasm which that critical dictum would demand. This great work, in fact, is to be regarded as poetical, only when, losing sight of that vital requisite in all works of Art, Unity, we view it merely as a series of minor poems. If, to preserve its Unity — its totality of effect or impression — we read it (as would be necessary) at a single sitting, the result is but a constant alternation of excitement and depression. After a passage of what we feel to be true poetry, there follows, inevitably, a passage of platitude which no critical prejudgment can force us to admire; but if, upon completing the work, we read it again, omitting the first book — that is to say, commencing with the second — we shall be surprised at now finding that admirable which we before condemned — that damnable which we had previously so much admired. It follows from all this that the ultimate, aggregate, or absolute effect of even the best epic under the sun, is a nullity: — and this is precisely the fact.

In regard to the Iliad, we have, if not positive proof, at least very good reason for believing it intended as a series of lyrics; but, granting the epic intention, I can say only that the work is based in an imperfect sense of art. The modern epic is, of the supposititious ancient model, but an inconsiderate and blindfold imitation. But the day of these artistic anomalies is over. If, at any time, any very long poem *were* popular in reality, which I doubt, it is at least clear that no very long poem will ever be popular again.

That the extent of a poetical work is, *ceteris paribus*, the measure of its merit, seems undoubtedly, when we thus state it, a proposition sufficiently absurd — yet we are indebted for it to the Quarterly Reviews. Surely there can be nothing in mere *size*, abstractly considered — there can be nothing in mere *bulk*, so far as a volume is concerned, which has so continuously elicited admiration from these saturnine pamphlets! A mountain, to be sure, by the mere sentiment of physical magnitude which it conveys, *does* impress us with a sense of the sublime — but no man is impressed after *this* fashion by the material grandeur of even "The Columbiad." Even the Quarterlies have not instructed us to be so impressed by it. *As yet*, they have not *insisted* on our estimating Lamartine by the cubic foot, or Pollok by the pound — but what else are we to *infer* from their continual prating about "sustained effort?" If, by "sustained effort," any little gentleman has accomplished an epic, let us frankly commend him for the effort — if this indeed be a thing commendable — but let us forbear praising the epic on the effort's account. It is to be hoped that common sense, in the time to come, will prefer deciding upon a work of art, rather by the impression it makes, by the effect it produces, than by the time it took to impress the effect, or by the amount of "sustained effort" which had been found necessary in effecting the impression. The fact is, that perseverance is one thing, and genius quite another; nor can all the Quarterlies in Christendom confound them. By and by, this proposition, with many which I have been just urging, will be received as self-evident. In the meantime, by being generally condemned as falsities, they will not be essentially damaged as truths.

On the other hand, it is clear that a poem may be improperly brief. Undue brevity degenerates into mere epigrammatism. A *very* short poem, while now and then producing a brilliant or vivid, never produces a profound or enduring effect. There must be the steady pressing down of the stamp upon the wax. De Béranger has wrought innumerable things, pungent and spirit-stirring; but, in general, they have been too imponderous to stamp themselves deeply into the public attention; and thus, as so many feathers of fancy, have been blown aloft only to be whistled down the wind.

A remarkable instance of the effect of undue brevity in depressing a poem — in keeping it out of the popular view — is afforded by the following exquisite little Serenade.

I arise from dreams of thee
  In the first sweet sleep of night,
When the winds are breathing low,
  And the stars are shining bright;
I arise from dreams of thee,
  And a spirit in my feet
Hath led me — who knows how? —
  To thy chamber-window, sweet!

The wandering airs, they faint
  On the dark, the silent stream —
The Champak odors fail
  Like sweet thoughts in a dream;
The nightingale's complaint,
  It dies upon her heart,
As I must die on thine,
  O, beloved as thou art!

O, lift me from the grass!
  I die, I faint, I fail!
Let thy love in kisses rain
  On my lips and eyelids pale.
My cheek is cold and white, alas!
  My heart beats loud and fast:
Oh! press it close to thine again,
  Where it will break at last!

Very few, perhaps, are familiar with these lines — yet no less a poet than Shelley is their author. Their warm, yet delicate and ethereal imagination will be appreciated by all — but by none so thoroughly as by him who has himself arisen from sweet dreams of one beloved, to bathe in the aromatic air of a southern midsummer night.

One of the finest poems by Willis — the very best, in my opinion, which he has ever written — has, no doubt, through this same defect of undue brevity, been kept back from its proper position, not less in the critical than in the popular view.

The shadows lay along Broadway,
  'Twas near the twilight-tide —
And slowly there a lady fair
  Was walking in her pride.
Alone walked she; but, viewlessly,
  Walked spirits at her side.

Peace charmed the street beneath her feet,
  And Honor charmed the air;
And all astir looked kind on her,
  And called her good as fair —
For all God ever gave to her
  She kept with chary care.

She kept with care her beauties rare
  From lovers warm and true —
For her heart was cold to all but gold,
  And the rich came not to woo —
But honored well are charms to sell
  If priests the selling do.

Now walking there was one more fair—
  A slight girl, lily-pale;
And she had unseen company
  To make the spirit quail—
'Twixt Want and Scorn she walked forlorn,
  And nothing could avail.

No mercy now can clear her brow
  For this world's peace to pray;
For, as love's wild prayer dissolved in air,
  Her woman's heart gave way! —
But the sin forgiven by Christ in Heaven
  By man is cursed alway!

In this composition we find it difficult to recognize the Willis who has written so many mere "verses of society." The lines are not only richly ideal, but full of energy; while they breathe an earnestness — an evident sincerity of sentiment — for which we look in vain throughout all the other works of this author.

While the epic mania — while the idea that, to merit in poetry, prolixity is indispensable — has, for some years past, been gradually dying out of the public mind, by mere dint of its own absurdity — we find it succeeded by a heresy too palpably false to be long tolerated, but one which, in the brief period it has already endured, may be said to have accomplished more in the corruption of our Poetical Literature than all its other enemies combined. I allude to the heresy of *The Didactic*. It has been assumed, tacitly and avowedly, directly and indirectly, that the ultimate object of all Poetry is Truth. Every poem, it is said, should inculcate a moral; and by this moral is the poetical merit of the work to be adjudged. We Americans, especially, have patronized this happy idea; and we Bostonians, very especially, have developed it in full. We have taken it into our heads that to write a poem simply for the poem's sake, and to acknowledge such to have been our design, would be to confess ourselves radically wanting in the true Poetic dignity and force: — but the simple fact is, that, would we but permit ourselves to look into our own souls, we should immediately there discover that under the sun there neither exists nor *can* exist any work more thoroughly dignified — more supremely noble than this very poem — this poem *per se* — this poem which is a poem and nothing more — this poem written solely for the poem's sake.

With as deep a reverence for the True as ever inspired the bosom of man, I would, nevertheless, limit, in some measure, its modes of inculcation. I would limit to enforce them. I would not enfeeble them by dissipation. The demands of Truth are severe. She has no sympathy with the myrtles. All *that* which is so indispensable in Song, is precisely all *that* with which *she* has nothing whatever to do. It is but making her a flaunting paradox, to wreathe her in gems and flowers. In enforcing a truth, we need severity rather than efflorescence of language. We must be simple, precise, terse. We must be cool, calm, unimpassioned. In a word, we must be in that mood which, as nearly as possible, is the exact converse of the poetical. *He* must be blind, indeed, who does not perceive the radical and chasmal differences between the truthful and the poetical modes of inculcation. He must be theory-mad beyond redemption who, in spite of these differences, shall still persist in attempting to reconcile the obstinate oils and waters of Poetry and Truth.

Dividing the world of mind into its three most immediately obvious distinctions, we have the Pure Intellect, Taste, and the Moral Sense. I place Taste in the middle, because it is just this position, which, in the mind, it occupies. It holds intimate relations with either extreme; but from the Moral Sense is separated by so faint a difference that Aristotle has not hesitated to place some of its operations among the virtues themselves. Nevertheless, we find the *offices* of the trio marked with a sufficient distinction. Just as the Intellect concerns itself with Truth, so Taste informs us of the Beautiful while the Moral Sense is regardful of Duty. Of this latter, while Conscience teaches the obligation, and Reason the expediency, Taste contents herself with displaying the charms: — waging war upon Vice solely on the ground of her deformity — her disproportion — her animosity to the fitting, to the appropriate, to the harmonious — in a word, to Beauty.

An immortal instinct, deep within the spirit of man, is thus, plainly, a sense of the Beautiful. This it is which administers to his delight in the manifold forms, and sounds, and odors, and sentiments amid which he exists. And just as the lily is repeated in the lake, or the eyes of

Amaryllis in the mirror, so is the mere oral or written repetition of these forms, and sounds, and colors, and odors, and sentiments, a duplicate source of delight. But this mere repetition is not poetry. He who shall simply sing, with however glowing enthusiasm, or with however vivid a truth of description, of the sights, and sounds, and odors, and colors, and sentiments, which greet *him* in common with all mankind — he, I say, has yet failed to prove his divine title. There is still a something in the distance which he has been unable to attain. We have still a thirst unquenchable, to allay which he has not shown us the crystal springs. This thirst belongs to the immortality of Man. It is at once a consequence and an indication of his perennial existence. It is the desire of the moth for the star. It is no mere appreciation of the Beauty before us — but a wild effort to reach the Beauty above. Inspired by an ecstatic prescience of the glories beyond the grave, we struggle, by multiform combinations among the things and thoughts of Time, to attain a portion of that Loveliness whose very elements, perhaps, appertain to eternity alone. And thus when by Poetry — or when by Music, the most entrancing of the Poetic moods — we find ourselves melted into tears — we weep then — not as the Abbate Gravina supposes — through excess of pleasure, but through a certain, petulant, impatient sorrow at our inability to grasp *now*, wholly, here on earth, at once and for ever, those divine and rapturous joys, of which *through* the poem, or *through* the music, we attain to but brief and indeterminate glimpses.

The struggle to apprehend the supernal Loveliness —

this struggle, on the part of souls fittingly constituted — has given to the world all *that* which it (the world) has ever been enabled at once to understand and *to feel* as poetic.

The Poetic Sentiment, of course, may develop itself in various modes — in Painting, in Sculpture, in Architecture, in the Dance — very especially in Music — and very peculiarly, and with a wide field, in the composition of the Landscape Garden. Our present theme, however, has regard only to its manifestation in words. And here let me speak briefly on the topic of rhythm. Contenting myself with the certainty that Music, in its various modes of metre, rhythm, and rhyme, is of so vast a moment in Poetry as never to be wisely rejected — is so vitally important an adjunct, that he is simply silly who declines its assistance, I will not now pause to maintain its absolute essentiality. It is in Music, perhaps, that the soul most nearly attains the great end for which, when inspired by the Poetic Sentiment, it struggles — the creation of supernal Beauty. It *may* be, indeed, that here this sublime end is, now and then, attained *in fact.* We are often made to feel, with a shivering delight, that from an earthly harp are stricken notes which *cannot* have been unfamiliar to the angels. And thus there can be little doubt that in the union of Poetry with Music in its popular sense, we shall find the widest field for the Poetic development. The old Bards and Minnesingers had advantages which we do not possess — and Thomas Moore, singing his own songs, was, in the most legitimate manner, perfecting them as poems.

To recapitulate, then: — I would define, in brief, the Poetry of words as *The Rhythmical Creation of Beauty.*

Its sole arbiter is Taste. With the Intellect or with the Conscience, it has only collateral relations. Unless incidentally, it has no concern whatever either with Duty or with Truth.

A few words, however, in explanation. *That* pleasure which is at once the most pure, the most elevating, and the most intense, is derived, I maintain, from the contemplation of the Beautiful. In the contemplation of Beauty we alone find it possible to attain that pleasurable elevation, or excitement, *of the soul*, which we recognize as the Poetic Sentiment, and which is so easily distinguished from Truth, which is the satisfaction of the Reason, or from Passion, which is the excitement of the heart. I make Beauty, therefore — using the word as inclusive of the sublime — I make Beauty the province of the poem, simply because it is an obvious rule of Art that effects should be made to spring as directly as possible from their causes: — no one as yet having been weak enough to deny that the peculiar elevation in question is at least *most readily* attainable in the poem. It by no means follows, however, that the incitements of Passion, or the precepts of Duty, or even the lessons of Truth, may not be introduced into a poem, and with advantage; for they may subserve, incidentally, in various ways, the general purposes of the work: — but the true artist will always contrive to tone them down in proper subjection to that *Beauty* which is the atmosphere and the real essence of the poem.

I cannot better introduce the few poems which I shall present for your consideration, than by the citation of the Proem to Mr. Longfellow's "Waif":

The day is done, and the darkness
  Falls from the wings of Night,
As a feather is wafted downward
  From an Eagle in his flight.

I see the lights of the village
  Gleam through the rain and the mist,
And a feeling of sadness comes o'er me,
  That my soul cannot resist;

A feeling of sadness and longing,
  That is not akin to pain,
And resembles sorrow only
  As the mist resembles the rain.

Come, read to me some poem,
  Some simple and heartfelt lay,
That shall soothe this restless feeling,
  And banish the thoughts of day.

Not from the grand old masters,
  Not from the bards sublime,
Whose distant footsteps echo
  Through the corridors of Time.

For, like strains of martial music,
  Their mighty thoughts suggest
Life's endless toil and endeavor;
  And to-night I long for rest.

Read from some humbler poet,
  Whose songs gushed from his heart,
As showers from the clouds of summer,
  Or tears from the eyelids start;

Who through long days of labor,
  And nights devoid of ease,
Still heard in his soul the music
  Of wonderful melodies.

Such songs have power to quiet
  The restless pulse of care,
And come like the benediction
  That follows after prayer.

Then read from the treasured volume
  The poem of thy choice,
And lend to the rhyme of the poet
  The beauty of thy voice.

And the night shall be filled with music,
  And the cares that infest the day,
Shall fold their tents, like the Arabs,
  And as silently steal away.

With no great range of imagination, these lines have been justly admired for their delicacy of expression. Some of the images are very effective. Nothing can be better than —

——— The bards sublime,
Whose distant footsteps echo
  Down the corridors of Time.

The idea of the last quatrain is also very effective. The poem, on the whole, however, is chiefly to be admired for the graceful *insouciance* of its metre, so well in accordance with the character of the sentiments, and especially for the *ease* of the general manner. This "case," or naturalness, in a literary style, it has long been the fashion to regard as ease in appearance alone — as a point of really difficult attainment. But not so: — a natural manner is difficult only to him who should never meddle with it — to the unnatural. It is but the result of writing with the understanding, or with the instinct, that *the tone*, in composition, should always be that which the mass of mankind would adopt — and must perpetually vary, of course, with the occasion. The author who, after the fashion of "The North American Review," should be, upon *all* occasions, merely "quiet," must necessarily upon *many* occasions, be simply silly, or stupid; and has no more right to be considered "easy," or "natural," than a Cockney exquisite, or than the sleeping Beauty in the wax-works.

Among the minor poems of Bryant, none has so much impressed me as the one which he entitles "June." I quote only a portion of it:

There through the long, long summer hours,
　　The golden light should lie,
And thick young herbs and groups of flowers
　　Stand in their beauty by.
The oriole should build and tell
His love-tale, close beside my cell;
　　The idle butterfly
Should rest him there, and there be heard
The housewife-bee and humming-bird.

And what, if cheerful shouts at noon,
　　Come, from the village sent,
Or songs of maids, beneath the moon,
　　With fairy laughter blent?
And what, if in the evening light,
Betrothed lovers walk in sight
　　Of my low monument?
I would the lovely scene around
Might know no sadder sight nor sound.

I know, I know I should not see
　　The season's glorious show,
Nor would its brightness shine for me,
　　Nor its wild music flow;

But if, around my place of sleep,
The friends I love should come to weep,
    They might not haste to go.
Soft airs, and song, and light, and bloom
Should keep them lingering by my tomb.

These to their softened hearts should bear
    The thought of what has been,
And speak of one who cannot share
    The gladness of the scene;
Whose part in all the pomp that fills
The circuit of the summer hills,
    Is — that his grave is green;
And deeply would their hearts rejoice
To hear again his living voice.

The rhythmical flow, here, is even voluptuous — nothing could be more melodious. The poem has always affected me in a remarkable manner. The intense melancholy which seems to well up, perforce, to the surface of all the poet's cheerful sayings about his grave, we find thrilling us to the soul — while there is the truest poetic elevation in the thrill. The impression left is one of a pleasurable sadness.

And if, in the remaining compositions which I shall introduce to you, there be more or less of a similar tone always apparent, let me remind you that (how or why we know not) this certain taint of sadness is inseparably connected with all the higher manifestations of true Beauty. It is, nevertheless,

A feeling of sadness and longing
  That is not akin to pain,
And resembles sorrow only
  As the mist resembles the rain.

The taint of which I speak is clearly perceptible even in a poem so full of brilliancy and spirit as the "Health" of Edward Coate Pinkney:

I fill this cup to one made up
  Of loveliness alone,
A woman, of her gentle sex
  The seeming paragon;
To whom the better elements
  And kindly stars have given
A form so fair, that, like the air,
  'Tis less of earth than heaven.

Her every tone is music's own,
  Like those of morning birds,
And something more than melody
  Dwells ever in her words;
The coinage of her heart are they,
  And from her lips each flows
As one may see the burdened bee
  Forth issue from the rose.

Affections are as thoughts to her,
  The measures of her hours;
Her feelings have the fragrancy,
  The freshness of young flowers;
And lovely passions, changing oft,
  So fill her, she appears
The image of themselves by turns, —
  The idol of past years!

Of her bright face one glance will trace
  A picture on the brain,
And of her voice in echoing hearts
  A sound must long remain;

But memory, such as mine of her,
So very much endears,
When death is nigh, my latest sigh
Will not be life's but hers.

I fill this cup to one made up
Of loveliness alone,
A woman, of her gentle sex
The seeming paragon —
Her health! and would on earth there stood
Some more of such a frame,
That life might be all poetry,
And weariness a name.

It was the misfortune of Mr. Pinkney to have been born too far south. Had he been a New Englander, it is probable that he would have been ranked as the first of American lyrists, by that magnanimous cabal which has so long controlled the destinies of American Letters, in conducting the thing called "The North American Review." The poem just cited is especially beautiful; but the poetic elevation which it induces, we must refer chiefly to our sympathy in the poet's enthusiasm. We pardon his hyperboles for the evident earnestness with which they are uttered.

It was by no means my design, however, to expatiate upon the *merits* of what I should read you. These will necessarily speak for themselves. Boccalini, in his "Advertisements from Parnassus," tells us that Zoilus once presented Apollo a very caustic criticism upon a very admirable book: — whereupon the god asked him for the beauties of the work. He replied that he only busied himself about the errors. On hearing this,

Apollo, handing him a sack of unwinnowed wheat, bade him pick out *all the chaff* for his reward.

Now this fable answers very well as a hit at the critics — but I am by no means sure that the god was in the right. I am by no means certain that the true limits of the critical duty are not grossly misunderstood. Excellence, in a poem especially, may be considered in the light of an axiom, which need only be properly *put*, to become self-evident. It is *not* excellence if it require to be demonstrated as such: — and thus, to point out too particularly the merits of a work of Art, is to admit that they are *not* merits altogether.

Among the "Melodies" of Thomas Moore, is one whose distinguished character as a poem proper, seems to have been singularly left out of view. I allude to his lines beginning — "Come rest in this bosom." The intense energy of their expression is not surpassed by anything in Byron. There are two of the lines in which a sentiment is conveyed that embodies the *all in all* of the divine passion of love — a sentiment which, perhaps, has found its echo in more, and in more passionate, human hearts than any other single sentiment ever embodied in words:

Come, rest in this bosom, my own stricken deer,
Though the herd have fled from thee, thy home is still here;
Here still is the smile that no cloud can o'ercast,
And a heart and a hand all thy own to the last.

Oh! what was love made for, if 'tis not the same
Through joy and through torment, through glory and shame?
I know not, I ask not, if guilt 's in that heart,
I but know that I love thee, whatever thou art.

Thou hast called me thy angel in moments of bliss,
And thy angel I'll be, 'mid the horrors of this, —
Through the furnace, unshrinking, thy steps to pursue,
And shield thee, and save thee, — or perish there too!

It has been the fashion, of late days, to deny Moore imagination, while granting him fancy — a distinction originating with Coleridge — than whom no man more fully comprehended the great powers of Moore. The fact is, that the fancy of this poet so far predominates over all his other faculties, and over the fancy of all other men, as to have induced, very naturally, the idea that he is fanciful *only*. But never was there a greater mistake. Never was a grosser wrong done the fame of a true poet. In the compass of the English language I can call to mind no poem more profoundly — more weirdly *imaginative*, in the best sense, than the lines commencing — "I would I were by that dim lake," — which are the composition of Thomas Moore. I regret that I am unable to remember them.

One of the noblest — and, speaking of fancy, one of the most singularly fanciful of modern poets, was Thomas Hood. His "Fair Ines" had always, for me, an inexpressible charm.

O saw ye not fair Ines?
  She's gone into the West,
To dazzle when the sun is down,
  And rob the world of rest:
She took our daylight with her,
  The smiles that we love best,
With morning blushes on her cheek,
  And pearls upon her breast.

O turn again, fair Ines,
  Before the fall of night,
For fear the moon should shine alone,
  And stars unrivalled bright;
And blessed will the lover be
  That walks beneath their light,
And breathes the love against thy cheek
  I dare not even write!

Would I had been, fair Ines,
  That gallant cavalier,
Who rode so gaily by thy side,
  And whispered thee so near!
Were there no bonny dames at home,
  Or no true lovers here,
That he should cross the seas to win
  The dearest of the dear?

I saw thee, lovely Ines,
  Descend along the shore,
With bands of noble gentlemen,
  And banners waved before;
And gentle youth and maidens gay,
  And snowy plumes they wore;
It would have been a beauteous dream,
  If it had been no more!

Alas, alas, fair Ines,
  She went away with song,
With Music waiting on her steps,
  And shoutings of the throng;
But some were sad and felt no mirth,
  But only Music's wrong,
In sounds that sang farewell, farewell,
  To her you've loved so long.

Farewell, farewell, fair Ines;
  That vessel never bore
So fair a lady on its deck,
  Nor danced so light before, —
Alas, for pleasure on the sea,
  And sorrow on the shore!
The smile that blest one lover's heart
  Has broken many more!

"The Haunted House," by the same author, is one of the truest poems ever written — one of the *truest* — one of the most unexceptionable — one of the most thoroughly artistic, both in its theme and in its execution. It is, moreover, powerfully ideal — imaginative. I regret that its length renders it unsuitable for the purposes of this Lecture. In place of it, permit me to offer the universally appreciated "Bridge of Sighs."

One more Unfortunate,
Weary of breath,
Rashly importunate,
Gone to her death!

Take her up tenderly,
Lift her with care; —
Fashioned so slenderly,
Young, and so fair!

Look at her garments
Clinging like cerements;
Whilst the wave constantly
Drips from her clothing;
Take her up instantly,
Loving, not loathing. —

Touch her not scornfully;
Think of her mournfully,
Gently and humanly;
Not of the stains of her,
All that remains of her
Now, is pure womanly.

Make no deep scrutiny
Into her mutiny
Rash and undutiful;
Past all dishonor,
Death has left on her
Only the beautiful.

Still, for all slips of hers,
One of Eve's family —
Wipe those poor lips of hers
Oozing so clammily.
Loop up her tresses
Escaped from the comb,
Her fair auburn tresses;
Whilst wonderment guesses
Where was her home?

Who was her father?
Who was her mother?
Had she a sister?
Had she a brother?
Or was there a dearer one
Still, and a nearer one
Yet, than all other?

Alas! for the rarity
Of Christian charity
Under the sun!
Oh! it was pitiful!
Near a whole city full,
Home she had none.

Sisterly, brotherly,
Fatherly, motherly,
Feelings had changed:
Love, by harsh evidence,
Thrown from its eminence;
Even God's providence
Seeming estranged.

Where the lamps quiver
So far in the river,
With many a light
From window and casement,
From garret to basement,
She stood, with amazement,
Houseless by night.

The bleak wind of March
Made her tremble and shiver;
But not the dark arch,
Or the black flowing river:
Mad from life's history,
Glad to death's mystery,
Swift to be hurled —
Anywhere, anywhere
Out of the world!

In she plunged boldly,
No matter how coldly
The rough river ran, —
Over the brink of it,
Picture it, — think of it,
Dissolute Man!
Lave in it, drink of it
Then, if you can!

Take her up tenderly,
Lift her with care;
Fashioned so slenderly,
Young, and so fair!

Ere her limbs frigidly
Stiffen too rigidly,
Decently, — kindly, —
Smooth, and compose them;
And her eyes, close them,
Staring so blindly!

Dreadfully staring
Through muddy impurity,
As when with the daring
Last look of despairing
Fixed on futurity.

Perishing gloomily,
Spurred by contumely,
Cold inhumanity,
Burning insanity,
Into her rest, —
Cross her hands humbly,
As if praying dumbly,
Over her breast!
Owning her weakness,
Her evil behaviour,
And leaving, with meekness,
Her sins to her Saviour!

The vigor of this poem is no less remarkable than its pathos. The versification, although carrying the fanciful to the very verge of the fantastic, is nevertheless admirably adapted to the wild insanity which is the thesis of the poem.

Among the minor poems of Lord Byron, is one which

has never received from the critics the praise which it undoubtedly deserves:

Though the day of my destiny's over,
  And the star of my fate hath declined,
Thy soft heart refused to discover
  The faults which so many could find;
Though thy soul with my grief was acquainted,
  It shrunk not to share it with me,
And the love which my spirit hath painted
  It never hath found but in *thee.*

Then when nature around me is smiling,
  The last smile which answers to mine,
I do not believe it beguiling,
  Because it reminds me of thine;
And when winds are at war with the ocean,
  As the breasts I believed in with me,
If their billows excite an emotion,
  It is that they bear me from *thee.*

Though the rock of my last hope is shivered,
  And its fragments are sunk in the wave,
Though I feel that my soul is delivered
  To pain — it shall not be its slave.
There is many a pang to pursue me:
  They may crush, but they shall not contemn —
They may torture, but shall not subdue me —
  'Tis of *thee* that I think — not of them.

Though human, thou didst not deceive me,
  Though woman, thou didst not forsake,
Though loved, thou forborest to grieve me,
  Though slandered, thou never couldst shake, —
Though trusted, thou didst not disclaim me,
  Though parted, it was not to fly,
Though watchful, 'twas not to defame me,
  Nor mute, that the world might belie.

Yet I blame not the world, nor despise it,
  Nor the war of the many with one —
If my soul was not fitted to prize it,
  'Twas folly not sooner to shun:
And if dearly that error hath cost me,
  And more than I once could foresee,
I have found that whatever it lost me,
  It could not deprive me of *thee.*

From the wreck of the past, which hath perished,
  Thus much I at least may recall,
It hath taught me that what I most cherished
  Deserved to be dearest of all:
In the desert a fountain is springing,
  In the wide waste there still is a tree,
And a bird in the solitude singing,
  Which speaks to my spirit of *thee.*

Although the rhythm here is one of the most difficult, the versification could scarcely be improved. No nobler *theme* ever engaged the pen of poet. It is the soul-elevating idea, that no man can consider himself entitled to complain of Fate while, in his adversity, he still retains the unwavering love of woman.

From Alfred Tennyson — although in perfect sincerity I regard him as the noblest poet that ever lived — I have left myself time to cite only a very brief specimen. I call him, and *think* him the noblest of poets — *not* because the impressions he produces are, at *all* times, the most profound — *not* because the poetical excitement which he induces is, at *all* times, the most intense — but because it *is*, at all times, the most ethereal — in other words, the most elevating and the most pure. No poet is so little of the earth, earthy. What I am about to read is from his last long poem, "The Princess":

> Tears, idle tears, I know not what they mean,
> Tears from the depth of some divine despair
> Rise in the heart, and gather to the eyes,
> In looking on the happy Autumn-fields,
> And thinking of the days that are no more.
>
> Fresh as the first beam glittering on a sail,
> That brings our friends up from the underworld,
> Sad as the last which reddens over one
> That sinks with all we love below the verge
> So sad, so fresh, the days that are no more.
>
> Ah, sad and strange as in dark summer dawns
> The earliest pipe of half-awakened birds
> To dying ears, when unto dying eyes
> The casement slowly grows a glimmering square;
> So sad, so strange, the days that are no more.
>
> Dear as remembered kisses after death,
> And sweet as those by hopeless fancy feigned
> On lips that are for others; deep as love,
> Deep as first love, and wild with all regret;
> O Death in Life, the days that are no more.

Thus, although in a very cursory and imperfect manner, I have endeavored to convey to you my conception of the Poetic Principle. It has been my purpose to suggest that, while this Principle itself is, strictly and simply, the Human Aspiration for Supernal Beauty, the manifestation of the Principle is always found in *an elevating excitement of the Soul* — quite independent of that passion which is the intoxication of the Heart — or of that Truth which is the satisfaction of the Reason. For, in regard to Passion, alas! its tendency is to degrade, rather than to elevate the

Soul. Love, on the contrary — Love — the true, the divine Eros — the Uranian, as distinguished from the Dionæan Venus — is unquestionably the purest and truest of all poetical themes. And in regard to Truth — if, to be sure, through the attainment of a truth, we are led to perceive a harmony where none was apparent before, we experience, at once, the true poetical effect — but this effect is referable to the harmony alone, and not in the least degree to the truth which merely served to render the harmony manifest.

We shall reach, however, more immediately a distinct conception of what the true Poetry is, by mere reference to a few of the simple elements which induce in the Poet himself the true poetical effect. He recognizes the ambrosia which nourishes his soul, in the bright orbs that shine in Heaven — in the volutes of the flower — in the clustering of low shrubberies — in the waving of the grain-fields — in the slanting of tall, Eastern trees — in the blue distance of mountains — in the grouping of clouds — in the twinkling of half-hidden brooks — in the gleaming of silver rivers — in the repose of sequestered lakes — in the star-mirroring depths of lonely wells. He perceives it in the songs of birds — in the harp of Æolus — in the sighing of the night-wind — in the repining voice of the forest — in the surf that complains to the shore — in the fresh breath of the woods — in the scent of the violet — in the voluptuous perfume of the hyacinth — in the suggestive odor that comes to him, at eventide, from far-distant, undiscovered islands, over dim oceans, illimitable and unexplored. He owns it in all noble thoughts — in all unworldly motives — in all holy impulses — in all chivalrous, generous, and self-sacrificing deeds. He feels it in the beauty of woman — in the grace of her step — in the lustre of her eye — in the melody of her voice — in her soft laughter — in her sigh — in the harmony of the rustling of her robes. He deeply feels it in her winning endearments — in her burning enthusiasms — in her gentle charities — in her meek and devotional endurances — but above all — ah, far above all — he kneels to it — he worships it in the faith, in the purity, in the strength, in the altogether divine majesty — of her *love.*

Let me conclude — by the recitation of yet another brief poem — one very different in character from any that I have before quoted. It is by Motherwell, and is called "The Song of the Cavalier." With our modern and altogether rational ideas of the absurdity and impiety of warfare, we are not precisely in that frame of mind best adapted to sympathize with the sentiments, and thus to appreciate the real excellence of the poem. To do this fully, we must identify ourselves, in fancy, with the soul of the old cavalier.

Then mounte! then mounte, brave gallants, all,
  And don your helmes amaine:
Deathe's couriers, Fame and Honour, call
  Us to the field againe.
No shrewish teares shall fill our eye
  When the sword-hilt 's in our hand, —
Heart-whole we'll part, and no whit sighe
  For the fayrest of the land;
Let piping swaine, and craven wight,
  Thus weepe and puling crye,
Our business is like men to fight,
  And hero-like to die!

Marginalia

In getting my books, I have been always solicitous of an ample margin; this not so much through any love of the thing in itself, however agreeable, as for the facility it affords me of pencilling suggested thoughts, agreements, and differences of opinion, or brief critical comments in general. Where what I have to note is too much to be included within the narrow limits of a margin, I commit it to a slip of paper, and deposit it between the leaves; taking care to secure it by an imperceptible portion of gum tragacanth paste.

All this may be whim; it may be not only a very hackneyed, but a very idle practice; — yet I persist in it still; and it affords me pleasure; which is profit, in despite of Mr. Bentham, with Mr. Mill on his back.

This making of notes, however, is by no means the making of mere *memoranda* — a custom which has its disadvantages, beyond doubt. "*Ce que je mets sur papier*," says Bernardin de St. Pierre, "*je remets de ma mémoire et par conséquence je l'oublie ;*" — and, in fact, if you wish to forget anything upon the spot, make a note that this thing is to be remembered.

But the purely marginal jottings, done with no eye to the Memorandum Book, have a distinct complexion, and not only a distinct purpose, but none at all; this it is which imparts to them a value. They have a rank somewhat above the chance and desultory comments of literary chit-chat — for these latter are not unfrequently "talk for talk's sake," hurried out of the mouth; while the *marginalia* are deliberately pencilled, because the mind of the reader wishes to unburthen itself of a *thought;* — however flippant — however silly — however trivial — still a thought indeed, not merely a thing that might have been a thought in time, and under more favorable circumstances. In the *marginalia*, too, we talk only to ourselves; we therefore talk freshly — boldly — originally — with *abandonnement* — without conceit — much after the fashion of Jeremy Taylor, and Sir Thomas Browne, and Sir William Temple, and the anatomical Burton, and that most logical analogist, Butler, and some other people of the old day, who were too full of their matter to have any room for their manner, which, being thus left out of question, was a capital manner, indeed, — a model of manners, with a richly marginalic air.

The circumscription of space, too, in these pencillings, has in it something more of advantage than of inconvenience. It compels us (whatever diffuseness of idea we may clandestinely entertain), into Montesquieu-ism, into Tacitus-ism (here I leave out of view the concluding portion of the "Annals") — or even into Carlyle-ism — a thing which, I have been told, is not to be confounded with your ordinary affectation and bad grammar. I say "bad grammar," through sheer obstinacy, because the grammarians (who should know better) insist upon it that I should not. But then grammar is not what these grammarians will have it; and, being merely the analysis of language, with the result of this analysis, must be good or bad just as the analyst is sage or silly — just as he is a Horne Tooke or a Cobbett.

But to our sheep. During a rainy afternoon, not long ago, being in a mood too listless for continuous study, I sought relief from *ennui* in dipping here and there, at random, among the volumes of my library — no very large one, certainly, but sufficiently miscellaneous; and, I flatter myself, not a little *recherché.*

Perhaps it was what the Germans call the "brain-scattering" humor of the moment; but, while the picturesqueness of the numerous pencil-scratches arrested my attention, the helter-skelter-iness of commentary amused me. I found myself at length forming a wish that it had been some other hand than my own which had so bedevilled the books, and fancying that, in such case, I might have derived no inconsiderable pleasure from turning them over. From this the transition-thought (as Mr. Lyell, or Mr. Murchison, or Mr. Featherstonhaugh would have it) was natural enough: — there might be something even in *my* scribblings which, for the mere sake of scribbling, would have interest for others.

The main difficulty respected the mode of transferring the notes from the volumes — the context from the text — without detriment to that exceedingly frail fabric of intelligibility in which the context was imbedded. With all appliances to boot, with the printed pages at their back, the commentaries were too often like Dodona's oracles — or those of Lycophron Tenebrosus — or the essays of the pedant's pupils, in Quintilian, which were "necessarily excellent, since even he (the pedant) found it impossible to comprehend them" : — what, then, would become of it — this context — if transferred? — if translated? Would it not rather be *traduit* (traduced) which is the French synonym, or *overzezet* (turned topsy-turvy) which is the Dutch one?

I concluded, at length, to put extensive faith in the acumen and imagination of the reader: — this as a general rule. But, in some instances, where even faith would not remove mountains, there seemed no safer plan than so to re-model the note as to convey at least the ghost of a conception as to what it was all about. Where, for such conception, the text itself was absolutely necessary, I could quote it; where the title of the book commented upon was indispensable, I could name it. In short, like a novel-hero dilemma'd, I made up my mind "to be guided by circumstances," in default of more satisfactory rules of conduct.

As for the multitudinous opinion expressed in the subjoined *farrago* — as for my present assent to all, or dissent from any portion of it — as to the possibility of my having, in some instances, altered my mind — or as to the impossibility of my not having altered it often — these are points upon which I say nothing, because upon these there can be nothing cleverly said. It may be as well to observe, however, that just as the goodness of your true pun is in the direct ratio of its intolerability, so is nonsense the essential sense of the Marginal Note.

*

*   *

In general, we should not be overscrupulous about

niceties of phrase, when the matter in hand is a dunce to be gibbeted. Speak out! — or the person may not understand you. He is to be hung? Then hang him by all means; but make no bow when you mean no obeisance, and eschew the droll delicacy of the Clown in the Play — "Be so good, sir, as to rise and be put to death."

This is the only true principle among men. Where the gentler sex is concerned, there seems but one course for the critic — speak if you can commend — be silent, if not; for a woman will never be brought to admit a non-identity between herself and her book, and "a well-bred man" says, justly, that excellent old English moralist, James Puckle, in his "Gray Cap for a Green Head," "a well-bred man will never *give himself the liberty* to speak ill of women."

How many good books suffer neglect through the inefficiency of their beginnings! It is far better that we commence irregularly — immethodically — than that we fail to arrest attention; but the two points, method and pungency, may always be combined. At all risks, let there be a few vivid sentences *imprimis*, by way of the electric bell to the telegraph.

The great force derivable from repetition of particular vowel sounds in verse, is little understood, or quite overlooked, even by those versifiers who dwell most upon what is commonly called "alliteration." How richly melodious are these lines of Milton's "Comus!"

May thy *brim*med waves for *this*
Their full *tri*bute never *miss* —
May thy *billows roll ashore*
The beryl and the *golden ore !*

— and yet it seems especially singular that, with the full and noble volume of the long ō resounding in his ears, the poet should have written, in the last line, "beryl," when he might so well have written "onyx."

*

* *

The defenders of this pitiable stuff, uphold it on the ground of its truthfulness. Taking the thesis into question, this truthfulness is the one overwhelming defect. An original idea that — to laud the accuracy with which the stone is hurled that knocks us in the head. A little less accuracy might have left us more brains. And here are critics absolutely commending the truthfulness with which only the disagreeable is conveyed ! In my view, if an artist must paint decayed cheeses, his merit will lie in their looking as little like decayed cheeses as possible.

*

* *

I am not sure that Tennyson is not the greatest of poets. The uncertainty attending the public conception of the term "poet" alone prevents me from demonstrating that he *is*. Other bards produce effects which are, now and then, otherwise produced than by what we call poems; but Tennyson an effect which only a poem does. His alone are idiosyncratic poems. By the enjoyment or non-enjoyment of the "Morte D'Arthur," or of the "Œnone," I would test any one's ideal sense.

There are passages in his works which rivet a conviction I had long entertained, that the *indefinite* is an element in the true ποίησις. Why do some persons fatigue themselves in attempts to unravel such phantasy-pieces as the "Lady of Shalott"? As well unweave the "*ventum textilem.*" If the author did not deliberately propose to himself a suggestive indefinitiveness of meaning, with the view of bringing about a definitiveness of vague and therefore of spiritual *effect* — this, at least, arose from the silent analytical promptings of that poetic genius which, in its supreme development, embodies all orders of intellectual capacity.

I *know* that indefinitiveness is an element of the true music — I mean of the true musical expression. Give to it any undue decision — imbue it with any very determinate tone — and you deprive it, at once, of its ethereal, its ideal, its intrinsic and essential character. You dispel its luxury of dream. You dissolve the atmosphere of the mystic upon which it floats. You exhaust it of its breath of faëry. It now becomes a tangible and easily appreciable idea — a thing of the earth, earthy. It has not, indeed, lost its power to please, but all which I consider the distinctiveness of that power. And to the uncultivated talent, or to the unimaginative apprehension, this deprivation of its most delicate grace will be, not unfrequently, a recommendation. A determinateness of expression is sought — and often by composers who should know better — is sought as a beauty rather than rejected as a blemish. Thus we have, even from high authorities, attempts at absolute *imitation* in music. Who can forget the silliness of the "Battle of Prague"? What man of taste but must laugh at the interminable drums, trumpets, blunderbusses, and thunder? "*Vocal* music," says L'Abbate Gravina, who would have said the same thing of instrumental, "ought to imitate the natural language of the human feelings and passions, rather than the warblings of Canary birds, which our singers, nowadays, affect so vastly to mimic with their quaverings and boasted cadences." This is true only so far as the "rather" is concerned. If any music must imitate anything, it were assuredly better to limit the imitation as Gravina suggests.

Tennyson's shorter pieces abound in minute rhythmical lapses sufficient to assure me that — in common with all poets living or dead — he has neglected to make precise investigation of the principles of metre; but, on the other hand, so perfect is his rhythmical instinct in general, that, like the present Viscount Canterbury, he seems *to see with his ear*.

It is the curse of a certain order of mind, that it can never rest satisfied with the consciousness of its ability to do a thing. Still less is it content with doing it. It must both know and show how it was done.

In a critical mood I would speak of these stanzas [of Mrs. Amelia Welby which have just been quoted] thus:

— The subject has *nothing* of originality: — A widower muses by the grave of his wife. Here then is a great demerit; for originality of theme, if not absolutely first sought, should be sought among the first. Nothing is more clear than this proposition, although denied by the chlorine critics (the grass-green). The desire of the new is an element of the soul. The most exquisite pleasures grow dull in repetition. A strain of music enchants. Heard a second time it pleases. Heard a tenth, it does not displease. We hear it a twentieth, and ask ourselves why we admired. At the fiftieth it induces ennui — at the hundredth disgust.

Mrs. Welby's theme is, therefore, radically faulty so far as originality is concerned; — but of common themes, it is one of the very best among the class *passionate*. True passion is prosaic — homely. Any strong mental emotion stimulates *all* the mental faculties; thus grief the imagination: — but in proportion as the effect is strengthened, the cause surceases. The excited fancy triumphs — the grief is subdued — chastened, — is no longer grief. In this mood we are poetic, and it is clear that a poem now written will be poetic in the exact ratio of its dispassion. A passionate poem is a contradiction in terms. When I say, then, that Mrs. Welby's stanzas are good among the class *passionate* (using the term commonly and falsely applied), I mean that her tone is properly subdued, and is not so much the tone of passion, as of a gentle and melancholy regret, interwoven with a pleasant sense of the natural loveliness surrounding the lost in the tomb, and a memory of her human beauty while alive. — Elegiac poems should either assume this character, or dwell purely on the beauty (moral or physical) of the departed — or, better still, utter the notes of triumph. I have endeavored to carry out this latter idea in some verses which I have called "Lenore."

Those who object to the proposition — that poetry and passion are discordant — would, thus, cite Mrs. Welby's poem as an instance of a passionate one. It is precisely similar to the hundred others which have been cited for like purpose. But it is *not* passionate; and for this reason (with others having regard to her fine genius) it *is* poetical. The critics upon this topic display an amusing *ignoratio elenchi.*

*

* *

Men of genius are far more abundant than is supposed. In fact, to appreciate thoroughly the work of what we call genius, is to possess all the genius by which the work was produced. But the person appreciating may be utterly incompetent to reproduce the work, or anything similar, and this solely through lack of what may be termed the constructive ability — a matter quite independent of what we agree to understand in the term "genius" itself. This ability is based, to be sure, in great part, upon the faculty of analysis, enabling the artist to get full view of the machinery of his proposed effect, and thus work it and regulate it at will; but a great deal depends also upon properties strictly moral — for example, upon patience, upon concentrativeness, or the power of holding the attention steadily to the one purpose, upon self-dependence and contempt for all opinion which is opinion and no more — in especial, upon energy or industry. So vitally important is this last, that it may well be doubted if anything to which we have been accustomed to give the title of a "work of genius" was ever accomplished without it; and it is chiefly because this quality and genius are nearly incompatible, that "works of genius" are few, while mere men of genius are, as I say, abundant. The Romans, who excelled us in acuteness of *observation*, while falling below us in induction from facts observed, seem to have been so fully aware of the inseparable connection between industry and a "work of genius" as to have adopted the error that industry, in great measure, was genius itself. The highest compliment is intended by a Roman when, of an epic, or anything similar, he says that it is written *industriâ mirabili* or *incredibili industriâ.*

*

* *

All true men must rejoice to perceive the decline of the miserable rant and cant against originality, which was so much in vogue a few years ago among a class of microscopical critics, and which at one period threatened to degrade all American literature to the level of Flemish art.

Of puns it has been said that those most dislike who are least able to utter them; but with far more of truth may it be asserted that invectives against originality proceed only from persons at once hypocritical and commonplace. I say hypocritical — for the love of novelty is an indisputable element of the moral nature of man; and since to be original is merely to be novel, the dolt who professes a distaste for originality, in letters or elsewhere, proves in no degree his aversion for the thing itself, but merely that uncomfortable hatred which ever arises in the heart of an envious man for an excellence he cannot hope to attain.

*

* *

"Here is a man who is a scholar and an artist, who knows precisely how every effect has been produced by every great writer, and who is resolved to reproduce them. But the heart passes by his pitfalls and traps, and carefully-planned springs, to be taken captive by some simple fellow who expected the event as little as did his prisoner."[1]

Perhaps I err in quoting these words as the author's own — they are in the mouth of one of his interlocutors — but whoever claims them, they are poetical and no more. The error is exactly that common one of separating practice from the theory which includes it. In all cases, if the practice fail, it is because the theory is imperfect. If Mr. Lowell's heart be not caught in the pitfall or trap, then the pitfall is ill-concealed and the trap is not properly baited or set. One who has *some artistical ability* may know how to do a thing, and even show how to do it, and yet fail in doing it after all; but the artist and the man of some artistic ability must not be confounded. He only is the former who can carry his most shadowy precepts into successful application. To say that a critic could not have written the work which he criticises, is to put forth a contradiction in terms.

[1] Lowell's "Conversations."

The farce of this big book is equaled only by the farce of the rag-tag-and-bobtail "embassy from the whole earth" introduced by the crazy Prussian into the hall of the French National Assembly. The author is the Anacharsis Clootz of American letters.

*

* *

I would have no difficulty in filling two ordinary novel volumes with just such concise parallels as these [referring to a series of parallels, or "nuts from memory for Outis," which have just been propounded]. Nevertheless, I am clearly of opinion that of one hundred plagiarisms of this character, seventy-five would be, not accidental, but unintentional. The poetic sentiment implies an abnormally keen appreciation of poetic excellence, with an unconscious assimilation of it into the poetic entity, so that an admired passage, being forgotten and afterwards reviving through an exceedingly shadowy train of association, is supposed by the plagiarizing poet to be really the coinage of his own brain. An uncharitable world, however, will never be brought to understand all this, and the poet who commits a plagiarism is, if not criminal, at least unlucky; and equally in either case does critical justice require the right of property to be traced home. Of two persons, one is to suffer — it matters not what — and there can be no question as to who should be the sufferer.

*

* *

The conclusion of the Proem in Mr. Longfellow's late "Waif" is exceedingly beautiful. The whole poem is remarkable in this, that one of its principal excellences arises from what is, generically, a demerit. No error, for example, is more certainly fatal in poetry than defective *rhythm ;* but here the *slipshodiness* is so thoroughly in unison with the nonchalant air of the thoughts — which, again, are so capitally applicable to the thing done (a mere introduction of other people's fancies) — that the effect of the looseness of rhythm becomes palpable, and we see at once that here is a case in which to be *correct* would be inartistic. Here are three of the quatrains—

"I see the lights of the village
  Gleam through the rain and the mist,
And a feeling of sadness comes over me
  That my soul cannot resist —

"A feeling of sadness and longing
  That is not akin to pain,
And *resembles sorrow only*
  As the mists resemble the rain.

* * * * * *

"And the night shall be filled with music,
  And the cares that infest the day
Shall fold their tents like the Arabs,
  And as silently steal away."

Now these lines are not to be scanned. They are referable to no true principles of rhythm. The general idea is that of a succession of anapæsts; yet not only is this idea confounded with that of dactyls, but this succession is improperly interrupted at all points — improperly, because by unequivalent feet. The partial prosaicism thus brought about, however, (without any interference with the mere melody,) becomes a beauty solely through the nicety of its adaptation to the *tone* of the poem, and of this tone, again, to the matter in hand. In his keen sense of this adaptation, (which conveys the notion of what is vaguely termed "ease,") the reader so far loses sight of the rhythmical imperfection that he can be convinced of its existence only by treating in the same rhythm (or, rather, lack of rhythm) a subject of different tone — a subject in which decision shall take the place of nonchalance.

Now, undoubtedly, I intend all this as complimentary to Mr. Longfellow; but it was for the utterance of these very opinions in the "New York Mirror" that I was accused, by some of the poet's friends, of inditing what they think proper to call "strictures" on the author of "Outre-mer."

*

* *

When we attend less to "authority" and more to principles, when we look *less* at merit and *more* at demerit, (instead of the converse, as some persons suggest,) we shall then be better critics than we are. We must neglect our models and study our capabilities. The mad eulogies on what occasionally has, in letters, been well done, spring from our imperfect comprehension of what it is possible for us to do better. "A man who has never seen the sun," says Calderon, "cannot be blamed for thinking that no glory can exceed that of the moon; a man who has seen neither moon nor sun, cannot be blamed for expatiating on the incomparable effulgence of the morning star." Now, it is the business of the critic so to soar that he shall *see the sun*, even although its orb be far below the ordinary horizon.

*

* *

The effect derivable from well-managed rhyme is very imperfectly understood. Conventionally "rhyme" implies merely close similarity of sound at the ends of verse, and it is really curious to observe how long mankind have been content with their limitation of the idea. What, in rhyme, first and principally pleases, may be referred to the human sense or appreciation of *equality* — the common element, as might be easily shown, of all the gratification we derive from music in its most extended sense — very especially in its modifications of metre and rhythm. We see, for example, a crystal, and are immediately interested by the equality between the sides and angles of one of its faces — but on bringing to view a second face, in all respects similar to our first, our pleasure seems to be *squared* — on bringing to view a third, it appears to be *cubed*, and so on: I have no doubt, indeed, that the delight experienced, if measurable, would be found to have exact mathematical relations, such, or nearly such, as I suggest — that is to say, as far as a certain point, beyond which there would be a decrease, in similar relations. Now here, as the ultimate result of analysis, we reach the sense of mere *equality*, or rather the human delight in this sense; and it was an instinct, rather than a clear comprehension of this delight as a principle, which, in the first instance, led the poet to attempt an increase of the effect arising from the mere similarity (that is to say equality) between two sounds — led him, I say, to attempt increasing this effect by making a secondary equalization, in placing the rhymes at equal distances — that is, at the ends of lines of equal length. In this manner, rhyme and the termination of the line grew connected in men's thoughts — grew into a conventionalism — the principle being lost sight of altogether. And it was simply because Pindaric verses had, before this epoch, existed — *i. e.* verses of unequal length — that rhymes were subsequently found at unequal distances. It was for this reason solely, I say — for none more profound — rhyme had come to be regarded as of right appertaining to the end of verse — and here we complain that the matter has finally rested.

But it is clear that there was much more to be considered. So far, the sense of equality alone, entered the effect; or, if this equality was slightly varied, it was varied only through an accident — the accident of the existence of Pindaric metres. It will be seen that the rhymes were always anticipated. The eye, catching the end of a verse, whether long or short, expected, for the ear, a rhyme. The great element of unexpectedness was not dreamed of — that is to say, of novelty — of originality. "But," says Lord Bacon, (how justly!) "there is no exquisite beauty without some strangeness in the proportions." Take away this element of strangeness — of unexpectedness — of novelty — of originality — call it what we will — and all that is ethereal in loveliness is lost at once. We lose — we miss the unknown — the vague — the uncomprehended, because offered before we have time to examine and comprehend. We lose, in short, all that assimilates the beauty of earth with what we dream of the beauty of Heaven.

Perfection of rhyme is attainable only in the combination of the two elements, Equality and Unexpectedness. But as evil cannot exist without good, so unexpectedness must arise from expectedness. We do not contend for mere arbitrariness of rhyme. In the first place, we must have equi-distant or regularly recurring rhymes, to form the basis, expectedness, out of which arises the element, unexpectedness, by the introduction of rhymes, not arbitrarily, but with an eye to the greatest amount of unexpectedness. We should not introduce them, for example, at such points that the entire line is a multiple of the syllables preceding the points. When, for instance, I write —

And the silken, sad, uncertain rustling of each purple curtain,

I produce more, to be sure, but not remarkably more than the ordinary effect of rhymes regularly recurring at the end of lines; for the number of syllables in the whole verse is merely a multiple of the number of syllables preceding the rhyme introduced at the middle, and there is still left, therefore, a certain degree of expectedness. What there is of the element unexpectedness, is addressed, in fact, to the eye only — for the ear divides the verse into two ordinary lines, thus —

And the silken, sad, uncertain
Rustling of each purple curtain.

I obtain, however, the whole effect of unexpectedness, when I write —

Thrilled me, *filled* me with fantastic terrors never felt before.

N. B. It is very commonly supposed that rhyme, as it now ordinarily exists, is of modern invention — but see the "Clouds" of Aristophanes. Hebrew verse, however, did *not* include it — the terminations of the lines, where most distinct, never showing anything of the kind.

*

* *

Some Frenchman — possibly Montaigne — says: "People talk about thinking, but for my part I never think, except when I sit down to write." It is this never thinking, unless when we sit down to write, which is the cause of so much indifferent composition. But perhaps there is something more involved in the Frenchman's observation than meets the eye. It is certain that the mere act of inditing, tends, in a great degree, to the logicalization of thought. Whenever, on account of its vagueness, I am dissatisfied with a conception of the brain, I resort forthwith to the pen, for the purpose of obtaining, through its aid, the necessary form, consequence and precision.

How very commonly we hear it remarked, that such and such thoughts are beyond the compass of words! I do not believe that any thought, properly so called, is out of the reach of language. I fancy, rather, that where difficulty in expression is experienced, there is, in the intellect which experiences it, a want either of deliberateness or of method. For my own part, I have never had a thought which I could not set down in words, with even more distinctness than that with which I conceived it: — as I have before observed, the thought is logicalized by the effort at (written) expression.

There is, however, a class of fancies, of exquisite delicacy, which are *not* thoughts, and to which, *as yet,* I have found it absolutely impossible to adapt language. I use the word *fancies* at random, and merely because I must use *some* word; but the idea commonly attached to the term is not even remotely applicable to the shadows of shadows in question. They seem to me rather psychal than intellectual. They arise in the soul (alas, how rarely!) only at its epochs of most intense tranquillity — when the bodily and mental health are in perfection — and at those mere points of time where the confines of the waking world blend with those of the world of dreams. I am aware of these "fancies" only when I am upon the very brink of sleep, with the consciousness that I am so. I have satisfied myself that this condition exists but for an inappreciable *point* of time — yet it is crowded with these "shadows of shadows"; and for absolute *thought* there is demanded time's *endurance.*

These "fancies" have in them a pleasurable ecstasy as far beyond the most pleasurable of the world of wakefulness, or of dreams, as the Heaven of the Northman theology is beyond its Hell. I regard the visions, even as they arise, with an awe which, in some measure, moderates or tranquilizes the ecstasy — I so regard them, through a conviction (which seems a portion of the ecstasy itself) that this ecstasy, in itself, is of a character supernal to the Human Nature — is a glimpse of the spirit's outer world; and I arrive at this conclusion — if this term is at all applicable to instantaneous intuition — by a perception that the delight experienced has, as its element, but *the absoluteness of novelty.* I say the absoluteness — for in these fancies — let me now term them psychal impressions — there is really nothing even approximate in character to impressions ordinarily received. It is as if the five senses were supplanted by five myriad others alien to mortality.

Now, so entire is my faith in the *power of words*, that, at times, I have believed it possible to embody even the evanescence of fancies such as I have attempted to describe. In experiments with this end in view, I have proceeded so far as, first, to control (when the bodily and mental health are good) the existence of the condition: — that is to say, I can now (unless when ill) be sure that the condition will supervene, if I so wish it, at the point of time already described: of its supervention, until lately, I could never be certain, even under the most favorable circumstances. I mean to say, merely, that now I can be sure, when all circumstances are favorable, of the supervention of the condition, and feel even the capacity of inducing or compelling it: — the favorable circumstances, however, are not the less rare — else had I compelled, already, the Heaven into the Earth.

I have proceeded so far, secondly, as to prevent the lapse from *the point* of which I speak — the point of blending between wakefulness and sleep — as to prevent at will, I say, the lapse from this border-ground into the dominion of sleep. Not that I can *continue* the condition — not that I can render the point more than a point — but that I can startle myself from the point into wakefulness — *and thus transfer the point itself into the realm of Memory* — convey its impressions, or more properly their recollections, to a situation where (although still for a very brief period) I can survey them with the eye of analysis.

For these reasons — that is to say, because I have been enabled to accomplish thus much — I do not altogether despair of embodying in words at least enough of the fancies in question to convey, to certain classes of intellect, a shadowy conception of their character.

In saying this I am not to be understood as supposing that the fancies, or psychal impressions, to which I allude, are confined to my individual self — are not, in a word, common to all mankind — for on this point it is quite impossible that I should form an opinion — but nothing can be more certain than that even a partial record of the impressions would startle the universal intellect of mankind, by the *supremeness of the novelty* of the material employed, and of its consequent suggestions. In a word — should I ever write a paper on this topic, the world will be compelled to acknowledge that, at last, I have done an original thing.

*

* *

"The artist belongs to his work, not the work to the artist"—Novalis.[1] In nine cases out of ten it is pure waste of time to attempt extorting sense from a German apothegm; — or, rather, any sense and every sense may be extorted from all of them. If in the sentence above quoted, the intention is to assert that the artist is the

[1] The nom-de-plume of Von Hardenberg.

slave of his theme, and must conform to it his thoughts, I have no faith in the idea, which appears to me that of an essentially prosaic intellect. In the hands of the *true* artist the theme, or "work," is but a mass of clay, of which anything (within the compass of the mass and quality of clay) may be fashioned at will or according to the skill of the workman. The clay is, in fact, the slave of the artist. It belongs to him. His genius, to be sure, is manifested very distinctively in *the choice* of the clay. It should be neither fine nor coarse, abstractly — but just so fine or so coarse — just so plastic or so rigid — as may best serve the purposes of the thing to be wrought — of the idea to be made out, or, more exactly, of the impression to be conveyed. There *are* artists, however, who fancy only the *finest* material, and who, consequently, produce only the *finest* ware. It is generally very transparent and excessively brittle.

*

* *

As a descriptive poet, Mr. Street is to be highly commended. He not only describes with force and fidelity — giving us a clear conception of the thing described — but never describes what, to the poet should be nondescript. He appears however not at any time to have been aware that *mere* description is not poetry at all. We demand creation — ποίησις. About Mr. Street there seems to be no spirit. He is all matter — substance — what the chemist would call "simple substance" — and exceedingly simple it is.

*

* *

If need were, I should have little difficulty, perhaps,

in defending a certain apparent dogmatism to which I am prone, on the topic of versification.

"What is Poetry?" notwithstanding Leigh Hunt's rigmarolic attempt at answering it, is a query that, with great care and deliberate agreement beforehand on the exact value of certain leading words, *may*, possibly, be settled to the partial satisfaction of a few analytical intellects, but which, in the existing condition of metaphysics, never *can* be settled to the satisfaction of the majority; for the question is purely metaphysical, and the whole science of metaphysics is at present a chaos, through the impossibility of fixing the meanings of the words which its very nature compels it to employ. But as regards versification, this difficulty is only partial; for although one-third of the topic may be considered metaphysical, and thus may be mooted at the fancy of this individual or of that, still the remaining two thirds belong, undeniably, to the mathematics. The questions ordinarily discussed with so much gravity in regard to rhythm, metre, etc., are susceptible of positive adjustment by demonstration. Their laws are merely a portion of the Median laws of form and quantity — of relation. In respect, then, to any of these ordinary questions — these sillily moot points which so often arise in common criticism — the prosodist would speak as weakly in saying "this or that proposition is *probably* so and so, or *possibly* so and so," as would the mathematician in admitting that, in his humble opinion, or if he were not greatly mistaken, any two sides of a triangle were, together, greater than the third side. I must add, however, as some palliation of the discussions referred to, and of the objections so often urged with a sneer to "particular theories of versification binding no one but their inventor" — that there is really extant no such work as a Prosody *Raisonnée*. The Prosodies of the schools are merely collections of vague *laws*, with their more vague exceptions, based upon no principles whatever, but extorted in the most speculative manner from the usages of the ancients, who had *no* laws beyond those of their ears and fingers. "And these were sufficient," it will be said, "since 'The Iliad' is melodious and harmonious beyond anything of modern times." Admit this: — but neither do we write in Greek, nor has the invention of modern times been as yet exhausted. An analysis based on the natural laws of which the bard of Scios was ignorant, would suggest multitudinous improvements to the best passages of even "The Iliad" — nor does it in any manner follow from the suppostitious fact that Homer found in his ears and fingers a satisfactory system of rules (the point which I have just denied) — nor does it follow, I say, from this, that the rules which *we* deduce from the Homeric *effects* are to supersede those immutable principles of time, quantity, etc. — the mathematics, in short, of music — which must have stood to these Homeric effects in the relation of *causes* — the *mediate* causes of which these "ears and fingers" are simply the *intermedia*.

*

* *

A book[1] which puzzles me beyond measure, since,

[1] Human Magnetism: Its Claim to Dispassionate Inquiry. Being an Attempt to show the Utility of its Application for the Relief of Human Suffering. By W. Newnham, M. R. S. L., Author of the Reciprocal Influence of Body and Mind. Wiley & Putnam.

while agreeing with its general conclusions, (except where it discusses *prévision*,) I invariably find fault with the reasoning through which the conclusions are attained. I think the treatise grossly illogical throughout. For example: — the origin of the work is thus stated in an introductory chapter.

"About twelve months since, I was asked by some friends to write a paper against Mesmerism — and I was furnished with materials by a highly esteemed quondam pupil, which proved incontestably that under some circumstances the operator might be duped — that hundreds of enlightened persons might equally be deceived — and certainly went far to show that the pretended science was wholly a delusion — a system of fraud and jugglery by which the imaginations of the credulous were held in thraldom through the arts of the designing. Perhaps in an evil hour I assented to the proposition thus made — but on reflection I found that the facts before me only led to the *direct proof* that certain phenomena might be counterfeited; and the existence of counterfeit coin is rather a proof that there is somewhere the genuine standard gold to be imitated."

This fallacy here lies in a mere variation of what is called "begging the question." Counterfeit coin is said to prove the existence of genuine: — this, of course, is no more than the truism that there can be no counterfeit where there is no genuine — just as there can be no badness where there is no goodness — the terms being purely relative. But *because* there can be no counterfeit where there is no original, does it in any manner follow that any undemonstrated original exists? In seeing a spurious coin we know it to be such by comparison with coins *admitted* to be genuine; but were *no* coins admitted to be genuine, how should we establish the counterfeit, and what right should we have to talk of counterfeits at all? Now, in the case of Mesmerism, our author is merely *begging the admission.* In saying that the existence of counterfeit proves the existence of real Mesmerism, he demands that the real *be admitted.* Either he demands this or there is no shadow of force in his proposition — for it is clear that *we can pretend to be* that which is not. A man, for instance, may feign himself a sphynx or a griffin, but it would never do to regard as thus demonstrated the actual existence of either griffins or sphynxes. A word alone — the word "counterfeit" — has been sufficient to lead Mr. Newnham astray. People cannot properly be said to "counterfeit" prévision, etc., but to *feign* these phenomena.

Dr. Newnham's argument, of course, is by no means original with *him*, although he seems to pride himself on it as if it were. Dr. More says: "That there should be so universal a fame and fear of that which never was, nor is, nor can be ever in the world, is to me the greatest miracle of all. If there had not been, at some time or other, true miracles, it had not been so easy to impose on the people by false. The alchemist would never go about to sophisticate metals, to pass them off for true gold and silver, unless that such a thing was acknowledged as true gold and silver in the world."

This is precisely the same idea as that of Dr. Newnham, and belongs to that extensive class of argumentation which is *all point* — deriving its whole effect from epigrammatism. That the belief in ghosts, or in a Deity, or in a future state, or in anything else credible or incredible — that any such belief is universal, demonstrates nothing more than that which needs no demonstration — the human unanimity — the identity of construction in the human brain — an identity of which the inevitable result must be, upon the whole, similar deductions from similar *data*.

Most especially do I disagree with the author of this book in his (implied) disparagement of the work of Chauncey Hare Townshend — a work to be valued properly only in a day to come.

*

* *

This book ["Thiodolf, the Icelander, and Aslauga's Knight"] could never have been popular out of Germany. It is too simple — too direct — too obvious — too *bald* — not sufficiently complex — to be relished by any people who have *thoroughly* passed the first (or impulsive) epoch of literary civilization. The Germans have not yet passed this first epoch. It must be remembered that *during the whole of the middle ages they lived in utter ignorance of the art of writing*. From so total a darkness, of so late a date, they could not, *as a nation*, have as yet fully emerged into the second or critical epoch. Individual Germans have been critical in the best sense — but the masses are unleavened. Literary Germany thus presents the singular spectacle of the impulsive spirit surrounded by the critical, and, of course, in some measure influenced thereby. England, for example, has advanced far, and France much farther, into the critical epoch ; and their effect on the German mind is seen in the wildly anomalous condition of the German literature at large. That this latter will be improved by age, however, should never be maintained. As the impulsive spirit subsides, and the critical uprises, there will appear the polished insipidity of the later England, or that ultimate *throe* of taste which has found its best exemplification in Sue. At present the German literature resembles no other on the face of the earth — for it is the result of certain conditions which, before this individual instance of their fulfillment, have never been fulfilled. And this anomalous state to which I refer is the source of our anomalous criticism upon what that state produces — is the source of the grossly conflicting opinions about German letters. For my own part, I admit the German vigor, the German directness, boldness, imagination, and some other qualities of impulse, just as I am willing to admit and admire these qualities in the first (or impulsive) epochs of British and French letters. At the German criticism, however, I cannot refrain from laughing all the more heartily, all the more seriously I hear it praised. Not that, in detail, it affects me as an absurdity — but in the adaptation of its details. It abounds in brilliant bubbles of *suggestion*, but these rise and sink and jostle each other, until the whole vortex of thought in which they originate is one indistinguishable chaos of froth. The German criticism is *unsettled*, and can only be settled by time. At present it suggests without demonstrating, or convincing, or effecting any definite purpose under the sun. We read it, rub our foreheads, and ask

"What then?" I am not ashamed to say that I prefer even Voltaire to Goethe, and hold Macaulay to possess more of the true critical spirit than Augustus William and Frederick Schlegel combined.

"Thiodolf" is called by Fouqué his "most *successful* work." He would not have spoken thus had he considered it his *best.* It is admirable of its kind — but its kind can *never* be appreciated by Americans. It will affect them much as would a grasp of the hand from a man of ice. Even the exquisite "Undine" is too chilly for our people, and, generally, for our epoch. We have less imagination and warmer sympathies than the age which preceded us. It would have done Fouqué more ready and fuller justice than ours.

Has any one remarked the striking similarity in tone between "Undine" and the "Libussa" of Musæus?

*

* *

About the "Antigone," as about all the ancient plays, there seems to me a certain *baldness*, the result of inexperience in art, but which pedantry would force us to believe the result of a studied and supremely artistic simplicity. Simplicity, indeed, is a very important feature in all true art — but *not* the simplicity which we see in the Greek drama. That of the Greek sculpture is everything that can be desired, because here the art in itself is simplicity in itself and in its elements. The Greek sculptor chiseled his forms from what he saw before him every day, in a beauty nearer to perfection than any work of any Cleomenes in the world. But in the drama, the direct, straightforward, *un-German* Greek had no Nature so immediately presented from which to make copy. He did what he could — but I do not hesitate to say that that was exceedingly little worth. The profound sense of one or two tragic, or rather, melodramatic elements (such as the idea of inexorable Destiny) — this sense gleaming at intervals from out the darkness of the ancient stage, serves, in the very imperfection of its development, to show, not the dramatic ability, but the dramatic *in*-ability of the ancients. In a word, the simple arts spring into perfection at their origin; the complex as inevitably demand the long and painfully progressive experience of ages. To the Greeks, beyond doubt, their drama *seemed* perfection — it fully answered, to them, the dramatic end, excitement — and this fact is urged as proof of their drama's perfection in itself. It need only be said, in reply, that their art and their sense of art were, necessarily, on a level.

*

* *

The more there are great excellences in a work, the less am I surprised at finding great demerits. When a book is said to have many faults, nothing is decided, and I cannot tell, by this, whether it is excellent or execrable. It is said of another that it is without fault; if the account be just, the work *cannot* be excellent. —*Trublet.*

The "*cannot*" here is much too positive. The opinions of Trublet are wonderfully prevalent, but they are none the less demonstrably false. It is merely the *indolence* of genius which has given them currency. The truth seems to be that genius of the highest order lives in a state of perpetual vacillation between ambition and *the scorn of it.* The ambition of a great intellect is at best negative. It struggles — it labors — it creates —not because excellence is desirable, but because to be excelled where there exists a sense of the power to excel, is unendurable. Indeed I cannot help thinking that the *greatest* intellects (since these most clearly perceive the laughable absurdity of human ambition) remain contentedly "mute and inglorious." At all events, the *vacillation* of which I speak is the prominent feature of genius. Alternately inspired and depressed, its inequalities of mood are stamped upon its labors. This is the truth, generally — but it is a truth very different from the assertion involved in the "cannot" of Trublet. Give to genius a sufficiently enduring *motive*, and the result will be harmony, proportion, beauty, perfection — all, in this case, synonymous terms. Its supposed "inevitable" irregularities shall not be found : — for it is clear that the susceptibility to impressions of beauty — that susceptibility which is the most important element of genius — implies an equally exquisite sensitiveness and aversion to deformity. The motive — the *enduring* motive — has indeed, hitherto, fallen *rarely* to the lot of genius ; but I could point to several compositions which, " without any fault," are yet " excellent " — supremely so. The world, too, is on the threshold of an epoch, wherein, with the aid of a calm philosophy, such compositions shall be ordinarily the work of that genius which is *true.* One of the first and most essential steps, in overpassing this threshold, will serve to kick out of the world's way this very idea of

Trublet — this untenable and paradoxical idea of the incompatibility of genius with *art*.

*

* *

In Colton's "American Review" for October, 1845, a gentleman, well known for his scholarship, has a forcible paper on "The Scotch School of Philosophy and Criticism." But although the paper is "forcible," it presents the most singular admixture of error and truth — the one dove-tailed into the other, after a fashion which is novel, to say the least of it. Were I to designate in a few words what the whole article demonstrated, I should say "the folly of not beginning at the beginning — of neglecting the giant Moulineau's advice to his friend Ram." Here is a passage from the essay in question:

"The Doctors [Campbell and Johnson] both charge Pope with error and inconsistency: — error in supposing that *in English*, of metrical lines unequal in the number of syllables and pronounced in equal times, the longer suggests celerity (this being the principle of the Alexandrine) — inconsistency, in that Pope himself uses the same contrivance to convey the contrary idea of slowness. But why in English? It is not and cannot be disputed that, in the Hexameter verse of the Greeks and Latins — which is the model in this matter — what is distinguished as the 'dactylic line' was uniformly applied to express velocity. How was it to do so? Simply from the fact of being pronounced in an equal time with, while containing a greater number of syllables or 'bars' than the ordinary or average measure; as, on the other hand, the spondaic line, composed of the minimum number, was, upon the same principle, used to indicate slowness. So, too, of the Alexandrine in English versification. No, says Campbell, there is a difference: the Alexandrine is not in fact, like the dactylic line, pronounced in the common time. But does this alter the principle? What is the rationale of Metre, whether the classical hexameter or the English heroic?"

I have written an essay on the "Rationale of Verse," in which the whole topic is surveyed *ab initio*, and with reference to general and immutable principles. To this essay (which will soon appear) I refer Mr. Bristed. In the meantime, without troubling myself to ascertain whether Doctors Johnson and Campbell are wrong, or whether Pope is wrong, or whether the reviewer is right or wrong, at this point or at that, let me succinctly state what is *the truth* on the topics at issue.

And first; the same principles, in *all* cases, govern *all* verse. What is true in English is true in Greek.

Secondly; in a series of lines, if one line contains more syllables than the law of the verse demands, and if, nevertheless, this line is pronounced in the same time, upon the whole, as the rest of the lines, then this line suggests celerity — on account of the increased rapidity of enunciation required. Thus in the Greek Hexameter the dactylic lines — those most abounding in dactyls — serve best to convey the idea of rapid motion. The spondaic lines convey that of slowness.

Thirdly; it is a gross mistake to suppose that the Greek dactylic line is "the model in this matter" — the matter of the English Alexandrine. The Greek dactylic line is of the same number of feet — bars — beats — pulsations — as the ordinary dactylic-spondaic lines among which it occurs. But the Alexandrine is longer by one foot — by one pulsation — than the pentameters among which it arises. For its pronunciation it demands *more time*, and therefore, *ceteris paribus*, it would well serve to convey the impression of length, or duration, and thus, indirectly, of slowness. I say *ceteris paribus*. But, by varying conditions, we can effect a total change in the impression conveyed. When the idea of slowness is conveyed by the Alexandrine, it is not conveyed by any slower enunciation of syllables — that is to say, it is not *directly* conveyed — but indirectly, through the idea of *length* in the whole line. Now, if we wish to convey, by means of an Alexandrine, the impression of velocity, we readily do so by giving rapidity to our enunciation of the syllables composing the several feet. To effect this, however, we must have *more* syllables, or we shall get through the whole line too quickly for the intended time. To get more syllables, all we have to do, is to use in place of iambuses, what our prosodies call anapæsts.[1] Thus, in the line,

> Flies o'er the unbending corn and skims along the main,

[1] I use the prosodial word "anapæst," merely because here I have no space to show what the reviewer will admit I have distinctly shown in the essay referred to — viz: that the additional syllable introduced, does *not* make the foot an anapæst, or the equivalent of an anapæst, and that, if it did, it would spoil the line. On this topic, and on all topics connected with verse, there is not a prosody in existence which is not a mere jumble of the grossest error.

the syllables "*the unbend*" form an anapæst and, demanding unusual rapidity of enunciation, in order that we may get them in in the ordinary time of an iambus, serve to suggest celerity. By the elision of *e* in *the*, as is customary, the whole of the intended effect is lost; for *th' unbend* is nothing more than the usual iambus. In a word, wherever an Alexandrine expresses celerity, we shall find it to contain one or more anapæsts — the more anapæsts, the more decided the impression. But the tendency of the Alexandrine consisting merely of the usual iambuses, is to convey slowness — although it conveys this idea feebly, on account of conveying it indirectly. It follows, from what I have said, that the common pentameter, interspersed with anapæsts, would better convey celerity than the Alexandrine interspersed with them in a similar degree; — and it unquestionably does.

*

* *

For all the rhetorician's rules
Teach nothing but to name the tools. — HUDIBRAS.

What these oft-quoted lines go to show is, that a falsity in verse will travel faster and endure longer than a falsity in prose. The man who would sneer or stare at a silly proposition nakedly put, will admit that "there is a good deal in that" when "*that*" is the point of an epigram shot in the ear. The rhetorician's rules — if they *are* rules — teach him not only to name his tools, but to use his tools, the capacity of his tools — their extent — their limit; and from an examination of the nature of the tools (an examination forced on him by their constant presence)

— force him, also, into scrutiny and comprehension of the material on which the tools are employed, and thus, finally, suggest and give birth to new material for new tools.

*

* *

That punctuation is important all agree; but how few comprehend the extent of its importance! The writer who neglects punctuation, or mis-punctuates, is liable to be misunderstood — this, according to the popular idea, is the sum of the evils arising from heedlessness or ignorance. It does not seem to be known that, even where the sense is perfectly clear, a sentence may be deprived of half its force — its spirit — its point — by improper punctuation. For the want of merely a comma, it often occurs that an axiom appears a paradox, or that a sarcasm is converted into a sermonoid.

There is *no* treatise on the topic — and there is no topic on which a treatise is more needed. There seems to exist a vulgar notion that the subject is one of pure conventionality, and cannot be brought within the limits of intelligible and consistent *rule*. And yet, if fairly looked in the face, the whole matter is so plain that its *rationale* may be read as we run. If not anticipated, I shall, hereafter, make an attempt at a magazine paper on "The Philosophy of Point."

In the meantime let me say a word or two of *the dash*. Every writer for the press, who has any sense of the accurate, must have been frequently mortified and vexed at the distortion of his sentences by the printer's now general substitution of a semicolon, or comma, for the dash of the MS. The total or nearly total disuse of the latter point, has been brought about by the revulsion consequent upon its excessive employment about twenty years ago. The Byronic poets were *all* dash. John Neal, in his earlier novels, exaggerated its use into the grossest abuse — although his very error arose from the philosophical and self-dependent spirit which has always distinguished him, and which will even yet lead him, if I am not greatly mistaken in the man, to do something for the literature of the country which the country "will not willingly," and cannot possibly, "let die."

Without entering now into the *why*, let me observe that the printer may always ascertain when the dash of the MS. is properly and when improperly employed, by bearing in mind that this point represents *a second thought — an emendation.* In using it just above I have exemplified its use. The words "an emendation" are, speaking with reference to grammatical construction, put in *ap*position with the words "a second thought." Having written these latter words, I reflected whether it would not be possible to render their meaning more distinct by certain other words. Now, instead of erasing the phrase "a second thought," which is of *some* use — which *partially* conveys the idea intended — which advances me *a step toward* my full purpose — I suffer it to remain, and merely put a dash between it and the phrase "an emendation." The dash gives the reader a choice between two, or among three or more expressions, one of which may be more forcible than another, but all of which help out the idea. It stands, in general, for these words — "*or, to make my meaning more distinct.*" This force *it* *has* — and this force no other point can have; since all other points have well-understood uses quite different from this. Therefore, the dash *cannot* be dispensed with.

It has its phases — its variation of the force described; but the one principle — that of second thought or emendation — will be found at the bottom of all.

*

* *

There are few cases in which mere popularity should be considered a proper test of merit; but the case of song-writing is, I think, one of the few. In speaking of song-writing, I mean, of course, the composition of brief poems with an eye to their adaptation for music in the vulgar sense. In this ultimate destination of the song proper, lies its essence — its genius. It is the strict reference to music — it is the dependence upon modulated expression — which gives to this branch of letters a character altogether *unique*, and separates it, in great measure and in a manner not sufficiently considered, from ordinary literature; rendering it independent of merely ordinary proprieties; allowing it, and in fact demanding for it, a wide latitude of Law; absolutely, insisting upon a certain wild license and *indefinitiveness* — an indefinitiveness recognized by every musician who is not a mere fiddler, as an important point in the philosophy of his science — as the *soul*, indeed, of the sensations derivable from its practice — sensations which bewilder while they enthral — and which would *not* so enthral if they did not so bewilder.

The sentiments deducible from the conception of sweet sound simply, are out of the reach of analysis — although referable, possibly, in their last result, to that merely mathematical recognition of *equality* which seems to be *the root of all Beauty.* Our impressions of harmony and melody in conjunction, are more readily analyzed; but one thing is certain — that the *sentimental* pleasure derivable from music, is nearly in the ratio of its indefinitiveness. Give to music any undue *decision* — imbue it with any very *determinate* tone — and you deprive it, at once, of its ethereal, its ideal, and, I sincerely believe, of its intrinsic and essential character. You dispel its dream-like luxury: — you dissolve the atmosphere of the mystic in which its whole nature is bound up: — you exhaust it of its breath of faëry. It then becomes a tangible and easily appreciable thing — a conception of the earth, earthy. It will not, to be sure, lose *all* its power to please, but all that I consider the *distinctiveness* of that power. And to the *over*-cultivated talent, or to the unimaginative apprehension, this deprivation of its more delicate *nare* will be, not unfrequently, a recommendation. A *determinateness* of expression is sought — and sometimes by composers who should know better — is sought as a beauty, rather than rejected as a blemish. Thus we have, even from high authorities, attempts at absolute *imitation* in musical sounds. Who can forget, or cease to regret, the many errors of this kind into which some great minds have fallen, simply through over-estimating the triumphs of *skill.* Who can help lamenting the Battles of Prague? What man of taste is not ready to laugh, or to weep, over their "guns, drums, trumpets, blunderbusses and thunder"? "Vocal music," says L'Abbate Gravina, "ought to imitate the natural language of the human feelings and passions, rather than the warblings of Canary birds, which our singers, nowadays, affect so vastly to mimic with their quaverings and boasted cadences." This is true only so far as the "rather" is concerned. If *any* music must imitate *anything*, it were, undoubtedly, better that the imitation should be limited as Gravina suggests.

That *indefinitiveness* which is, at least, *one* of the essentials of true music, must, of course, be kept in view by the song-writer; while, by the critic, it should always be considered in his estimate of the *song*. It is, in the author, a consciousness — sometimes merely an instinctive appreciation, of this necessity for the indefinite, which imparts to all songs, rightly conceived, that free, affluent, and *hearty* manner, little scrupulous about niceties of phrase, which cannot be better expressed than by the hackneyed French word *abandonnement*, and which is so strikingly exemplified in both the serious and joyous ballads and carols of our old English progenitors. Wherever verse has been found most strictly married to music, this feature prevails. It is thus the essence of all antique song. It is the soul of Homer. It is the spirit of Anacreon. It is even the genius of Æschylus. Coming down to our own times, it is the vital principle in De Béranger. Wanting this quality, no song-writer was ever truly popular, and, for the reasons assigned, no song-writer need ever expect to be so.

These views properly understood, it will be seen how baseless are the ordinary objections to songs proper, on the score of "conceit," (to use Johnson's word,) or of hyperbole, or on various other grounds tenable enough in respect to poetry not designed for music. The "conceit," for example, which some envious rivals of *Morris* have so much objected to —

> Her heart and morning broke together
> In the storm —

this "conceit" is merely in keeping with the essential spirit of the song proper. To all reasonable persons it will be sufficient to say that the fervid, hearty, free-spoken songs of Cowley and of Donne — more especially of Cunningham, of Harrington and of Carew — abound in precisely similar things; and that they are to be met with, plentifully, in the polished pages of Moore and of Béranger, who introduce them with thought and retain them after mature deliberation.

Morris is, very decidedly, our best writer of songs — and, in saying this, I mean to assign him a high rank as *poet*. For my own part, I would much rather have written the best *song* of a nation than its noblest *epic*. One or two of Hoffman's songs have merit — but they are sad echoes of Moore, and even if this were not so (everybody knows that it *is* so) they are totally deficient in the real song-essence. "*Woodman spare that Tree*" and "*By the Lake where droops the Willow*" are compositions of which any poet, living or dead, might justly be proud. By these, if by nothing else, Morris is *immortal.* It is quite impossible to put down such things by sneers. The affectation of contemning them is of no avail — unless to render manifest the envy of those who affect the contempt. As mere *poems*, there are several of Morris's compositions equal, if not superior, to either of those just mentioned, but as *songs* I much doubt whether these latter have ever been surpassed. In quiet grace and unaffected tenderness, I know no American poem which excels the following:

Where Hudson's wave o'er silvery sand
  Winds through the hills afar,
Old Crow-nest like a monarch stands,
  Crowned with a single star.
And there, amid the billowy swells
  Of rock-ribbed, cloud-capped earth,
My fair and gentle Ida dwells,
  A nymph of mountain birth.

The snow-flake that the cliff receives —
  The diamonds of the showers —
Spring's tender blossoms, buds and leaves —
  The sisterhood of flowers —
Morn's early beam — eve's balmy breeze —
  Her purity define: —
But Ida's dearer far than these
  To this fond breast of mine.

My heart is on the hills; the shades
  Of night are on my brow.
Ye pleasant haunts and silent glades
  My soul is with you now.
I bless the star-crowned Highlands where
  My Ida's footsteps roam: —
Oh, for a falcon's wing to bear —
  To bear me to my home.

*
*   *

If ever mortal "wreaked his thoughts upon expression," it was *Shelley*. If ever poet sang — as a bird sings — earnestly — impulsively — with utter abandonment — to himself solely — and for the mere joy of his own song — that poet was the author of "The Sensitive Plant." Of Art — beyond that which is instinctive with Genius — he either had little or disdained all. He *really* disdained that Rule which is an emanation from Law, because his own soul was Law in itself. His rhapsodies are but the rough notes — the stenographic memoranda of poems — memoranda which, because they were all-sufficient for his own intelligence, he cared not to be at the trouble of writing out in full for mankind. In all his works we find no conception thoroughly wrought. For this reason he is the most fatiguing of poets. Yet he wearies in saying too little rather than too much. What, in him, seems the diffuseness of one idea, is the conglomerate concision of many: and this species of concision it is, which renders him obscure. With such a man, to imitate was out of the question. It would have served no purpose; for he spoke to his own spirit alone, which would have comprehended no alien tongue. Thus he was profoundly original. His quaintness arose from intuitive perception of that truth to which Bacon alone has given distinct utterance: — "There is no exquisite Beauty which has not some strangeness in its proportions." But whether obscure, original, or quaint, Shelley had no *affectations*. He was at all times sincere.

From his *ruins*, there sprang into existence, affronting the Heavens, a tottering and fantastic *pagoda*, in which the salient angles, tipped with mad jangling bells, were the idiosyncratic *faults* of the original — faults which cannot be considered such in view of his purposes, but which are monstrous when we regard his works as addressed to mankind. A "school" arose — if that absurd term must still be employed — a school — a system of *rules* — upon the basis of the Shelley who had none. Young men innumerable, dazzled with the glare and bewildered by the *bizarrerie* of the lightning that flickered through the clouds of "Alastor," had no trouble whatever in heaping up imitative vapors, but, for the lightning, were forced to be content with its *spectrum*, in which the *bizarrerie* appeared without the fire. Nor were mature minds unimpressed by the contemplation of a greater and more mature; and thus, gradually, into this school of all Lawlessness, — or obscurity, quaintness and exaggeration — were interwoven the out of place didacticism of Wordsworth, and the more anomalous metaphysicianism of Coleridge. Matters were now fast verging to their worst; and at length, in *Tennyson* poetic inconsistency attained its extreme. But it was precisely this extreme (for the greatest truth and the greatest error are scarcely two points in a circle) which, following the law of all extremes, wrought in him (Tennyson) a natural and inevitable revulsion; leading him first to contemn, and secondly to investigate, his early manner, and finally to winnow, from its magnificent elements, the truest and purest of all poetical styles. But not even yet is the process complete; and for this reason in part, but chiefly on account of the mere fortuitousness of that mental and moral combination which shall unite in one person (if *ever* it shall) the Shelleyan *abandon* and the Tennysonian poetic sense, with the most profound Art (based both in

Instinct and *Analysis*) and the sternest Will properly to blend and rigorously to control all — chiefly, I say, because such combination of seeming antagonisms will be only a "happy chance" — the world has never yet seen the noblest poem which, possibly, *can* be composed.

*
* *

There lies a deep and sealèd well
Within yon leafy forest hid,
Whose pent and lonely waters swell
Its confines chill and drear amid.

This putting the adjective after the noun is, merely, an inexcusable Gallicism; but the putting the preposition after the noun is alien to all language and in opposition to all its principles. Such things, in general, serve only to betray the versifier's poverty of resource; and, when an inversion of this kind occurs, we say to ourselves, "Here the poet lacked the skill to make out his line without distorting the natural or colloquial order of the words." Now and then, however, we must refer the error not to deficiency of skill, but to something far less defensible — to an idea that such things belong to the essence of poetry — that it needs them to distinguish it from prose — that we are poetical, in a word, very much in the ratio of our unprosaicalness at these points. Even while employing the phrase "poetic license," — a phrase which has to answer for an infinity of sins — people who think in this way seem to have an indistinct conviction that the license in question *involves a necessity of being adopted.* The true artist will avail himself of no "license" whatever. The very word will disgust him; for it says—"Since you seem unable to manage without these peccadillo advantages, you must have them, I suppose; and the world, half-shutting its eyes, will do its best not to see the awkwardness which they stamp upon your poem."

Few things have greater tendency than inversion, to render verse feeble and ineffective. In most cases where a line is spoken of as "forcible," the force may be referred to directness of expression. A vast majority of the passages which have become household through frequent quotation, owe their popularity either to this directness, or, in general, to the scorn of "poetic license." In short as regards verbal construction, *the more prosaic* a poetical style is, the better. Through this species of prosaicism, Cowper, with scarcely one of the higher poetical elements, came very near making his age fancy him the equal of Pope; and to the same cause are attributable three-fourths of that unusual point and force for which Thomas Moore is distinguished. It is the *prosaicism* of these two writers to which is owing their especial *quotability*.

*

* *

The *pure Imagination* chooses, from *either Beauty or Deformity*, only the most combinable things hitherto uncombined; the compound, as a general rule, partaking, in character, of beauty, or sublimity, in the ratio of the respective beauty or sublimity of the things combined—which are themselves still to be considered as atomic—that is to say, as previous combinations. But, as often analogously happens in physical chemistry, so not unfrequently does it occur in this chemistry of the intellect, that the admixture of two elements results in a something that has nothing of the qualities of one of them, or even nothing of the qualities of either. . . . Thus, the range of Imagination is unlimited. Its materials extend throughout the universe. Even out of deformities it fabricates that *Beauty* which is at once its sole object and its inevitable test. But, in general, the richness or force of the matters combined; the facility of discovering combinable novelties worth combining; and, especially the absolute "chemical combination" of the completed mass — are the particulars to be regarded in our estimate of Imagination. It is this thorough harmony of an imaginative work which so often causes it to be undervalued by the thoughtless, through the character of *obviousness* which is superinduced. We are apt to find ourselves asking *why* it is that these combinations have never been imagined before.

*

* *

Quaintness, within reasonable limits, is not only *not* to be regarded as affectation, but has its proper uses, in aiding a fantastic effect. Miss Barrett will afford me two examples. In some lines to a Dog, she says:

Leap! thy broad tail waves a light.
Leap! thy slender feet are bright,
  Canopied in fringes.
Leap! those tasselled ears of thine
Flicker strangely fair and fine
  Down their golden inches.

And again—in the "Song of a Tree-Spirit."

The Divine impulsion cleaves
In dim movements to the leaves
Dropt and lifted—dropt and lifted
In the sun-light greenly sifted —
In the sun-light and the moon-light
Greenly sifted through the trees.
Ever wave the Eden trees
In the night-light and the moon-light
With a ruffling of green branches
Shaded off to resonances
Never stirred by rain or breeze.

The thoughts here belong to a high order of poetry, but could not have been wrought into effective expression, without the aid of those repetitions — those unusual phrases — those *quaintnesses*, in a word, which it has been too long the fashion to censure, indiscriminately, under the one general head of "affectation." No poet will fail to be pleased with the two extracts I have here given ; but no doubt there are some who will find it hard to reconcile the psychal impossibility of refraining from admiration, with the too-hastily attained mental conviction that, critically, there is nothing to admire.

*
* *

When a man of genius speaks of "the difficult" he means, simply, "the impossible."

*
* *

Not only do I think it paradoxical to speak of a man of *genius* as personally ignoble, but I confidently maintain that the *highest* genius is but the loftiest moral nobility.

*

* *

Were I called on to define, *very* briefly, the term "Art," I should call it "the reproduction of what the Senses perceive in Nature through the veil of the soul." The mere imitation, however accurate, of what *is* in Nature, entitles no man to the sacred name of "Artist." Denner was no artist. The grapes of Zeuxis were *in*-artistic — unless in a bird's-eye view; and not even the curtain of Parrhasius could conceal his deficiency in point of genius. I have mentioned "the *veil* of the soul." Something of the kind appears indispensable in Art. We can, at any time, double the true beauty of an actual landscape by half closing our eyes as we look at it. The naked Senses sometimes see too little — but then *al-ways* they see too much.

*

* *

To see distinctly the machinery — the wheels and pinions — of any work of Art is, unquestionably, of itself, a pleasure, but one which we are able to enjoy only just in proportion as we do *not* enjoy the legitimate effect designed by the artist: — and, in fact, it too often happens that to reflect analytically upon Art, is to reflect after the fashion of the mirrors in the temple of Smyrna, which represent the fairest images as deformed.

*

* *

In the tale proper — where there is no space for development of character or for great profusion and variety of incident — mere *construction* is, of course, far more imperatively demanded than in the novel. Defective plot, in this latter, may escape observation, but in the tale, never. Most of our tale-writers, however, neglect the distinction. They seem to begin their stories without knowing how they are to end; and their ends, generally, — like so many governments of Trinculo — appear to have forgotten their beginnings.

Appendix

Including detached passages, selected, from reviews too long to be printed entire, as valuable either for themselves or for comparison with preceding texts.

It cannot, we think, be a matter of doubt with any reflecting mind, that at least one-third of the *reverence*, or of the *affection*, with which we regard the elder poets of Great Britain, should be credited to what is, in itself, a thing [distinct] from poetry — we mean to the simple love of the antique — and that again a third of even the proper *poetic sentiment* inspired by these writings should be ascribed to a fact which, while it has a strict connection with poetry in the abstract, and also with the particular poems in question, must not be looked upon as a merit appertaining to the writers of the poems. Almost every devout reader of the old English bards, if demanded his opinion of their productions, would mention vaguely, yet with perfect sincerity, a sense of dreamy, wild, indefinite, and he would perhaps say, undefinable delight. Upon being required to point out the source of this so shadowy pleasure, he would be apt to speak of the quaint in phraseology and of the grotesque in rhythm. And this quaintness and grotesqueness are, as we have elsewhere endeavored to show, very powerful, and if well managed, very admissible adjuncts to Ideality. But in the present instance they arise independently of the author's will, and are matters altogether apart from his intention. The

American Monthly has forcibly painted the general character of the old English Muse. She was a maid, frank, guileless, and perfectly sincere, and although very learned at times, still very learned without art. No general error evinces a more thorough confusion of ideas than the error of supposing Donne and Cowley metaphysical in the sense wherein Wordsworth and Coleridge are so.

With the two former ethics were the end — with the two latter the means. The poet of the *Creation* wished, by highly artificial verse, to inculcate what he considered moral truth — he of the *Auncient Mariner* to infuse the *Poetic Sentiment* through channels suggested by mental analysis. The one finished by complete failure what he commenced in the grossest misconception — the other by a path which could not possibly lead him astray, arrived at a certainty and intensity of triumph which is not the less brilliant and glorious because concentrated among the very few who have the power to perceive it. It will now be seen that even the "metaphysical verse" of Cowley is no more than evidence of the straightforward simplicity and single-heartedness of the man. And he was in all this but a type of his school — for we may as well designate in this way the entire class of writers whose poems are bound up in the volume before us, and throughout all of whom runs a very perceptible general character. They used but little art in composition. Their writings sprang immediately from the soul — and partook intensely of the nature of that soul. It is not difficult to perceive the tendency of this glorious *abandon*. To elevate immeasurably all the energies of mind — but again — so to mingle the greatest possible fire, force, delicacy, and all good things, with the lowest possible bathos, baldness, and utter imbecility, as to render it not a matter of doubt, but of certainty, that the average results of mind in such a school, will be found inferior to those results in one (ceteris paribus) more artificial: Such, we think, is the view of the older English Poetry, in which a very calm examination will bear us out. The quaintness in manner of which we were just speaking, is an adventitious advantage. It formed no portion of the poet's intention. Words and their rhythm have varied. Verses which affect us to-day with a vivid delight, and which in some instances, may be traced to this one source of grotesqueness and to none other, must have worn in the days of their construction an air of a very commonplace nature. This is no argument, it will be said, against the poems *now*. Certainly not — we mean it for the poets *then*. The notion of *power*, of excessive *power*, in the English antique writers should be put in its proper light. This is all we desire to see done. — From review of *The Book of Gems*, 1836.

*

* *

The word *plot*, as commonly accepted, conveys but an indefinite meaning. Most persons think of it as a simple *complexity;* and into this error even so fine a critic as Augustus William Schlegel has obviously fallen, when he confounds its idea with that of the mere *intrigue* in which the Spanish dramas of Cervantes and Calderon abound. But the greatest involution of incident will not result in plot; which, properly defined, is *that in which no part can be displaced without ruin to the whole.* It may be described as a building so dependently constructed, that to change the position of a single brick is to overthrow the entire fabric. In this definition and description, we of course refer only to that infinite perfection which the true artist bears ever in mind — that unattainable goal to which his eyes are always directed, but of the possibility of attaining which he still endeavors, if wise, to cheat himself into the belief. The reading world, however, is satisfied with a less rigid construction of the term. It is content to think that plot a good one, in which none of the *leading* incidents can be *removed* without *detriment* to the mass.

. . . . . .

We have defined the word *plot* in a definition of our own to be sure, but in one which we do not the less consider substantially correct; and we have said that it has been a main point with Mr. Bulwer in his last novel, "Night and Morning," to work up his plot as near perfection as possible. We have asserted, too, that his design is well accomplished; but we do not the less assert that it has been conceived and executed in error.

The interest of plot, referring, as it does, to cultivated thought in the reader, and appealing to considerations analogous with those which are the essence of sculptural taste, is by no means a popular interest; although it has the peculiarity of being appreciated in its atoms by all, while in its totality of beauty it is comprehended but by the few. The pleasure which the many derive from it is disjointed, ineffective, and evanescent; and even in the case of the critical reader it is a pleasure which may be purchased too dearly. A good tale may be written without it. Some of the finest fictions in the world have neglected it altogether. We see nothing of it in "Gil Blas," in the "Pilgrim's Progress," or in "Robinson Crusoe." Thus it is not an essential in story-telling at all; although, well managed, within proper limits, it is a thing to be desired. At best it is but a secondary and rigidly artistical merit, for which no merit of a higher class — no merit founded in nature — should be sacrificed.

. . . . . .

Very little reflection might have sufficed to convince Mr. Bulwer that narratives, even one-fourth as long as the one now lying upon our table, are *essentially* inadapted to that nice and complex adjustment of incident at which he has made this desperate attempt. In the wire-drawn romances which have been so long fashionable (God only knows how or why) the pleasure we derive (if any) is a composite one, and made up of the respective sums of the various pleasurable sentiments experienced in perusal. Without excessive and fatiguing exertion, inconsistent with legitimate interest, the mind cannot comprehend at one time and in one survey the numerous individual items which go to establish the whole. Thus the high ideal sense of the *unique* is sure to be wanting; for, however absolute in itself be the unity of the novel, it must inevitably fail of appreciation. We speak now of that species of unity which is alone worth the attention of the critic — the unity or totality of *effect*.

But we could never bring ourselves to attach any idea of merit to mere *length* in the abstract. A long story does not appear to us necessarily twice as good as one only half so long. The ordinary talk about "continuous and sustained effort" is pure twaddle and nothing more. Perseverance is one thing and genius is another, — whatever Buffon or Hogarth may assert to the contrary, — and notwithstanding that, in many passages of the dogmatical literature of old Rome, such phrases as "*diligentia maxima*," "*diligentia mirabilis*" can be construed only as "great talent" or "wonderful ability." Now if the author of "Ernest Maltravers," implicitly following authority like *les moutons de Panurge*, *will* persist in writing long romances because long romances have been written before, — if, in short, he cannot be satisfied with the brief tale (a species of composition which admits of the highest development of artistical power in alliance with the wildest vigor of imagination), — he must then content himself, perforce, with a more simply and more rigidly narrative form. — From review of Bulwer's *Night and Morning*, 1841.

*

* *

But when we come to speak of the excellences of the tale, these defects appear really insignificant. It embodies more *originality* in every point, but in character especially, than any single work within our knowledge. There is the grandfather — a truly profound conception; the gentle and lovely Nelly — we have discoursed of her before; Quilp, with mouth like that of the panting dog (a bold idea which the engraver has neglected to embody), with his hilarious antics, his cowardice, and his very petty and spoilt-child-like malevolence; Dick Swiveller, that prince of good-hearted, good-for-nothing, lazy, luxurious, poetical, brave, romantically generous, gallant, affectionate, and not over-and-above honest, "glorious Apollos"; the marchioness, his bride; Tom Codlin and his partner; Miss Sally Brass, that "fine fellow"; the pony that had an opinion of its own; the boy that stood upon his head; the sexton; the man at the forge; not forgetting the dancing dogs and baby Nubbles. There are other, admirably drawn characters; but we note these for their remarkable originality, as well as their wonderful keeping, and the glowing colors in which they are painted. We have heard some of them called caricatures, but the charge is grossly ill-founded. No critical principle is more firmly based in reason than that a certain amount of exaggeration is essential in the proper depicting of truth itself. We do not paint an object to be true, but to appear true to the beholder. Were we to copy nature with accuracy, the object copied would seem unnatural. The columns of the Greek temples, which convey the idea of absolute proportion, are very considerably thicker just beneath the capital than at the base. We regret that we have not left ourselves space in which to examine this whole question as it deserves. We must content ourselves with saying that caricature seldom exists (unless in so gross a form as to disgust at once) where the component parts are *in keeping;* and that the laugh excited by it, in any case, is radically distinct from that induced by a properly artistical *incongruity* — the source of all mirth. Were these creations of Mr. Dickens really caricatures, they would not live in public estimation beyond the hour of their first survey. We regard them as *creations*, (that is to say, as original combinations of character), only not all of the highest order, because the elements employed are not always of the highest. In the instances of Nelly, the grandfather, the Sexton, and the man of the furnace, the force of the creative intellect could scarcely have been engaged with nobler material, and the result is that these personages belong to the most august regions of the *Ideal.* — From review of Dickens's *The Old Curiosity Shop*, 1841.

*

* *

Macaulay has obtained a reputation which, although deservedly great, is yet in a remarkable measure undeserved. The few who regard him merely as a terse, forcible, and logical writer, full of thought, and abounding in original views — often sagacious and never otherwise than admirably expressed — appear to us precisely in the right. The many who look upon him as not only all this, but as a comprehensive and profound thinker, little prone to error, err essentially themselves. The source of the general mistake lies in a very singular consideration, yet in one upon which we do not remember ever to have heard a word of comment. We allude to a tendency in the public mind towards logic for logic's sake; a liability to confound the vehicle with the conveyed; an aptitude to be so dazzled by the luminousness with which an idea is set forth as to mistake it for the luminousness of the idea itself. The error is one exactly analogous with that which leads the immature poet to think himself sublime wherever he is obscure, because obscurity is a source of the sublime, thus confounding obscurity of expression with the expression of obscurity. In the case of Macaulay — and we may say, *en passant*, of our own Channing — we assent to what he says, too often because we so very clearly understand what it is that he intends to say. Comprehending vividly the points and the sequence of his argument, we fancy that we are concurring in the argument itself. It is not every mind which is at once able to analyze the satisfaction it receives from such Essays as we see here. If it were merely *beauty* of style for which they were distinguished, — if they were remarkable only for rhetorical flourishes, — we would not be apt to estimate these flourishes at more than their due value. We would not agree with the doctrines of the essayist on account of the elegance with which they were urged. On the contrary, we would be inclined to disbelief. But when all ornament save that of simplicity is disclaimed, — when we are attacked by precision of language, by perfect accuracy of expression, by directness and singleness of thought, and above all by a logic the most rigorously close and consequential, — it is hardly a matter for wonder that nine of us out of ten are content to rest in the gratification thus received as in the gratification of absolute truth.— From review of Macaulay's *Essays*, 1841.

*

* *

In all commentating upon Shakespeare, there has been a radical error, never yet mentioned. It is the error of attempting to expound his characters — to account for their actions — to reconcile his inconsistencies — not as if they were the coinage of a human brain, but as if they had been actual existences upon earth. We talk of Hamlet the man, instead of Hamlet the *dramatis persona* — of Hamlet that God, in place of Hamlet that Shakespeare created. If Hamlet had really lived, and if the tragedy were an accurate record of his deeds, from this record (with some trouble) we might, it is true, reconcile his inconsistencies and settle to our satisfaction his true character. But the task becomes the purest absurdity when we deal only with a phantom. It is not (then) the inconsistencies of the acting man which we have as a subject of discussion — (although we proceed as if it were, and thus *inevitably* err,) but the whims and vacillations — the conflicting energies and indolences of the poet. It seems to us little less than a miracle, that this obvious point should have been overlooked.

While on this topic we may as well offer an ill-considered opinion of our own as to the *intention of the poet* in the delineation of the Dane. It must have been well known to Shakespeare, that a leading feature in certain more intense classes of intoxication, (from whatever cause,) is an almost irresistible impulse to counterfeit a farther degree of excitement than actually exists. Analogy would lead any thoughtful person to suspect the same impulse in madness — where beyond doubt it is manifest. This, Shakespeare *felt* — not thought. He felt it through his marvellous power of *identification* with humanity at large — the ultimate source of his magical influence upon mankind. He wrote of Hamlet as if Hamlet he were; and having, in the first instance, imagined his hero excited to partial insanity by the disclosures of the ghost — he (the poet) *felt* that it was natural he should be impelled to exaggerate the insanity.— From review of Hazlitt's *Characters of Shakespeare*, 1845.

*

* *

In defence of allegory, (however, or for whatever object, employed,) there is scarcely one respectable word to be said. Its best appeals are made to the fancy — that is to say, to our sense of adaptation, not of matters proper, but of matters improper for the purpose, of the real with the unreal; having never more of intelligible connection than has something with nothing, never half so much of effective affinity as has the substance for the shadow. The deepest emotion aroused within us by the happiest allegory, *as* allegory, is a very, very imperfectly satisfied sense of the writer's ingenuity in overcoming a difficulty we should have preferred his not having attempted to overcome. The fallacy of the idea that allegory, in any of its moods, can be made to enforce a truth — that metaphor, for example, may illustrate as well as embellish an argument — could be promptly demonstrated: the converse of the supposed fact might be shown, indeed, with very little trouble — but these are topics foreign to my present purpose. One thing is clear, that if allegory ever establishes a fact, it is by dint of overturning a fiction. Where the suggested meaning runs through the obvious one in a *very* profound undercurrent so as never to interfere with the upper one without our own volition, so as never to show itself unless *called* to the surface, there only, for the proper uses of fictitious narrative, is it available at all. Under the best circumstances, it must always interfere with that unity of effect which to the artist, is worth all the allegory in the world. Its vital injury, however, is rendered to the most vitally important point in fiction — that of earnestness or verisimilitude. That "The Pilgrim's Progress" is a ludicrously over-rated book, owing its seeming popularity to one or two of those accidents in critical literature which by the critical are sufficiently well understood, is a matter upon which no two thinking people disagree; but the pleasure derivable from it, in any sense, will be found in the direct ratio of the reader's capacity to smother its true purpose, in the direct ratio of his ability to keep the allegory out of sight, or of his *in*-ability to comprehend it. Of allegory properly handled, judiciously subdued, seen only as a shadow or by suggestive glimpses, and making its nearest approach to truth in a not obtrusive and therefore not unpleasant *appositeness*, the "Undine" of De La Motte Fouqué is the best, and undoubtedly a very remarkable specimen. — From review of Hawthorne's *Twice Told Tales*, 1847.

*

* *

That the imagination has not been unjustly ranked as supreme among the mental faculties, appears from the intense consciousness, on the part of the imaginative man, that the faculty in question brings his soul often to a glimpse of things supernal and eternal — to the very verge of the *great secrets*. There are moments, indeed, in which he perceives the faint perfumes, and hears the melodies of a happier world. Some of the most profound knowledge — perhaps all *very* profound knowledge — has originated from a highly stimulated imagination. Great intellects *guess* well. The laws of Kepler were, professedly, *guesses*. — From *A Chapter of Suggestions*, 1845.

*

* *

An excellent magazine paper might be written upon the subject of the progressive steps by which any great work of art — especially of literary art — attained completion. How vast a dissimilarity always exists between the germ and the fruit — between the work and its original conception! Sometimes the original conception is abandoned, or left out of sight altogether. Most authors sit down to write with *no* fixed design, trusting to the inspiration of the moment; it is not, therefore, to be wondered at, that *most* books are valueless. Pen should never touch paper, until at least a well-digested *general* purpose be established. In fiction, the *dénouement* — in all other composition the intended *effect*, should be definitely considered and arranged, before writing the first word; and *no* word should be then written which does not tend, or form a part of a sentence which tends to the development of the *dénouement*, or to the strengthening of the effect. Where *plot* forms a portion of the contemplated interest, too much preconsideration cannot be had. *Plot* is very imperfectly understood, and has never been rightly defined. Many persons regard it as mere complexity of incident. In its most rigorous acceptation, it is *that from which no component atom can be removed, and in which none of the component atoms can be displaced, without ruin to the whole;* and although a sufficiently good plot may be constructured, without attention to the whole rigor of this definition, still it is the definition which the true artist should always keep in view, and always endeavor to consummate in his works. Some authors appear, however, to be totally deficient in constructiveness, and thus, even with plentiful invention, fail signally in plot. Dickens belongs to this class. His "Barnaby Rudge" shows not the least ability to *adapt*. Godwin and Bulwer are the best constructors of plot in English literature. The former has left a preface to his "Caleb Williams," in which he says that the novel was *written backwards;* the author first completing the second volume, in which the hero is involved in a maze of difficulties, and then casting about him for sufficiently probable cause of these difficulties, out of which to concoct volume the first. This mode cannot surely be recommended, but evinces the idiosyncrasy of Godwin's mind. Bulwer's "Pompeii" is an instance of admirably managed plot. His "Night and Morning," sacrifices to *mere* plot interests of far higher value.—From *A Chapter of Suggestions*, 1845.

*

* *

The last selection of my Tales was made from about 70, by Wiley and Putnam's reader, Duyckinck. He has what he thinks a taste for ratiocination, and has accordingly made up the book mostly of analytic stories. But this is not *representing* my mind in its various phases — it is not giving me fair play. In writing these Tales one by one, at long intervals, I have kept the book-unity always in mind — that is, each has been composed with reference to its effect as part of *a whole*. In this view, one of my chief aims has been the widest diversity of subject, thought, & especially *tone* and manner of handling. Were all my tales now before me in a large volume and as the composition of another — the merit which would principally arrest my attention would be the wide *diversity and variety*. You would be surprised to hear me say that (omitting one or two of my first efforts) I do not consider any one of my stories *better* than another. There is a vast variety of kinds and, in degree of value, these kinds vary — but each tale is equally good *of its kind*. The loftiest kind is that of the highest imagination — and, for this reason only, "Ligeia" may be called my *best* tale. I have much improved this last since you saw it and I mail you a copy, as well as a copy of my best specimen of analysis — "The Philosophy of Composition." — From letter to P. P. Cooke, 1846.

NOTES

References to Poe's *Works* are to the Virginia edition. In references to the text of the present volume the first number refers to page, the second to line. For the convenience of the reader references are in many cases made both to the present text and to the complete *Works*.

LETTER TO B—— (1836)

1: 1. This letter dated "West Point, ——, 1831," and beginning, "Dear B——," was prefixed to the *Poems*, New York, 1831. With slight changes it was reprinted in the *Southern Literary Messenger*, July, 1836, with the following note by Poe: "These detached passages form part of the preface to a small volume printed some years ago for private circulation. They have vigor and much originality — but of course we shall not be called upon to endorse all the writer's opinions." The text of 1836 is here followed; for the text of 1831 see *Works*, Stedman and Woodberry, vol. x, p. 144.

1: 2, *no poet*. The critic, according to Poe, must be a poet; a good poet is not, however, necessarily a good critic. Cf. *Works*, vol. xi, p. 150: "A poet is necessarily neither a critical nor an impartial judge of poetry." Also *Works*, vol. xvi, p. 101: "Poets are by no means, necessarily judges of poetry, but nothing is more certain than that, to be a judge of poetry, it is necessary at least to have the poetic sentiment, if not the poetic power — the 'vision,' if not the 'faculty divine';" — and *Works*, vol. xvi, p. 66 (**266**: 14): "To appreciate thoroughly the work of what we call genius, is to possess all the genius by which the work was produced." Cf. also *Works*, vol. xvi, p. 69 (**268**: 6).

3: 7, *Milton.* "We commonly hear and read that Milton preferred his *Paradise Regained* to his *Paradise Lost.* There is no warrant whatever for that idea, but only for the fact that he did not like his shorter epic to be decried in comparison with his longer." — Masson, *Life*, vol. vi, p. 655.

3: 22, *singular heresy.* Cf. **234**: 2, note.

3: 31, *Aristotle.* Poe makes this statement in other places; cf. *Works*, vol. xi, p. 12; vol. xii, p. 15. He apparently misquotes and misunderstands Aristotle, whose expression lends no support to didactic poetry. Cf. *Poetics*, IX, 3: *διὸ καὶ φιλοσοφώτερον καὶ σπουδαιότερον ποίησις ἱστορίας ἐστίν*; "Poetry, therefore, is a more philosophical and a higher thing than history." Poe, however, errs with Wordsworth, from whom he may have got this idea; cf. *Preface to Lyrical Ballads*, 1800: "Aristotle, I have been told, has said, that Poetry is the most philosophic of all writing: it is so: its object is truth," etc. Poe's reference to Aristotle is casual and second-hand; his purpose is to combat Wordsworth and the "heresy of the Lake School." Several passages in the "Letter to B——" suggest that Poe wrote it after a critical reading of Wordsworth's prefaces and Coleridge's *Biographia.* Cf. *Biographia*, chap. xv: "No man was ever yet a great poet, without being at the same time a profound philosopher." Cf. also Shelley, *Defence of Poetry*: "Shakespeare, Dante, and Milton are philosophers of the very loftiest power."

4: 25, *Melmoth the Wanderer*, a tale by Charles Robert Maturin, 1820.

4: 29, *poetry a study.* This is evidently a protest against a passage in Wordsworth's *Essay Supplementary to the Preface* (1815): "And, lastly, there are many, who, having been enamored of this [poetical] art in their youth, have found leisure, after youth was spent, to cultivate general literature; in which poetry has continued to be comprehended *as a study.* Into the above classes the Readers of poetry may be divided; Critics abound in them all; but from the last only can opinions be collected of absolute value."

6: 25, *Of genius.* The quotation is from the *Essay Supple-*

mentary to the Preface, 1815 (in *Prose Works*, ed. Knight, vol. ii, p. 251).

7: 12, "*Temora*." See *Essay Supplementary to the Preface* (vol. ii, p. 245).

7: 21, *And now she's at.* The lines, from *The Idiot Boy*, are not consecutive and are somewhat garbled. The second passage, from *The Pet Lamb*, is also slightly misquoted, and made ridiculous by the dashes.

8: 13, *his preface; i. e.*, the *Preface to the Lyrical Ballads*, 1800. Poe takes some liberties in quotation.

8: 22, *immortality to a wagon.* See Wordsworth's *Waggoner.*

8: 23, *the bee Sophocles.* A. W. Schlegel in his *Lectures on Dramatic Art*, vii, refers to the fact that Sophocles was called the "Attic Bee"; the point is interesting as evidence to show that Poe read Schlegel. Poe has many references to Schlegel; cf., for example, *Works*, vol. viii, p. 126; vol. x, p. 65 (**58**: 19); vol. xi, p. 79 (**84**: 2); vol. xiii, p. 43; and see Introduction.

9: 23, *A poem.* Poe evidently takes as a starting-point Coleridge's definition in the *Biographia Literaria*, chap. xiv: "A poem is that species of composition, which is opposed to works of science, by proposing for its immediate object pleasure, not truth; and from all other species (having this object in common with it) it is discriminated by proposing to itself such delight from the whole, as is compatible with a distinct gratification from each component part." Poe's distinction between poem and romance is suggested by the context in Coleridge. Cf. also Coleridge's definition in *Lectures*, 1818; and Wordsworth's distinction between "poetry and matter of fact, or science," in *Preface to Lyrical Ballads* (*Prose Works*, vol. i, p. 56, note).

Poe's definition in the *Letter to B——* (1831) contains the germ of the conception of poetry which he held throughout, and to which he gave final statement in the *Poetic Principle* (1850). Cf. **234**: 2, **263**: 4, **295**: 21, **236**: 22, and notes.

9: 26, *indefinite.* Poe uses this criterion throughout; see **263**: 4, note. Poe may have got both the word and the idea from Wordsworth and Coleridge; see **54**: 14, note.

DRAKE'S CULPRIT FAY (1836)

11: 1. What follows is from a review of Drake's *Culprit Fay and Other Poems* and Halleck's *Alnwick Castle with other Poems*, which appeared in the *Southern Literary Messenger*, April, 1836. Drake, whose poems were published posthumously in 1836, was hailed as a great American poet. Poe attempts to determine his poetical merits. The review is an admirable example of sanity and sound critical method. The present edition omits a summary of the plot of the *Culprit Fay*, and, at the end, several pages reviewing Drake's minor poems and the poems of Halleck.

12: 20, *true theatre of the biblical histrio.* A favorite idea of Poe; cf. **65**: 24.

15: 19, *Ideality.* The term of phrenology, which Poe, like others of his age, took seriously. "Craniology is worth some consideration, although it is merely in its rudiments and guesses yet." — Coleridge, *Table Talk*, June 24, 1827. Poe hopes that phrenology will be helpful to criticism; cf. *Works*, vol. xi, p. 65.

16: 4, *with the passions.* Cf. **238**: 20, note.

16: note 2, *What the Deity imagines.* Perhaps an echo of Coleridge, *Biographia Literaria*, chap. xiii: "The primary imagination I hold to be the living power and prime agent of all human perception, and as a repetition in the finite mind of the eternal act of creation in the infinite I AM." Cf. **103**: 16.

16: note 2, *Bielfeld.* This encyclopædic work, to which Poe is fond of referring, contains sections — "Of the polite arts in general," "Poetry," "On versification" — which Poe read attentively and drew upon for ideas. The demonstration to which Poe refers may be found in Book II, chap. i, § vii, of the English translation (London, 1770). For other references to Bielfeld see *Works*, vol. x, pp. 47, 62; vol. xi, p. 74; vol. xiv, p. 39; vol xvi, pp. 13, 30.

18: 10, *Auncient Mariner.* Coleridge's spelling in the title of 1798 was "Ancyent Marinere"; in 1800 and subsequently "Ancient Mariner."

18: 18, *Mr. George Dearborn.* Drake's son-in-law, who brought out the volume of poems under review.

19: 24, *compendium of the narrative.* Omitted in this edition.

20 : note 1, *Chestnut color,* — from "A Celebration of Charis," ix.

23 : 21, *melancholy.* For the same idea cf. **156** : 4, **242** : 26, and *Works,* vol. xi, p. 24. Poe may have got the idea from A. W. Schlegel : "Several inquirers . . . have placed the essence of the northern poetry in melancholy." — *Lectures* (Bohn edition), p. 26.

26: note 1, *We have seen American poems.* Has Poe his own poems in mind ?

BRYANT'S POEMS (1837)

32 : 1. From a review of Bryant's *Poems,* in the *Southern Literary Messenger,* January, 1837. The present edition omits several pages from the middle of the review.

32 : 1, *Mr. Bryant's poetical reputation.* Poe paid full tribute to Bryant's genius. For other reviews see *Works,* vol. x, p. 85 ; vol. xiii, p. 125 ; also vol. viii, pp. vii, 1.

34 : 6, *time necessary.* The following acute analysis is in accord with the theory later developed in *The Rationale of Verse.* Cf. **190** : 25 and note.

38 : 15, *first book of the Dunciad.* The last three are from the second book.

MOORE'S ALCIPHRON (1840)

53 : 1. A review in *Burton's Gentleman's Magazine,* January, 1840.

What Poe here says of Drake and of fancy and imagination is drawn from his review of Drake's *Culprit Fay ;* cf. **19** : 8 ff. The theory of fancy and imagination receives further development in the review of Willis ; cf. **103** : 9 ff.

53 : 3, *Anacreon Moore.* Moore published *Odes of Anacreon* in 1800.

54 : 14, "*The fancy.*" Not apparently a direct quotation from the *Biographia ;* but a fair summary of Coleridge's famous distinction between the fancy and the imagination. Poe probably had in mind the following passages: "The imagination then I consider either as primary or secondary. The primary imagination I hold to be the living power and prime agent of all human perception, and as a repetition in the finite mind of the eternal act of creation in the infinite I AM. The secondary I consider as an echo of the former, co-existing with the conscious will, yet still as identical with the primary in the kind of its agency, and differing only in degree, and in the mode of its operation. It dissolves, diffuses, dissipates, in order to re-create; or where this process is rendered impossible, yet still, at all events, it struggles to idealize and to unify. It is essentially *vital*, even as all objects (as objects) are essentially fixed and dead. Fancy, on the contrary has no other counters to play with, but fixities and definites. The Fancy is indeed no other than a mode of memory emancipated from the order of time and space," etc. (*Biographia*, chap. xiii). "He [the Poet] diffuses a tone and spirit of unity, that blends, and (as it were) fuses, each into each, by that sympathetic and magical power to which we have exclusively appropriated the name of imagination" (chap. xiv). Cf. also the last half of Wordsworth's *Preface* of 1815, particularly the following, which may have set Poe thinking: "Fancy does not require that the materials which she makes use of should be susceptible of change in their constitution, from her touch; and, when they admit of modification, it is enough for her purpose if it be slight, limited, and evanescent. Directly the reverse of these, are the desires and demands of the Imagination. She recoils from everything but the plastic, the pliant, and the indefinite." Cf. the discussion beginning at **103**: 9.

54: 22, *unusual combinations*. Cf. **78**: 4, note.

55: 24, "*Lilian*." Tennyson's poem appeared in 1830.

62: 7, *of a prose relation*. Cf. *Marginalia* (**303**: 14): "As regards verbal construction, *the more prosaic* a poetical style is, the better." Also *Works*, vol. xiii, p. 103. This favorite idea of Poe may have come to him in perusal of Wordsworth's *Preface to the Lyrical Ballads*: "Not only the language of a large portion of every good poem, even of the most elevated character, must necessarily, except with reference to the meter, in no respect differ from that of good prose, but likewise some of the most interesting parts of the best poems will be found to be strictly the language of prose when prose is well written."

EXORDIUM (1842)

65: 1. From *Graham's Magazine*, January, 1 42, where it stood under the general title "Review of New Books."

65: 14, *Time was*. The following paragraph is a rewriting of the first paragraph of the review of Drake's *Culprit Fay*, published in the *Southern Literary Messenger*, April, 1836. See **11**: 8.

68: 3, *essay upon the subject matter of the publication*. Cf. the opposite view expressed by Coleridge in *Biographia Literaria*, chap. xxi.

69: 7, *Arcturus*. "Mr. Cornelius Mathews," Poe says in *The Literati*, "was one of the editors and originators of *Arcturus*, decidedly the very best magazine in many respects ever published in the United States." See also Poe's remarks on Mathews in a review of *The Fable for Critics*, *Works*, vol. xiii, p. 169.

71: 22, *Orphicism*, — referring to Alcott's "Orphic Sayings," published in the transcendental *Dial*, 1840–1844.

72: 22, *with Bulwer*. Poe quotes from a paper by Bulwer "Upon the Spirit of True Criticism," in *Critical and Miscellaneous Writings*, — reviewed by Poe in *Graham's Magazine* two months before (November, 1841). Cf. *Works*, vol. x, p. 213.

LONGFELLOW'S BALLADS (1842)

73: 1. A review in *Graham's Magazine*, April, 1842. A shorter notice of the *Ballads* appeared in *Graham's*, March, 1842 (see *Works*, vol. xi, p. 64). These two reviews are run together to form the essay which appears in the Griswold and Stedman-Woodberry editions. For other reviews of Longfellow see *Works*, vol. x, pp. 39, 71; vol. xii, p. 41; vol. xiii, p. 54.

73: 1, *hasty observations*, — to the effect that "it will always be impossible to construct an English hexameter," and that Longfellow's "didactics are all out of place." See *Works*, vol. xi, p. 64.

73: 7, *a similar objection.* Cf. **52**: 9.

74: 15, *Now with as deep a reverence.* The following exposition of poetry is repeated in *The Poetic Principle* (**234**: 21 ff.); see also notes on those pages. As usual Poe revised and changed his phrasing; it is instructive to compare the two passages. The citations from Bielfeld are omitted in *The Poetic Principle.*

78: 4, *novel combinations.* Poe believed that imagination, creation, originality (the terms are to him synonymous) consisted in novel combination. See discussion of this point in the Introduction. The following references cover the important passages on this subject: *Works*, vol. x, pp. 62 (**54**: 21), 126, 153; vol. xi, p. 96; vol. xii, p. 37 (**103**: 15); vol. xiv, p. 73.

78: 28, *Bielfeld's definition.* This, and also the observation on German terms which follows, will be found in *The Elements of Universal Erudition* (London, 1770), vol. ii, p. 194. Cf. p. **16**, and note thereon.

81: 4, "*Armstrong on Health.*" John Armstrong (1709–1779), physician and disciple of Thomson, published his didactic *Art of Preserving Health* in 1744.

81: 9, *Brainard's Poems.* Cf. *Works*, vol. xi, p. 23: "Of the merely humorous pieces we have little to say. Such things are not *poetry*. . . . Humor, with an exception to be made hereafter, is directly antagonistical to that which is the soul of the Muse proper; and the omni-prevalent belief, that melancholy is inseparable from the higher manifestations of the beautiful, is not without a firm basis in nature and in reason. But it so happens that humor and that quality which we have termed the soul of the Muse (imagination) are both essentially aided in their development by the same adventitious assistance — that of rhythm and of rhyme. Thus the only bond between humorous verse and poetry, properly so-called, is that they employ in common a certain tool."

83: 19, *poems of magnitude.* This germ develops into Poe's argument against the long poem in *The Poetic Principle*; cf. **228**: 12, note.

84: 2, *Schlegel.* A. W. Schlegel, in his *Lectures on Dramatic Art*, XVII, approves of De la Motte's substitution of "unity of interest" for "unity of action." Cf. *Works*, vol. viii, p. 126.

84: 21, *Moore's Alciphron.* The passage probably referred to will be found at **58**: 13.

87: 25, *Mr. Langtree.* In *Autography* (*Works*, vol. xv, p. 232) Poe praises S. D. Langtree as a "just, bold, and acute critic."

HAWTHORNE'S TWICE-TOLD TALES (1842)

91: 1. A review in *Graham's Magazine*, May, 1842. The *Twice-Told Tales* had been briefly noticed in *Graham's*, April, 1842. Another review, appearing in *Godey's Lady's Book*, November, 1847 (see *Works*, vol. xiii, p. 141), is partially a repetition of the earlier reviews. The reviews of May, 1842, and November, 1847, are run together, with omission of repeated passages, to form the essay in the Griswold and Stedman-Woodberry editions. On the authority of Griswold's text see *Nation*, Dec. 4, 1902, p. 445.

92: 28, *under-current of suggestion.* Refers to Poe's discussion of fancy and imagination in the review of *Alciphron*; see **59**: 23; also **165**: 17 and note.

93: 4, *The tale proper.* The following passage, repeated (with revision) in a later review of Hawthorne (*Works*, vol. xiii, p. 151), contains the best exposition of Poe's theory of the tale. Compare it with his theory of the poem, **228**: 1; also with *Works*, vol. ix, p. 46; vol. x, p. 116.

95: 3, *unique or single effect.* Cf. the expression of another master of the short story: "Let him [the fiction-writer] choose a motive, whether of character or of passion; carefully construct his plot so that every incident is an illustration of the motive and every property employed shall bear to it a near relation of congruity or contrast; avoid a sub-plot, unless, as sometimes in Shakespeare, the sub-plot be a reversion or complement of the main intrigue; . . . and allow neither himself in the narrative nor any character in the course of the dialogue, to utter one sentence that is not part and parcel of the business of the story or the discussion of the problem involved." — R. L. Stevenson, "A Humble Remonstrance" (*Memories and Portraits*).

95: 19, *rhythm*. Cf. **79**: 14, **81**; 30, **237**: 15.

96: 3, *the humorous*. Cf. note on **81**: 9; in the passage there quoted, however, Poe speaks of rhythm as *aiding* humorous effect.

99: 16, *something which resembles plagiarism*. Poe is apparently the plagiarist, if any one. "Howe's Masquerade" appeared in *The Democratic Review*, May, 1838, "William Wilson" in *Burton's Gentleman's Magazine*, October, 1839, and in *The Gift* for 1840.

N. P. WILLIS (1845)

102: 1. From the *Broadway Journal*, January 18, 1845. The two paragraphs beginning at **103**: 9 summarize the passage on the same subject in the review of Moore's *Alciphron*; see note on **53**: 1. The discussion is then broadened to include fantasy and humor, wit and sarcasm.

102: 5, *Proctor*. A misspelling of the name of Bryan Waller Procter (1787–1874)?

THE AMERICAN DRAMA (1845)

107: 1. From the *American Whig Review*, August, 1845. A brief notice of Willis's *Tortesa* had appeared in *Burton's Gentleman's Magazine*, August, 1839 (see *Works*, vol. x, p. 27).

107: 9, *de nier ce qui est*. Quoted at the close of *The Murders in the Rue Morgue*, where it is attributed to Rousseau, *Nouvelle Héloïse*.

108: 26, *the imitative arts*. Poe seems to use the word "imitative" vaguely or ambiguously. Does he mean arts reproductive of what exists in nature, or arts in which the tendency for one artist to follow another is strong? Or does he argue that an art reproductive in the first sense will be reproductive in the other? For a discussion of the imitative arts see Sidney Colvin, *Encyclopædia Britannica*, sub "Fine Arts."

110: 28, *Elizabethan routine.* It is strange that two such different minds as Poe and Emerson should have come to the same conclusion. Cf. *The American Scholar:* "Genius is always sufficiently the enemy of genius by over-influence. . . . The English dramatic poets have Shakespearized now for two hundred years."

118: 1, *P. S. and O. P.* "Prompter's Side" (right hand side facing audience), and "Opposite Prompter."

118: 20, *bedight*, — apparently in the sense of *named.* Perhaps a slip of the pen or misprint; Poe had already used the word correctly in *The Conqueror Worm* (1843):

> "An angel throng, bewinged, bedight
> In veils, and drowned in tears."

120: 1, *Bridgewater treatises.* This passage is reprinted by Poe from the *Marginalia*, in the *Democratic Review*, November, 1844. Poe reviewed one of the Bridgewater treatises in the *Southern Literary Messenger*, February, 1836; see *Works*, vol. viii, p. 206.

121: 8, *not an essential.* The fullest statement of Poe's theory on this point is to be found in a review of *Bulwer's Night and Morning* (1841), *Works*, vol. x, p. 120: "The interest of plot, referring, as it does, to cultivated thought in the reader, and appealing to considerations analogous with those which are the essence of sculptural taste, is by no means a popular interest; although it has the peculiarity of being appreciated in its atoms by all, while in its totality of beauty it is comprehended but by the few. The pleasure which the many derive from it is disjointed, ineffective, and evanescent; and even in the case of a critical reader it is a pleasure which may be purchased too dearly. A good tale may be written without it. Some of the finest fictions in the world have neglected it altogether. We see nothing of it in *Gil Blas*, in the *Pilgrim's Progress*, or in *Robinson Crusoe.* Thus it is not an essential in story-telling at all; although, well managed, within proper limits, it is a thing to be desired. At best it is but a secondary and rigidly artistical merit, for which no merit of a higher class — no merit founded in nature — should be sacrificed."

The last sentence is particularly interesting, as showing that Poe did not prize mere "artistical merits" above truth to nature. The same view of plot is taken in a review of Cooper's *Wyandotte* (1843), in *Works*, vol. xi, p. 209.

128: 28, *this general opinion.* The substance of this passage is from the "Letter to B——"; cf. **1**: 14 ff.

143: 4, *Nec Deus intersit.* From Horace, *Art of Poetry*, l. 191: "Nec deus intersit, nisi dignus vindice nodus inciderit."

PREFACE TO THE POEMS (1845)

149: 1. Prefixed to *The Raven and Other Poems*, New York, 1845. For a slight change in the text see *Works*, vol. vii, p. xlvii, note.

THE PHILOSOPHY OF COMPOSITION (1846)

150: 1. From *Graham's Magazine*, April, 1846.

150: 1, *Charles Dickens.* The note will be found in *Works*, vol. xvii, p. 107; Poe's examination of *Barnaby Rudge* in *Works*, vol. xi, p. 38. Although he had Dickens's letter "lying before him," Poe does not use Dickens's exact words.

150: 10, *what he himself acknowledges.* Godwin's account will be found in his preface to *Caleb Williams*, 1832: "I formed a conception of a book of fictitious adventure, that should in some way be distinguished by a very powerful interest. Pursuing this idea, I invented first the third volume of my tale, then the second, and last of all the first," etc. The passage is quite in Poe's ratiocinative style and may have suggested to him *The Philosophy of Composition.* Cf. *Works*, vol. xvi, p. 170: "to begin their works at the end."

151: 5, *effect.* Cf. what Poe says of preconceived effect in the review of Hawthorne, **95**: 3.

152: 16, *For my own part.* Cf. *Marginalia* (**264**: 21) where Poe is evidently thinking of himself: "It is the curse of a certain order of mind, that it can never rest satisfied with the consciousness of its ability to do a thing. Still less is it content with doing it. It must both know and show how it was done." This was published in December, 1844, more than a year before the *Philosophy of Composition* and before *The Raven* — indeed at about the time when *The Raven* was probably written.

153: 16, *a long poem.* Cf. *The Poetic Principle*, **228**: 12, review of Hawthorne, **93**: 25, and review of Longfellow's *Ballads*, **83**: 19.

153: 19, *excites, by elevating, the soul.* Cf. *The Poetic Principle*, **228**: 16.

154: 26, *Beauty is the sole legitimate province.* Cf. *The Poetic Principle*, **237**: 31, and note.

155: 22, *passion, or even truth.* Poe throughout takes the ground that passion and truth may be introduced provided they are "toned into proper subservience." Cf. **238**: 20, and note.

156: 4, *Melancholy.* Cf. **23**: 21, note.

158: 20, *the death, then, of a beautiful woman.* Cf. "the moral sentiment of beauty heightened in dissolution," **30**: 11.

160: 23, *My first object.* Cf. *Works*, vol. xi, p. 277: "Originality of theme, if not absolutely first sought, should be sought among the first. . . . The desire of the new is an element of the soul." Also *Works*, vol. xiii, p. 85: "In *all* cases of fictitious composition it [originality] should be the *first* object — by which we do not mean to say that it can ever be considered as the most important." Cf. **151**: 5, **267**: 26.

161: 3, *it must be elaborately sought.* Cf. *Peter Snook* (1836), *Works*, vol. xiv, p. 73: "There is no greater mistake than the supposition that a true originality is a mere matter of impulse or inspiration. To originate, is carefully, patiently, and understandingly to combine."

161: 9, *heptameter catalectic.* Poe must mean octameter catalectic; the alternate lines contain fifteen syllables.

161: 20, *nothing even remotely approaching this combination.* The resemblances between *The Raven* and *Lady Geraldine's Courtship* are too striking to be overlooked, — these resemblances extending to rhythm, phrasing, and what Poe himself calls "tone" (cf. **134**: 3). Though the date of composition of *The Raven* is undetermined (see *Works*, vol. vii, p. 211), certain facts suggest that Poe was reading Mrs. Browning's poem and writing *The Raven* at the same time. *Lady Geraldine's Courtship* appeared in the *Poems* of 1844, which Poe reviewed in the *Evening Mirror* in the autumn of 1844 and in the *Broadway Journal*, January 4 and 11, 1845 (see *Works*, vol. xii, p. 1). *The Raven* appeared a little later in the same periodicals, — in the *Evening Mirror*, January 29, 1845, and in the *Broadway Journal* in the same year. Metrically *The Raven* and *Lady Geraldine's Courtship* are very similar: both are in an eight-foot trochaic measure, the rhymes in some of Mrs. Browning's stanzas also corresponding to those in the first four lines of Poe's. For example, the following:

> With a murmurous stir uncertain, in the air the purple curtain
> Swelleth in and swelleth out around her motionless pale brows,
> While the gliding of the river sends a rippling noise for ever
> Through the open casement heightened by the moonlight's slant repose.
>
> Said he — " Vision of a lady ! stand there silent, stand there steady !
> Now I see it plainly, plainly now I cannot hope or doubt —
> There, the brows of mild repression, there the lips of silent passion,
> Curvèd like an archer's bow to send the bitter arrows out."
>
> Ever, evermore the while in a slow silence she kept smiling,
> And approached him slowly, slowly, in a gliding measured pace ;
> With her two white hands extended as if praying one offended,
> And a look of supplication gazing earnest in his face.

As in *The Raven*, the first and third lines have internal feminine rhyme at the fourth foot, and the second and fourth masculine rhyme with what Poe calls "cæsura." It is hard to believe that Poe, fresh from reading Mrs. Browning, was unconscious of the resemblance, or that he is justified in saying that "nothing even remotely approaching this combination has ever been attempted." Some readers may even feel that one object Poe may have had in writing the *Philosophy of Composition* was to convince the public that *The Raven* was original and independent by showing its genesis in his own mind.

163 : 5, *moment.* This reads *minute* in other versions of the poem.

165 : 17, *under current.* Cf. review of *Alciphron*, **59** : 23, where an under current of suggestion is spoken of as a mark of *ideality*; here it appears as imparting *richness*, which (Poe thinks) may be confounded with the ideal. Cf. also **84** : 19, **92** : 28.

THE RATIONALE OF VERSE (1848)

167 : 1. *The Rationale of Verse*, published in the *Southern Literary Messenger*, October and November, 1848, was an elaboration of "Notes on English Verse," published in *The Pioneer*, March, 1843. Poe also incorporated, in a review of Griswold's *Poets*, 1843, a "short notice of the art of versification"; for this see *Works*, vol. xi, p. 225. Cf. also the passage on versification in the review of Bryant, **33** : 22 ff.

167 : 6, *no topic in polite literature.* An opinion repeatedly expressed by Poe. Cf. *Works*, vol. xiii, p. 91 : "In common with a very large majority of American and, indeed, of European poets, Mrs. Smith seems to be totally unacquainted with the principles of versification — by which, of course, we mean its *rationale*. . . . There is not a prosody in existence which is worth the paper on which it is printed." Cf. also **281** : 3; **291** : Poe's note.

168 : 14, *irrational deference to antiquity.* Cf. Poe's opinion of the ancient plays, **286** : 17.

168 : 15, *nature of Truth.* A favorite idea of Poe; cf. *Letter to B——* (**5** : 11) : "As regards the greater truths men oftener err by seeking them at the bottom than at the top." In *The Purloined Letter* the Parisian police err because they are over-ingenious and overlook the obvious.

176 : 23, *enjoyment of equality.* Cf. *Marginalia* (**295** : 28) : "The sentiments deducible from the conception of sweet sound simply, are out of the reach of analysis — although referable, possibly, in their last result, to that merely mathematical recognition of *equality* which seems to be *the root of all Beauty*." Also **272** : 9.

178 : 20, *inferior or less capable Music.* Cf. what Poe says of music in the *Poetic Principle*, **236** : 22, **237** : 16, and note.

179: 4, "*The Principle of Variety in Uniformity.*" In his essay "What is Poetry?" prefixed to *Imagination and Fancy* (1844) Leigh Hunt defines poetry as "the utterance of a passion for truth, beauty, and power, embodying and illustrating its conceptions by imagination and fancy, and modifying its language on the principle of variety in uniformity." In the last part of the essay this principle is discussed. Cf. Coleridge, *Anima Poetæ* (Boston, 1895), p. 129: "Now, poetry produces two kinds of pleasure, one for each of the two master-movements or impulses of man, — the gratification of the love of variety, and the gratification of the love of uniformity," etc. Cf. also *Table Talk*, Dec. 27, 1831 ("multitude in unity"); and "On the Principles of Genial Criticism," *Biographia Literaria*, ed. Shawcross, vol. ii, p. 232 ("multeity in unity"). Poe perhaps treats Hunt's essay contemptuously because it contains ideas not in harmony with his own. Hunt, for example, identifies poetry with passion, and makes "continuity" one of the marks of the great poet. Cf. **280**: 3; and **274**: 3, "Perfection of rhyme is attainable only in the combination of the two elements, Equality and Unexpectedness," etc.

183: 16, *Parturiunt montes.* Misquoted from Horace, *Art of Poetry*, l. 139: "Parturient montes, nascetur ridiculus mus."

183: 18, *Litoreis ingens.* Virgil, *Æneid*, III, l. 390.

188: 13, *varying its application.* Cf. **158**: 29.

190: 25, *point of time.* A comparison of this passage with the review of Bryant (**33**: 22 ff.) shows that a part of Poe's theory of verse had been worked out eleven years earlier (1837). The example from Pope's *Dunciad* occurs in both passages.

193: 8, "*Orion.*" Poe published a very appreciative review of Horne's poem in *Graham's Magazine*, March, 1844; see *Works*, vol. xi, p. 249.

194: 19, *two consecutive equivalent feet.* "The suggestion of his [Poe's] being the first to use two initial inversions shows extraordinary ignorance of Milton, to go no farther." — Omond, *English Metrists*, p. 141.

196: 18, *Coleridge.* Poe probably has in mind the *Preface* of 1816 (see *Poetical Works*, ed. J. Dykes Campbell, p. 601): "I have only to add, that the metre of Christabel is not, properly speaking, irregular, though it may seem so from its being founded on a new principle: namely, that of counting in each line the accents, not the syllables. Though the latter may vary from seven to twelve, yet in each line the accents will be found to be only four. Nevertheless this occasional variation in number of syllables is not introduced wantonly, or for the mere ends of convenience, but in correspondence with some transition, in the nature of the imagery or passion." Cf. Robertson, *New Essays Toward a Critical Method*, p. 363.

198: 3, "*Christabel*." Poe does scant justice to Coleridge's poem as to his theory. That Poe's difficulties are not all imaginary, however, the reader may see by rereading the poem. What, for example, is Coleridge's metrical intention in the first of the following lines?

"Is the night chilly and dark?
The night is chilly, but not dark."

200: 18, *the cæsura*. Cf. **175**: 1. In the earlier discussion of versification (see *Works*, vol. xi, p. 228) Poe says: "All our Prosodists define the cæsura as a pause introduced for the purpose of producing harmony, in a single verse or couplet, between 'two members of the same verse,' by which the one is placed in direct comparison with the others. . . . We too use the cæsura as a pause — a pause compelled by the position of, and upon the foot — of the voice, which renders it equal in quantity to any of the larger feet, and at the same time gives to the close of the verse, where it is most frequently found, a singular richness, as well as sonorous fullness and force." In the review of Longfellow's *Ballads* (**87**: 3), dating 1842, Poe has a conception of the cæsura perhaps slightly different, speaking of Byron's line

Know ye the | land where the | cypress and | myrtle

as "formed of three dactyls and a cæsura." "The *myrtle*, at the close of Byron's line, is a double rhyme, and must be understood as one syllable." This reading Poe apparently abandoned later. On the subject of pauses see Alden, *English Verse*, p. 16, where the cæsura is defined in its ordinary sense as "a pause not counted out of the regular time of the rhythm, but corresponding to the pause between 'phrases' of music, and nearly always coinciding with syntactical or rhetorical divisions of the sentence."

202 : 27, *'Tis the land.* In quoting Poe transposes *land* and *clime*.

205 : 31, *false in point of melody.* J. J. Sylvester, *Laws of Verse*, notes that "*twine*, ending a line, takes after it a slight pause, which with the *and* would make out the value of a dactyl." See Robertson, *New Essays Toward a Critical Method*, p. 360; Omond, *English Metrists*, p. 139.

207 : 5, *hudsonizing.* Explained by reference to an article by Poe on H. N. Hudson, a lecturer on Shakespeare; he had, Poe says, among other bad points "an elocution that would disgrace a pig." See *Works*, vol. xiii, p. 27.

207 : 10, *rhythm.* Poe's etymology is false; it is from ῥυθμός, motion or flow.

224 : 13, *English hexameters.* Poe touches this subject in other places. Cf. **86 :** 28; also *Works*, vol. xi, p. 66; vol. xvi, p. 72.

224 : 22, *Professor Felton.* C. C. Felton, Professor of Greek at Harvard and friend of Longfellow. The "Frogpondian Professors" are those dwelling near the pond in Boston Common.

225 : 11, *Also the church within.* From *The Children of the Lord's Supper.* For "In which" (second line) read "When." The line when correctly quoted, however, contains the feet to which Poe objects.

THE POETIC PRINCIPLE (1850)

228 : 1. *The Poetic Principle*, originally a lecture delivered in 1848–1849 in Lowell, Providence, Richmond, and other places, was published posthumously in *Sartain's Union Magazine*, October, 1850.

228 : 12, *a long poem.* Poe insists on the brevity of the poem throughout, beginning in 1836. Cf. *Works*, vol. viii, p. 126. The point is more fully developed elsewhere; see **83 :** 19, **93 :** 7, **153 :** 16.

For the first statement of the same principle applied to fiction see *Works*, vol. ix, p. 46.

Cf. two expressions of Gray, with whom Poe has something in common: "The true lyric style, with all its flights of fancy, ornaments, and heightening of expression, and harmony of sound, is in its nature superior to every other style; which is just the cause why it could not be borne in a work of great length," etc. — Letter to Mason, December, 1756. "I have been used to write chiefly lyric poetry, in which, the poems being short, I have accustomed myself to polish every part of them with care; . . . the labor of this in a *long* poem would hardly be tolerable." — Mathias, *Observations*, p. 52.

228: 16, *excites, by elevating the soul.* Cf. *Philosophy of Composition*, **153**: 19, where the insertion of the comma gives a slightly different meaning.

228: 22, *half an hour, at the very utmost.* "Not to exceed in length what might be perused in an hour," is the limit set in an earlier discussion of the same point; see **93**: 10.

229: 10, *After a passage.* Cf. Coleridge, *Biographia Literaria*, chap. xiv: "A poem of any length neither can be, or ought to be, all poetry," etc.

230: 12, "*The Columbiad.*" Joel Barlow's great epic was the work of a lifetime. Begun in his college days, and published as *The Vision of Columbus*, 1787, it finally appeared in a large and sumptuous volume as *The Columbiad*, 1807.

230: 15. *Lamartine* was voluminous: *Jocelyn* and *La Chute d'un Ange* occupied four volumes in the original editions. Robert Pollok (1799–1827), a Scotchman, wrote a didactic poem, *The Course of Time.*

231: 14, *undue brevity.* Comparison with the examples given shows some of Poe's own poems to be unduly brief.

234: 2, *The Didactic.* Poe fought this "heresy" consistently throughout. The following references will enable the reader to collect Poe's most important expressions on this subject: *Works*, vol. vii, pp. xxxvii, xliii (**3**: 22; **10**: 8); vol. ix, p. 305 (**52**: 9); vol. x, p. 141; vol. xi, pp. 67, 68, 79 (**82**: 11), 84 (**89**: 10), 244,

247, 253, 254; vol. xii, p. 33; vol. xiii, p. 131. Beginning with his attack on the heresy of the Lake School in the *Preface* of 1831 Poe uniformly takes the position that "didactic subjects are utterly beyond, or rather beneath the province of true poesy." Cf. Shelley, *Defence of Poetry*, to the effect that the "eternal poets" do not make the mistake of "affecting a moral aim." — *Prose Works*, ed. Forman, vol. iii, p. 112.

234: 21, *With as deep a reverence.* Cf. **74**: 15 and note.

235: 15, *Aristotle.* In the *Ethics* Aristotle treats indifferently morals and what we should consider matters of taste. He did not separate the good and the beautiful.

236: 4, *mere repetition is not poetry.* This gives Poe's attitude toward realism. Cf. **89**: 10, **279**: 23, **306**: 6.

236: 15, *the desire of the moth for the star.* Quoted from Shelley, *One Word is too Often Profaned.*

236: 22, *by Music.* Cf. *The Rationale of Verse* (**178**: 19): "Verse which cannot be better designated than as an inferior or less capable music." In a letter to Lowell, July 2, 1844, Poe says: "I am profoundly excited by music. . . . Music is the perfection of the soul, or idea, of poetry. The *vagueness* of exaltation aroused by a sweet air (which should be strictly indefinite and never too strongly suggestive) is precisely what we should aim at in poetry." — Woodberry, *Poe*, p. 213. Cf. also what Poe says of music at **177**: 23; and E. Lauvrière, *Edgar Poe*, p. 353, note: "Nous savons son goût pour la musique, ses preférences pour les poètes chanteurs, Tennyson, Keats, Shelley; ses poèmes juvéniles comme ses théories poétiques sont pleines des mots: musique, melodie, harmonie; ses premiers succès en poésie, *Helen*, *Ligeia*, *Israfel*, sont d'heureuses manifestations de cette musique des vers qui ne fera que s'affirmer et se perfectionner par la suite. . . . Les tendances artistiques de Poe étaient, en leur fond intime, essentiellement musicales."

236: 24, *Abbate Gravina.* Probably Gianvincenzo Gravina, Italian critic, author of *Della Ragion Poetica* (1708). Cf. **264**: 5, **296**: 31.

237: 22, *unfamiliar to the angels.* Cf. *Israfel*, ll. 40–51:

Yes, Heaven is thine ; but this
  Is a world of sweets and sours ;
  Our flowers are merely — flowers,
And the shadow of thy perfect bliss
  Is the sunshine of ours.

If I could dwell
Where Israfel
  Hath dwelt, and he where I,
He might not sing so wildly well
  A mortal melody,
While a bolder note than this might swell
  From my lyre within the sky.

Cf. also Shelley, *Defence of Poetry:* "It is doubtful whether the alloy of costume, habit, &c., be not necessary to temper this planetary music to mortal ears." — *Prose Works*, ed. Forman, vol. iii, p. 110.

237: 31, *The Rhythmical Creation of Beauty*. Substantially the same definition occurs in other places, particularly in the review of Longfellow's *Ballads*, **80**: 20. Compare the following: "The sole legitimate object of a true poem is the *creation of beauty*." — *Works*, vol. xi, p. 244. "A poem, whose single object is the creation of Beauty — the novel collocation of old forms of the Beautiful and of the Sublime." — Vol. xi, p. 254. Cf. also **154**: 26 ff.; **304**: 8.

Robertson (*New Essays Toward a Critical Method*, p. 84, note) says: "It is remarkable that no one has ever pointed out that Poe's own excellent definition of poetry, 'the rhythmical creation of beauty,' is a condensation of a sentence by (of all men) Griswold." This statement, however, is doubtful, the facts being as follows. Griswold used the words in the preface to his *Poets and Poetry of America* (1842): "The creation of beauty, the manifestation of the real by the ideal, 'in words that move in metrical array,' is poetry." This preface is dated "Philadelphia, March, 1842." In the same month, if not earlier, Poe was writing the review of Longfellow's *Ballads* in which his definition first occurs — since this review appeared in *Graham's Magazine* for April, 1842. The dates do not justify the assertion that Poe was indebted to Griswold. Furthermore, in an anonymous review of Griswold's *Poets* in the Philadelphia *Saturday Museum*, 1842 (*Works*, vol. xi, p. 239), Poe says, after quoting the sentence from Griswold's preface given above: "Now what is this but a direct amplification by our poet [Griswold] of the definition of poetry — '*the rhythmical creation of beauty*' — which appeared in Mr. Poe's *critique* of Professor Longfellow's ballads, from which *we* know and *he* knows he stole it?" See also *Works*, vol. xi, p. 154. Poe would hardly make this charge so explicitly without some warrant? It should be noted, also, that Poe and Griswold were both in Philadelphia in March, 1842, and that Griswold soon succeeded Poe as editor of *Graham's Magazine*. Griswold, therefore, may have got the phrase in question directly from Poe before it appeared in print. It is likely that Poe got his famous definition, not from Griswold, but from A. W. Schlegel: see Introduction.

238: 20, *It by no means follows, however*. Poe takes the ground that truth and passion, while not proper subjects of poetry, may be introduced if strictly subordinated to the true poetic purpose. Cf. **16**: 4, **75**: 24, **155**: 22, **235**: 22, **254**: 31.

The best statement of his position may be found in the review of Horne's *Orion*: "The question . . . is not whether it be not possible to introduce didacticism, with effect, into a poem, or possible to introduce poetical images and measures, with effect, into a didactic essay. To do either the one or the other, would be merely to surmount a difficulty — would be simply a feat of literary sleight of hand. But the true question is, whether the author who shall attempt either feat, will not be laboring at a disadvantage. . . . Although we agree, for example, with Coleridge that poetry and *passion* are discordant, yet we are willing to permit Tennyson to bring, to the intense *passion* which prompted his 'Locksley Hall' the aid of that terseness and pungency which are derivable from rhythm and from rhyme. The effect he produces, however, is a purely passionate, and not, unless in detached passages of this magnificent philippic, a properly poetic effect." — *Works*, vol. xi, p. 254.

On passionate poetry the following is instructive: "Mrs. Welby's theme is . . . one of the very best among the class *passionate*. True passion is prosaic—homely. Any strong mental emotion stimulates *all* the mental faculties; thus grief the imagination:—but in proportion as the effect is strengthened, the cause surceases. The excited fancy triumphs—the grief is subdued—chastened,—is no longer grief. In this mood we are poetic, and it is clear that a poem now written will be poetic in the exact ratio of its dispassion. A passionate poem is a contradiction in terms."—*Works*, vol. xi, p. 277. Cf. also *Works*, vol. xiii, pp. 131, 160, 162. In the last two of these passages Poe writes almost as if passion were a proper ingredient of poetry; and in a review of Lowell (*Works*, vol. xiii, p. 168) he says: "The poetry of sentiment . . . to be sure is *not* the very loftiest order of verse; for it is far inferior to that of the imagination or that of the passions."

Poe regularly attributes to Coleridge the doctrine that "poetry and passion are discordant,"—apparently without authority. Coleridge, like the other early nineteenth century critics, considered passion "the all in all in poetry"; cf. *Biographia Literaria*, chap. xviii: "Now poetry, Mr. Wordsworth truly affirms, does always imply passion; which word must be here understood, in its most general sense, as an excited state of the feelings and faculties." Many other passages are to the same effect. For passages, however, indicating vaguely that Coleridge believed poetry to arise in the subsidence or control of passion see *Biographia*, ed. Shawcross, vol. ii, pp. 253, 15.

241: 30, *I know*. The line should read: "I know that I no more should see."

242: 26, *sadness is inseparably connected*. Cf. **23**: 21, and note. The quotation is from Longfellow's *The Day is Done*.

246: 7, *originating with Coleridge*. Cf. **54**: 14, note.

253: 23, *Alfred Tennyson*. In a review of Tennyson of 1842 (*Works*, vol. xi, p. 127) Poe's tone is disparaging. Elsewhere he speaks, as here, in terms of highest praise.

MARGINALIA (1844–1849)

257: 1, *Marginalia.* Poe published between 1836 and 1849 many articles made up of critical scraps, under this and other titles. The first article, entitled *Pinakidia* (*tablets* or *memoranda*), appeared in the *Southern Literary Messenger*, August, 1836; *Literary Small Talk* in the *American Museum*, January and February, 1839; *Fifty Suggestions* in *Graham's Magazine*, May and June, 1845; *A Chapter of Suggestions* in *The Opal*, 1845. The *Marginalia* appeared as follows: *Democratic Review*, November, December, 1844; *Godey's Lady's Book*, August, September, 1845 (with the title "Marginal Notes . . . a sequel to the *Marginalia* of the *Democratic Review*"); *Graham's Magazine*, March, 1846; *Democratic Review*, April, 1846; *Graham's Magazine*, November, December, 1846, January, February, March, 1848; *Southern Literary Messenger*, April, May, June, July, September, 1849. The article entitled *Marginalia* in *Graham's Magazine*, March, 1848, though under Poe's name and clearly Poe's, is not included in the Virginia edition; this article will be found in *Works*, Stedman and Woodberry, vol. vii, p. 238. The title *Marginalia*, properly belonging only to the articles given above, has been extended by editors of Poe to other scraps; see *Works*, vol. xvi, p. vii; and *Works*, Stedman and Woodberry, vol. vii, p. 355. Griswold, however, may have had some authority for his inclusions; see *Nation*, vol. 75, p. 446. Passages in *Marginalia* were often reprinted by Poe from earlier reviews, — sometimes reprinted in later ones.

258: 30, *the analysis of language.* Cf. *The Rationale of Verse*, **171**: 13.

260: 29, *In general.* Cf. *Works*, vol. xii, p. 1, where this passage is worked over to furnish the opening to a review of Mrs. Browning's poems.

263: 4, *the indefinite.* Cf. **9**: 26, **295**: 21, **297**: 8, and letter to Lowell, **236**: 22, note.

264: 5, *L' Abbate Gravina.* Cf. **236**: 24, note.

264: 21, *It is the curse.* Cf. **306**: 17.

264 : 25, *In a critical mood.* This passage is part only of a short review of Mrs. Welby's poems which Poe inserted in the *Marginalia.*

265 : 15, *class passionate.* See **238 :** 20, note.

268 : 18, *if the practice fail.* Cf. *Works*, vol. xi, p. 39.

269 : 12, *The poetic sentiment.* For the same idea elaborated see *Works*, vol. xii, p. 105, where Poe thus explains Longfellow's "plagiarisms."

271 : 12, *Mr. Longfellow.* See *Works*, vol. xii, p. 41, and references there given.

271 : 18, *less at merit.* Cf. *The Poetic Principle*, **244 :** 24 ff.

272 ; 3, *The effect derivable.* An interesting variant of passages in *The Rationale of Verse ;* cf. **176 :** 23 *et seq.*

273 : 24, *says Lord Bacon.* A favorite quotation with Poe, occurring in *Ligeia* and other places. The sentence, in Bacon's essay *Of Beauty*, reads: "There is no excellent beauty that hath not some strangeness in the proportion." Cf. Poe's discussion of *quaintness* as a means of producing artistic effect, *Works*, vol. xii, pp. 6, 20, 21, and **304 :** 20, note.

276 : 3, *a class of fancies.* The following passage throws light on Poe's poetry and imaginative tales.

276 : 28, *a character supernal.* Cf. **77 :** 30, **236 :** 31, **254 :** 27.

277 : 8, *the power of words.* In some of the tales, for example *Ligeia*, Poe evidently finds the power of words inadequate. He is forced constantly to the use of superlatives and expressions such as "more than passionate devotion," "melody more than mortal." He sometimes admits the weakness of words : "Words are impotent to convey any just idea of the fierceness of resistance with which he wrestled with the shadow"; "Through a species of unutterable horror and awe, for which the language of mortality has no sufficiently energetic expression," etc. Music, Poe believed, has powers of expression beyond words.

278 : 22, *The artist belongs.* This will be found in Sarah Austin's *Fragments of the German Prose Writers*, 1841, — a volume of miscellaneous translations which Poe seems to have used.

280 : 3, *Leigh Hunt's rigmarolic attempt.* In the prefatory essay to *Imagination and Fancy* (1844), "What is Poetry?" Cf. **179**: 4, and note.

286: 17, *About the "Antigone."* The passage is reprinted by Poe from an article in the *Broadway Journal*, April 12, 1845; see *Works*, vol. xii, p. 130.

287: 24, *Trublet* published *Literary and Moral Essays*, 1735.

289: 15, *Campbell and Johnson.* Johnson's observations will be found in the Life of Pope and in *Rambler*, No. 92; Campbell's in *The Philosophy of Rhetoric*, Book iii, ch. i, sec. iii.

295: 7, *There are few cases.* What follows is a revision of a ten years old review of George P. Morris; see *Burton's Gentleman's Magazine*, December, 1839; and *Works*, vol. x, p. 41.

295: 21, *indefinitiveness.* Cf. **263**: 4, and note.

296: 2, *equality.* Cf. **176**: 23, **272**: 9.

299: 29, *If ever mortal*, etc. A revision from the review of Mrs. Browning's *Poems;* cf. *Works*, vol. xii, p. 32.

300: 21, *His quaintness.* Cf. **273**: 24, note; and **304**: 20, note.

302: 11, *Gallicism.* Cf. *Works*, vol. xiii, p. 103; also **62**: 7, and note.

304: 20, *Quaintness.* Cf. **300**: 21. Stedman, *Poets of America*, p. 241, well analyzes the quaintness of Poe's own diction in *The Raven:* "This appears in the gravely quaint diction. . . . The grimness of fate is suggested by phrases which it requires a masterly hand to subdue to the meaning of the poem. 'Sir, said I, or madam,' 'this ungainly fowl,' and the like sustain the air of grotesqueness, and become a foil to the pathos, an approach to the tragical climax, of this unique production. Only genius can deal so closely with the grotesque, and make it add to the solemn beauty of structure an effect like that of the gargoyles seen by moonlight on the façade of Notre Dame."

306: 6, *mere imitation.* See **236**: 4 and note.

306: 17, *To see distinctly the machinery.* Cf. **264**: 21.